THE FRESHMAN READER

Essays and Casebook

THE FRESHMAN READER

Essays and Casebook

Kent Forrester
Jerry A. Herndon
Murray State University

Holt, Rinehart and Winston

New York / Chicago / San Francisco / Philadelphia
Montreal / Toronto / London / Sydney
Tokyo / Mexico City / Rio de Janeiro / Madrid

Library of Congress Cataloging in Publication Data

Main entry under title:

The Freshman reader.

  Includes index.
   1. College readers.   2. English language—Rhetoric.
I. Forrester, Kent.   II. Herndon, Jerry A.
PE1417.F73   1983   808'.0427   82-9328
ISBN 0-03-059296-8   AACR2

CBS COLLEGE PUBLISHING
Holt, Rinehart and Winston
The Dryden Press
Saunders College Publishing

For our Wives and Children:

Marie Forrester
Kelly
Annie
Alan

Patricia Herndon
Rose
Joel
Jay
Joanna
Melanie
Victoria
Susan

Preface

We know it's easy to lose sight of writing techniques if an essay has too many twists and tangles. We have therefore avoided the kind of essay that gets readers to their destination, but by a route so long, circuitous, and tiring that they can't quite grasp how they got there.

Instead, we have sought out essays that are brief and manageable. A few are as short as 400 to 500 words; about half are from 1,000 to 1,200. In each chapter, moreover, you should be able to find at least one very brief essay whose rhetorical methods are so apparent that it can be used as a clear and manageable model.

To further clarify the rhetorical methods, we have followed the introduction of each chapter with a model paragraph that illustrates, in miniature, what students will find in the four essays that follow it. If students will imitate these model paragraphs (and we have provided assignments for that purpose), they will be better prepared to confront the relative complexity of the full-blown essays.

We think we have included a nice mix of classic and contemporary essayists. What we searched for, at any rate, were essays that combine readability with humanistic concerns. The contemporary essayists we have included—lively writers like Loren Eiseley, Lewis Thomas, Joan Didion, and Jacob Bronowski—are noted for their humanistic concerns; the classic essayists, humanists such as Abraham Lincoln, Mark Twain, George Orwell, and Bertrand Russell—are noted for their crisp, readable prose.

Most of the essays are contemporary, culled from magazines like *Harper's*, *Newsweek* (we are fond of the "My Turn" column), and *Saturday Review*. Others are from lively books like Edward Abbey's *Desert Solitaire* and Tom Wolfe's *Mauve Gloves & Madmen, Clutter & Vine*.

The first and last chapters are special chapters. Chapter 1 begins with a short discussion of some of the issues dealt with in the book, and then immediately follows with two essays about language and freshman composition. Paul Roberts' "How to Say Nothing in Five Hundred Words" and Ken Macrorie's "Telling Truths" are written from two different vantage points, or sensibilities, so that you are free either to assign the essay you feel more comfortable with or to assign both essays and use them as points of departure. Whatever the method, we think you will find that Roberts' and Macrorie's essays are good ways to begin the semester. They raise many of the issues that instructors usually cover in the first few days of freshman composition.

The last chapter is also special. Instead of including a final section of "essays for further reading," we have designed what might be called a mini-casebook for our final chapter. Chapter 12, "The American Way of Death," is made up of ten essays that deal with the same narrow issue—American funeral customs. These essays can be used as the raw material for reports, documented argumentative essays, and other short research papers.

If you have tried these kinds of assignments in the classroom, you know how difficult it is to find in the usual freshman reader even two or three essays on a narrowly circumscribed issue; and you know that it seems impossible to find both sides of an issue represented in enough essays to allow students to experience realistically what it takes to write even a short documented report.

Of course, these essays don't have to be used that way. You might select just two opposing essays and have your students write a comparison theme. Or you might have them write a short argumentative theme, using one essay for support of their position and an opposing essay as the foil. However the essays are used, they will give your students the opportunity to analyze two sides of an issue.

The essays in Chapter 12 can also stand on their own. Our classroom experiences with Jessica Mitford's powerful (perhaps stomach-turning) "In the Hands of the Embalmer" have shown us that students are curious about the subject and eager to talk and write about "last things."

A FINAL NOTE

Over the years we have come to believe that there are no quick fixes in freshman composition, no ten-easy-steps-to-success tricks, no panaceas. And that includes our book.

But we think it can help, and we hope to make it better. Perhaps you can help. Maybe you have a favorite essay, one that has worked well for you in class, or one that you've always wanted to see in a freshman reader—perhaps an essay from *Sports Illustrated* or *Harper's* that has stuck in your mind over the years. Will you tell us about it?

Let us know too if there are essays in the book that don't work in class. While trying to decide what to include, we worried over some of the essays the way a dog worries a bone. As a matter of fact, our friendship almost went up in smoke during a couple of discussions about what should be dropped and what should be left in.

However, we did agree—at least before we started working on the book in earnest—that we were going to write better questions following the essays than *we* had seen in freshman readers. Then we discovered—to the utter destruction of our naiveté—that writing those questions is damnably difficult. As a matter of fact, those little questions gave us more trouble than anything else in the book. So if you have any good questions that we've overlooked, please let us know. In the second edition we'll give you credit.

Here's where we can be reached:

English Department
Murray State University
Murray, Kentucky 42071

For helping us prepare this first edition, we want to thank several people, beginning with two of our colleagues—Thayle Anderson and Charles Duke. The following teachers read the manuscript and offered many useful comments: Richard S. Beal (whose advice was particularly helpful); Raymond Brebach, Drexel University; Lynn Garrett, Louisiana State University; Francis A. Hubbard, University of Wisconsin; W. Michael Kleine, University of Minnesota; Mildred E. Kuester, Jefferson State Junior College; Miriam Youngerman Miller, University of New Orleans; and David Skwire, Cuyahoga Community College. Finally, we would like to thank these Holt editors, who helped make our work on the book a pleasure: Susan Katz, Nedah Abbott, Anne Boynton-Trigg, and Karen Mugler.

K.F.
J.A.H.

Contents

C H A P T E R O N E

First Things 1

Paul Roberts / *How to Say Nothing in Five Hundred Words* 5
An unlucky freshman writer guesses wrong on his first college theme.

Ken Macrorie / *Telling Truths* 17
A good writer tries to shake the habit of telling lies.

C H A P T E R T W O

Description 23

Edward Abbey / *The Spadefoot Toad* 28
Desert toads want to sing even when it might be the death of them.

George Orwell / *How It Feels to Be Shot* 32
It doesn't feel good. Then again, it's not as bad as you might think.

Rachel Carson / *The Abyss* 36
"Here and there a tooth still lies in the red-clay ooze of the deep sea, coated with a deposit of iron from a distant sun."

John Madson / *On the Trail of the Curly Cows* 40
What could be better than the free and carefree life of a buffalo hunter? Almost anything.

CHAPTER THREE

Narration 46

Loren Eiseley / *The Bird and the Snake* 50
In the desert a scientist watches a snake and a bird locked in a death struggle. Can he maintain his scientific detachment?

E. B. White / *Once More to the Lake* 54
A boy pulls up his cold, wet bathing suit, and his father feels the "chill of death."

Faye Moskowitz / *Linking "A" to "Aleph'* 61
How to learn actively from books by drawing on your "rich stores of memory and experience."

Bruce Catton / *A Watery Grave and the Stars* 67
Death beneath a frozen lake and stars on a Christmas Eve—these two images sum up the two sides of life, the horror and the glory.

CHAPTER FOUR

Illustration 73

Lewis Thomas / *On Natural Death* 76
A dying mouse lies languidly in a cat's mouth. Two men lie crushed in a jeep and feel no pain. These and other "astonishments" tell Thomas that nature is a wonder, not an abomination.

Joseph Campbell / *The Witch in the Nervous System* 80
Do images of chicken hawks sleep in the souls of chickens? Do witches sleep in the souls of children?

Joan Didion / *California Dreaming* 83
Floating on air in the Center for the Study of Democratic Institutions.

Nora Ephron / *Conundrum* 88
James Morris becomes Jan Morris and learns to giggle.

CHAPTER FIVE

Process 93

S. I. Hayakawa / *How Dictionaries Are Made* 98
The dictionary-maker is a recorder, not a lawgiver.

Hana Umlauf and Barry Youngerman / *An Exercise in Levitation* 101
How you and three others, using only two fingers apiece, can lift a large friend.

Joseph Wheelwright / *The Preying Tree* 103
> *The author puts together two trees and comes up with something that looks like a human. Well, sort of.*

Donald M. Murray / *The Maker's Eye: Revising Your Own Manuscripts* 106
> *Just when you think you're finished, the most important step remains.*

CHAPTER SIX

Comparison 112

Jacob Bronowski / *Man and the Grunion* 117
> *Man differs from the grunion in one significant way: He is not a captive of his environment—he changes it.*

E. M. Forster / *Voltaire and Frederick the Great* 120
> *Voltaire, the malicious but liberty-loving Frenchman, visits the cultured ruler Frederick the Great and learns that culture and tyranny can exist together very comfortably.*

Michael Levin / *How to Tell Bad from Worse* 125
> *"There is no one as dangerous as an idealist with a machine gun."*

P. S. Wood / *Female Athletes: They've Come a Long Way, Baby* 129
> *Women athletes, already better than men in long-distance swimming, are coming up fast in other sports as well.*

CHAPTER SEVEN

Classification 135

Faces in the Crowd 140
> *It's easy to spot the Heavy Metal rock fans. They're the ones who fight the bouncers and toss empty wine bottles.*

Martin Luther King, Jr. / *Three Ways of Responding to Oppression* 144
> *"The old law of an eye for an eye leaves everybody blind."*

Desmond Morris / *Communication Among the Naked Apes* 149
> *A cocktail party is a place where naked apes get together for grooming talk.*

Alexander Theroux / *The Candy Man* 153
> *Wherein the author comes up with some surprising categories of candy and makes some harsh comments about "trash" candies.*

CHAPTER EIGHT

Definition   158

Norman Cousins / *Where Hell Begins*   163
What is hell? Consider definitions by Menotti, T. S. Eliot, and others.

Roger Shuy / *Dialects: What They Are*   166
People from southern Illinois and people from northern Illinois can't stand one another's pronunciation of "greasy." Who is right?

Paul / *Tongues of Men and Angels*   171
Those without charity become sounding brass and tinkling cymbals.

William Faulkner / *The Nobel Prize Address*   173
Writers who forget the "old verities and truths of the heart" labor under a curse.

CHAPTER NINE

Cause and Effect   176

E. M. Forster / *My Wood*   180
The author's newly acquired property makes him feel heavy, large, restless, and possessive of his blackberries.

Mark Twain / *The War Prayer*   185
A messenger from God startles a group of worshippers by telling them that their prayers, the unspoken as well as the spoken parts, have been answered.

Tom Wolfe / *The Perfect Crime*   189
A hostage taker is captured, yet his crime is still perfect in his eyes. How can this be?

Lance Morrow / *Back to Reticence!*   195
Offensive slogans on T shirts, John McEnroe's tantrums, and other examples of insufferable behavior have gone too far. It's time to return to reticence and self-discipline.

CHAPTER TEN

Argumentation: Appeals to Reason   199

Bertrand Russell / *Do We Survive Death?*   205
Russell says we don't. Darn it.

D. Keith Mano / *Cruel Lib* 211

Liberation is cruel when the talents we thought were only hidden and waiting for release turn out to be nonexistent.

Judith Plotz / *Is a Crime Against the Mind No Crime at All?* 215

Does plagiarism stem from a "perverted ideal of creativity"? Plotz says it does.

C. S. Lewis / *The Law of Human Nature* 221

Is there a real, unvarying Right and Wrong? Lewis says there is.

CHAPTER ELEVEN

Argumentation: Appeals to Emotion 226

Martin Luther King, Jr. / *I Have a Dream* 231

"Free at last! free at last! thank God Almighty, we are free at last!"

Abraham Lincoln / *Second Inaugural Address* 236

"With malice toward none; with charity for all; with firmness in the right . . ."

Edward Abbey / *The Right to Arms* 239

Owning a gun is an affirmation of personal liberty.

David Berg / *The Right to Bear Arms* 244

Owning a gun is an act of cowardice and stupidity.

CHAPTER TWELVE

The American Way of Death: Pros and Cons 248

THE CONS

Al Morgan / *The Bier Barons* 252

Eighty miles of pipes, 100,000 shrubs, 370 loudspeakers that play continuous music—a new shopping mall? No. California's Forest Lawn cemetery.

Roul Tunley / *Can You Afford to Die?* 257

One mortician says he can embalm an elephant for $1.50. It will cost you a bit more.

Ruth Mulvey Harmer / *The High Cost of Dying* 261

The author agrees with an Episcopal minister who thinks that the traditional funeral ceremony is an "ugly survival of paganism."

Jessica Mitford / *In the Hands of the Embalmer* 267
   The author indelicately shows us what the embalmer is going to do to us if we let
   him.

Deborah Wolters / *Death, Here Is Thy Sting* 272
   The undertaker, like the realtor, has become a "professional," and the addition of
   that harmless-sounding noun is proving to be expensive to his customers.

THE PROS

J. H. Plumb / *De Mortuis* 276
   A historian shows that it is entirely appropriate that Checkers is buried in
   Slumberland.

William M. Lamers, Jr. / *Funerals Are Good for
People* 280
   A psychiatrist argues that the traditional funeral acts as a mechanism to allow
   mourners an emotional catharsis.

Ralph A. Head / *The Reality of Death: What Happens When
It Is Ignored?* 284
   The author argues that the traditional funeral is psychologically better for the
   survivors than memorial services.

Dotson Rader / *Four Undertakers* 288
   Four craftsmen give people a "better impression of death."

Richard Huntington and Peter Metcalf / *The Role of
the Mortician* 291
   The rituals of the traditional American funeral, according to these two
   anthropologists, are widespread and popular because the public demands them.

Suggestions for Writing 294

Index 303

CHAPTER ONE

First Things

This is a book about how to write well. It is not just about how to write a short essay, though that is the shape your writing will usually take. It is a book about how to write well in any kind of writing you do.

The principles discussed—organization, diction, comparison, and so forth—are principles that underlie all good writing, whether it be a short essay, a business letter, a technical report, or a history examination.

The principles that guided us in the creation of *The Freshman Reader* are rather simple:

1. People who study good writing often turn out to be good writers themselves. We have therefore collected essays by some of the best writers we know of for you to read.
2. People who consciously imitate good prose usually improve their own writing. To that end we have included a variety of excercises that ask you to imitate rhetorical techniques.
3. People who work to improve their vocabularies improve their vocabularies. Following most of the essays, therefore, you will find a list of words. Learn their meanings. This will help you to read more easily and express yourself more clearly.
4. People who learn to write by using various methods of exposition usually turn out to be versatile writers. We have therefore organized this book around basic rhetorical principles which are illustrated in the essays we have chosen.
5. People who write a lot improve the way they write. Following most of the essays, then, you will find a variety of suggestions for writing.

But before we get too deep into the book, we need to say a few things that you should keep in mind as you read.

First a note of caution: The methods of development that are used as chapter headings (Description, Narration, Illustration, and so forth) are merely *ways* of developing what you need to say, or your thesis. They are ways of shaping an idea as it moves down the page of an essay. Methods of development are, in effect, a craftsman's tools.

Naturally, the thing that a craftsman builds is the reason for his work, and his chisel and plane are only means to an end (though it's true that an occasional tool-loving craftsman elevates his tools to an end). A carpenter doesn't sit down and say to himself, "I think I'll build something with my chisel and plane today." Instead, he says, "I need to build a bookshelf today." Then he uses the tools that are necessary.

Likewise, a writer doesn't sit down and say, "I think I'll write an illustration essay." Instead, he first has something he wishes to say, and *then* he uses the rhetorical tools needed to do the job. Methods of development, then, are only the means to an end—the fulfillment of a communication purpose.

That purpose, the controlling idea behind a piece of writing, is called a thesis. Naturally, in the world outside the classroom, this thesis either emerges from within or is given to you by someone else. For instance, if you were to sit down to write a letter of complaint to the newspaper about the sudden disappearance of "The Wizard of Id" from the comic strip page, your thesis ("Bring back the Wizard of Id!") comes ready-made. It is indistinguishable from your need to write.

Theses also come ready-made on the job. Unless you end up as one of the resident essayists for *Newsweek*, your employer will give you your theses. ("Marie, write up a report on the initial consumer reaction to the widget.")

Composition classes resemble the outside world in at least one respect: They usually require that writers use theses given to them by someone else—in this case the instructor.

But there may be times—probably early in the semester—when you will be given only a subject, usually a single word or phrase. It will thus be your job to come up with a thesis, or statement *about* the subject. (A thesis, by the way, is also called a central idea, or even a statement of purpose.)

Let's say you are given the subject "electronic games" to write on. Obviously, "electronic games" is not a thesis, or central idea. It is not a statement *about* something. It is the *something*. It is not difficult, however, to come up with a statement about electronic games. To begin, you might dig down inside yourself and discover an attitude you have toward electronic games. Now translate that attitude, that generalized emotional response, into a thesis statement by answering this question: Why do I like (or dislike) electronic games? If the "Why?" can be broken down into analyzable parts, you probably have a satisfactory thesis. In simple form the process looks like this:

Subject	Attitude	Question	Thesis statement
electronic games	I like them.	Why?	I like them because they keep my mind sharp, give me a feeling of power, and keep my pockets free of change.

A special variety of thesis is the argumentative thesis. But instead of answering the question of why you like or dislike something, you answer the question of why you favor a certain side of an issue. Your answer is your thesis. For instance, if you believe that *Playboy* is a harmful publication (rather than a harmless or beneficent one), you should first ask, "Why do I hold such an opinion?" Your thesis, then, is the answer to that question. It might look something like this: "*Playboy* is a harmful publication because it encourages a lifestyle based on getting and spending, and because it demeans women by treating them as flesh without mind."

Not all theses, however, require a point of view, or attitude toward the subject. The purpose of certain kinds of essays may be merely to clarify a subject. A process essay, for instance, can consist of nothing more than an explanation of how something works—how a dictionary is made, how the U.S. Senate conducts its business, and so forth. Explaining the obscure, classifying the chaotic, precisely defining a commonly misunderstood word or an interesting abstraction—these reasons for writing are sometimes sufficient in themselves.

Of course, even these kinds of essays *can* express points of view, and they are often better when they do. Indeed, unless your classification essay, for instance, opens up your subject in such a way that your reader will see something in a new light, you had better provide your essay with a point of view.

There might even be times when you are given a completely open-ended assignment. ("Class, write a paper for next Monday.") At first glance this kind of assignment looks attractive, but you will find that total freedom is usually more of a burden than a blessing. All we can suggest is this: Find a subject that truly interests you, and then look to your heart for an attitude toward that subject.

Whatever the assignment, you will want to state your thesis as clearly as possible, usually in a single sentence, in your opening paragraph. There are good reasons for this: Once down in black and white, it will serve as a reminder to you to stay on track; it will also help your readers because it tells them what you are going to do (and readers need all the help you can give them).

In this book we have grouped essays into chapters based on methods of development. This might suggest that those essays that fall under, let's say, "Narration" are pure narration. Nothing could be further from the truth. Like alley cats, essays are mixed breeds. A writer might begin with pure description, continue with a short narrative, and end with a comparison.

What we have done is put essays that are *predominantly* one kind of development into individual chapters. Thus, though John Madson's "On the Trail of the Curly Cows" is partly a narrative essay, it is also heavily descriptive—and thus finds itself in the chapter titled "Description."

The two essays that follow—"How to Say Nothing in Five Hundred Words" and "Telling Truths"—are introductions, from two vantage points, to the study of writing. And though the authors differ in sensibility (Roberts' essay was published in the 1950s, Macrorie's in the 1970s), both essays are full of sound advice.

Sound advice, we know, sounds rather dreary—the kind of thing that one usually listens to with only half a mind. But Roberts and Macrorie write with such clarity and insight—and each has such a strong and distinctive "voice"—that *their* advice is almost a pleasure (if advice can ever be a pleasure).

It's the kind of advice that we would give in a first-day lecture if we could express it as well as they do. If you read Roberts and Macrorie with care and take to heart their advice, your experiences in composition will likely be softer, smoother, and altogether more satisfying.

But enough for now. Your instructor will have much more to say about theses, developmentally mixed essays, and the contents of at least one of the two opening essays. We just didn't want you to jump cold into the book.

How to Say Nothing in Five Hundred Words

Paul Roberts

In English Syntax *(1954) and* Patterns of English *(1956), Paul Roberts turned the work of descriptive linguists into practical English textbooks for the classroom. The following essay, a chapter from* Understanding English *(1958), is full of sensible and appropriate advice for freshman writers.*

Nothing About Something

It's Friday afternoon, and you have almost survived another week of classes. You are just looking forward dreamily to the week end when the English instructor says: "For Monday you will turn in a five-hundred word composition on college football."

Well, that puts a good big hole in the week end. You don't have any strong views on college football one way or the other. You get rather excited during the season and go to all the home games and find it rather more fun than not. On the other hand, the class has been reading Robert Hutchins in the anthology and perhaps Shaw's "Eighty-Yard Run," and from the class discussion you have got the idea that the instructor thinks college football is for the birds. You are no fool, you. You can figure out what side to take.

After dinner you get out the portable typewriter that you got for high school graduation. You might as well get it over with and enjoy Saturday and Sunday. Five hundred words is about two double-spaced pages with normal margins. You put in a sheet of paper, think up a title, and you're off:

Why College Football Should Be Abolished

College football should be abolished because it's bad for the school and also bad for the players. The players are so busy practicing that they don't have any time for their studies.

This, you feel, is a mighty good start. The only trouble is that it's only thirty-two words. You still have four hundred and sixty-eight to go, and you've pretty well exhausted the subject. It comes to you that you do your best thinking in the morning, so you put away the typewriter and go to the movies. But the next morning you have to do your washing and some math problems, and in the afternoon you go to the game. The English instructor turns up too, and you wonder if you've taken the right side after all. Saturday night you have a date, and Sunday morning you have to go to church. (You shouldn't let English assignments interfere with your religion.) What with one thing and another, it's ten o'clock Sunday night before you get out the typewriter again. You make a pot of coffee and start to fill out your views on college football. Put a little meat on the bones.

Why College Football Should Be Abolished

In my opinion, it seems to me that college football should be abolished. The reason why I think this to be true is because I feel that football is bad for the colleges in nearly every respect. As Robert Hutchins says in his article in our anthology in which he discusses college football, it would be better if the colleges had race horses and had races with one another, because then the horses would not have to attend classes. I firmly agree with Mr. Hutchins on this point, and I am sure that many other students would agree too.

One reason why it seems to me that college football is bad is that it has become too commercial. In the olden times when people played football just for the fun of it, maybe college football was all right, but they do not play football just for the fun of it now as they used to in the old days. Nowadays college football is what you might call a big business. Maybe this is not true at all schools, and I don't think it is especially true here at State, but certainly this is the case at most colleges and universities in America nowadays, as Mr. Hutchins points out in his very interesting article. Actually the coaches and alumni go around to the high schools and offer the high school stars large salaries to come to their colleges and play football for them. There was one case where a high school star was offered a convertible if he would play football for a certain college.

Another reason for abolishing college football is that it is bad for the players. They do not have time to get a college education, because they are so busy playing football. A football player has to practice every afternoon from three to six, and then he is so tired that he can't concentrate on his studies. He just feels like dropping off to sleep after dinner, and then the next day he goes to his classes without having studied and maybe he fails the test.

(Good ripe stuff so far, but you're still a hundred and fifty-one words from home. One more push.)

Also I think college football is bad for the colleges and the universities because not very many students get to participate in it. Out of a college of ten thousand students only seventy-five or a hundred play football, if that many. Football is what you might call a spectator sport. That means that most people go to watch it but do not play it themselves.

(Four hundred and fifteen. Well, you still have the conclusion, and when you retype it, you can make the margins a little wider.)

These are the reasons why I agree with Mr. Hutchins that college football should be abolished in American colleges and universities.

On Monday you turn it in, moderately hopeful, and on Friday it 4 comes back marked "weak in content" and sporting a big "D."

This essay is exaggerated a little, not much. The English instructor 5 will recognize it as reasonably typical of what an assignment on college football will bring in. He knows that nearly half of the class will contrive in five hundred words to say that college football is too commercial and bad for the players. Most of the other half will inform him that college football builds character and prepares one for life and brings prestige to the school. As he reads paper after paper all saying the same thing in almost the same words, all bloodless, five hundred words dripping out of nothing, he wonders how he allowed himself to get trapped into teaching English when he might have had a happy and interesting life as an electrician or a confidence man.

Well, you may ask, what can you do about it? The subject is one on 6 which you have few convictions and little information. Can you be expected to make a dull subject interesting? As a matter of fact, this is precisely what you are expected to do. This is the writer's essential task. All subjects, except sex, are dull until somebody makes them interesting. The writer's job is to find the argument, the approach, the angle, the wording that will take the reader with him. This is seldom easy, and it is particularly hard in subjects that have been much discussed: College Football, Fraternities, Popular Music, Is Chivalry Dead?, and the like. You will feel that there is nothing you can do with such subjects except repeat the old bromides. But there are some things you can do which will make your papers, if not throbbingly alive, at least less insufferably tedious than they might otherwise be.

Avoid the Obvious Content

Say the assignment is college football. Say that you've decided to 7 be against it. Begin by putting down the arguments that come to your mind: it is too commercial, it takes the students' minds off their studies, it is hard on the players, it makes the university a kind of circus instead of an intellectual center, for most schools it is financially ruin-ous. Can you think of any more arguments just off hand? All right. Now when you write your paper, *make sure that you don't use any of the material on this list.* If these are the points that leap to your mind, they will leap to everyone else's too, and whether you get a "C" or a "D" may depend on whether the instructor reads your paper early when he is fresh and tolerant or late, when the sentence "In my opinion, college football has become too commercial," inexorably repeated, has brought him to the brink of lunacy.

8   Be against college football for some reason or reasons of your own. If they are keen and perceptive ones, that's splendid. But even if they are trivial or foolish or indefensible, you are still ahead so long as they are not everybody else's reasons too. Be against it because the colleges don't spend enough money on it to make it worth while, because it is bad for the characters of the spectators, because the players are forced to attend classes, because the football stars hog all the beautiful women, because it competes with baseball and is therefore un-Amer-ican and possibly Communist inspired. There are lots of more or less unused reasons for being against college football.

9   Sometimes it is a good idea to sum up and dispose of the trite and conventional points before going on to your own. This has the advan-tage of indicating to the reader that you are going to be neither trite nor conventional. Something like this:

> We are often told that college football should be abolished because it has become too commercial or because it is bad for the players. These argu-ments are no doubt very cogent, but they don't really go to the heart of the matter.

Then you go to the heart of the matter.

Take the Less Usual Side

10   One rather simple way of getting interest into your paper is to take the side of the argument that most of the citizens will want to avoid. If the assignment is an essay on dogs, you can, if you choose, explain that dogs are faithful and lovable companions, intelligent, useful as guardians of the house and protectors of children, indispensable in police work—in short, when all is said and done, man's best friends. Or you can suggest that those big brown eyes conceal, more often than not, a vacuity of mind and an inconstancy of purpose; that the dogs you have known most intimately have been mangy, ill-tempered brutes, incapable of instruction; and that only your nobility of mind and fear of arrest prevent you from kicking the flea-ridden animals when you pass them on the street.

Naturally, personal convictions will sometimes dictate your 11
approach. If the assigned subject is "Is Methodism Rewarding to the
Individual?" and you are a pious Methodist, you have really no choice.
But few assigned subjects, if any, will fall in this category. Most of
them will lie in broad areas of discussion with much to be said on both
sides. They are intellectual exercises and it is legitimate to argue now
one way and now another, as debaters do in similar circumstances.
Always take the side that looks to you hardest, least defensible. It will
almost always turn out to be easier to write interestingly on that side.

This general advice applies where you have a choice of subjects. If 12
you are to choose among "The Value of Fraternities" and "My Favorite
High School Teacher" and "What I Think About Beetles," by all means
plump for the beetles. By the time the instructor gets to your paper,
he will be up to his ears in tedious tales about the French teacher at
Bloombury High and assertions about how fraternities build character
and prepare one for life. Your views on beetles, whatever they are, are
bound to be a refreshing change.

Don't worry too much about figuring out what the instructor thinks 13
about the subject so that you can cuddle up with him. Chances are his
views are no stronger than yours. If he does have convictions and you
oppose them, his problem is to keep from grading you higher than
you deserve in order to show he is not biased. This doesn't mean that
you should always cantankerously dissent from what the instructor
says; that gets tiresome too. And if the subject assigned is "My Pet
Peeve," do not begin, "My pet peeve is the English instructor who
assigns papers on 'my pet peeve.'" This was still funny during the War
of 1812, but it has sort of lost its edge since then. It is in general good
manners to avoid personalities.

Slip Out of Abstraction

If you will study the essay on college football . . . you will perceive 14
that one reason for its appalling dullness is that it never gets down to
particulars. It is just a series of not very glittering generalities: "football is bad for the colleges," "it has become too commercial," "football
is a big business," "it is bad for the players," and so on. Such round
phrases thudding against the reader's brain are unlikely to convince
him, though they may well render him unconscious.

If you want the reader to believe that college football is bad for the 15
players, you have to do more than say so. You have to display the evil.
Take your roommate, Alfred Simkins, the second-string center. Picture
poor old Alfy coming home from football practice every evening,
bruised and aching, agonizingly tired, scarcely able to shovel the
mashed potatoes into his mouth. Let us see him staggering up to the
room, getting out his econ textbook, peering desperately at it with his

good eye, falling asleep and failing the test in the morning. Let us share his unbearable tension as Saturday draws near. Will he fail, be demoted, lose his monthly allowance, be forced to return to the coal mines? And if he succeeds, what will be his reward? Perhaps a slight ripple of applause when the third-string center replaces him, a moment of elation in the locker room if the team wins, of despair if it loses. What will he look back on when he graduates from college? Toil and torn ligaments. And what will be his future? He is not good enough for pro football, and he is too obscure and weak in econ to succeed in stocks and bonds. College football is tearing the heart from Alfy Simkins and, when it finishes with him, will callously toss aside the shattered hulk.

16 This is no doubt a weak enough argument for the abolition of college football, but it is a sight better than saying, in three or four variations, that college football (in your opinion) is bad for the players.

17 Look at the work of any professional writer and notice how constantly he is moving from the generality, the abstract statement, to the concrete example, the facts and figures, the illustration. If he is writing on juvenile delinquency, he does not just tell you that juveniles are (it seems to him) delinquent and that (in his opinion) something should be done about it. He shows you juveniles being delinquent, tearing up movie theatres in Buffalo, stabbing high school principals in Dallas, smoking marijuana in Palo Alto. And more than likely he is moving toward some specific remedy, not just a general wringing of the hands.

18 It is no doubt possible to be *too* concrete, too illustrative or anecdotal, but few inexperienced writers err this way. For most the soundest advice is to be seeking always for the picture, to be always turning general remarks into seeable examples. Don't say, "Sororities teach girls the social graces." Say "Sorority life teaches a girl how to carry on a conversation while pouring tea, without sloshing the tea into the saucer." Don't say, "I like certain kinds of popular music very much." Say, "Whenever I hear Gerber Spinklittle play 'Mississippi Man' on the trombone, my socks creep up my ankles."

Get Rid of Obvious Padding

19 The student toiling away at his weekly English theme is too often tormented by a figure: five hundred words. How, he asks himself, is he to achieve this staggering total? Obviously by never using one word when he can somehow work in ten.

20 He is therefore seldom content with a plain statement like "Fast driving is dangerous." This has only four words in it. He takes thought, and the sentence becomes:

In my opinion, fast driving is dangerous.

Better, but he can do better still:

> In my opinion, fast driving would seem to be rather dangerous.

If he is really adept, it may come out:

> In my humble opinion, though I do not claim to be an expert on this complicated subject, fast driving, in most circumstances, would seem to be rather dangerous in many respects, or at least so it would seem to me.

Thus four words have been turned into forty, and not an iota of content has been added.

Now this is a way to go about reaching five hundred words, and if you are content with a "D" grade, it is as good a way as any. But if you aim higher, you must work differently. Instead of stuffing your sentences with straw, you must try steadily to get rid of the padding, to make your sentences lean and tough. If you are really working at it, your first draft will greatly exceed the required total, and then you will work it down, thus:

> It is thought in some quarters that fraternities do not contribute as much as might be expected to campus life.

> Some people think that fraternities contribute little to campus life.

> The average doctor who practices in small towns or in the country must toil night and day to heal the sick.

> Most country doctors work long hours.

> When I was a little girl, I suffered from shyness and embarrassment in the presence of others.

> I was a shy little girl.

> It is absolutely necessary for the person employed as a marine fireman to give the matter of steam pressure his undivided attention at all times.

> The fireman has to keep his eye on the steam gauge.

You may ask how you can arrive at five hundred words at this rate. Simply. You dig up more real content. Instead of taking a couple of obvious points off the surface of the topic and then circling warily around them for six paragraphs, you work in and explore, figure out the details. You illustrate. You say that fast driving is dangerous, and then you prove it. How long does it take to stop a car at forty and at eighty? How far can you see at night? What happens when a tire blows? What happens in a head-on collision at fifty miles an hour?

Pretty soon your paper will be full of broken glass and blood and headless torsos, and reaching five hundred words will not really be a problem.

Call a Fool a Fool

23   Some of the padding in freshman themes is to be blamed not on anxiety about the word minimum but on excessive timidity. The student writes, "In my opinion, the principal of my high school acted in ways that I believe every unbiased person would have to call foolish." This isn't exactly what he means. What he means is, "My high school principal was a fool." If he was a fool, call him a fool. Hedging the thing about with "in-my-opinion's" and "it-seems-to-me's" and "as-I-see-it's" and "at-least-from-my-point-of-view's" gains you nothing. Delete these phrases whenever they creep into your paper.

24   The student's tendency to hedge stems from a modesty that in other circumstances would be commendable. He is, he realizes, young and inexperienced, and he half suspects that he is dopey and fuzzy-minded beyond the average. Probably only too true. But it doesn't help to announce your incompetence six times in every paragraph. Decide what you want to say and say it as vigorously as possible, without apology and in plain words.

25   Linguistic diffidence can take various forms. One is what we call *euphemism*. This is the tendency to call a spade "a certain garden implement" or women's underwear "unmentionables." It is stronger in some eras than others and in some people than others but it always operates more or less in subjects that are touchy or taboo: death, sex, madness, and so on. Thus we shrink from saying "He died last night" but say instead "passed away," "left us," "joined his Maker," "went to his reward." Or we try to take off the tension with a lighter cliché: "kicked the bucket," "cashed in his chips," "handed in his dinner pail." We have found all sorts of ways to avoid saying *mad*: "mentally ill," "touched," "not quite right upstairs," "feeble-minded," "innocent," "simple," "off his trolley," "not in his right mind." Even such a now plain word as *insane* began as a euphemism with the meaning "not healthy."

26   Modern science, particularly psychology, contributes many poly-syllables in which we can wrap our thoughts and blunt their force. To many writers there is no such thing as a bad schoolboy. Schoolboys are maladjusted or unoriented or misunderstood or in need of guidance or lacking in continued success toward satisfactory integration of the personality as a social unit, but they are never bad. Psychology no doubt makes us better men or women, more sympathetic and tolerant, but it doesn't make writing any easier. Had Shakespeare been confronted with psychology, "To be or not to be" might have come out,

"To continue as a social unit or not to do so. That is the personality problem. Whether 'tis a better sign of integration at the conscious level to display a psychic tolerance toward the maladjustments and repressions induced by one's lack of orientation in one's environment or—" But Hamlet would never have finished the soliloquy.

Writing in the modern world, you cannot altogether avoid modern   27 jargon. Nor, in an effort to get away from euphemism, should you salt your paper with four-letter words. But you can do much if you will mount guard against those roundabout phrases, those echoing polysyllables that tend to slip into your writing to rob it of its crispness and force.

Beware of the Pat Expression

Other things being equal, avoid phrases like "other things being   28 equal." Those sentences that come to you whole, or in two or three doughy lumps, are sure to be bad sentences. They are no creation of yours but pieces of common thought floating in the community soup.

Pat expressions are hard, often impossible, to avoid, because they   29 come too easily to be noticed and seem too necessary to be dispensed with. No writer avoids them altogether, but good writers avoid them more often than poor writers.

By "pat expressions" we mean such tags as "to all practical intents   30 and purposes," "the pure and simple truth," "from where I sit," "the time of his life," "to the ends of the earth," "in the twinkling of an eye," "as sure as you're born," "over my dead body," "under cover of darkness," "took the easy way out," " when all is said and done," "told him time and time again," "parted the best of friends," "stand up and be counted," "gave him the best years of her life," "worked her fingers to the bone." Like other clichés, these expressions were once forceful. Now we should use them only when we can't possibly think of anything else.

Some pat expressions stand like a wall between the writer and   31 thought. Such a one is "the American way of life." Many student writers feel that when they have said that something accords with the American way of life or does not they have exhausted the subject. Actually, they have stopped at the highest level of abstraction. The American way of life is the complicated set of bonds between a hundred and eighty million ways. All of us know this when we think about it, but the tag phrase too often keeps us from thinking about it.

So with many another phrase dear to the politician: "this great land   32 of ours," "the man in the street," "our national heritage." These may prove our patriotism or give a clue to our political beliefs, but otherwise they add nothing to the paper except words.

Colorful Words

33 The writer builds with words, and no builder uses a raw material more slippery and elusive and treacherous. A writer's work is a constant struggle to get the right word in the right place, to find that particular word that will convey his meaning exactly, that will persuade the reader or soothe him or startle or amuse him. He never succeeds altogether—sometimes he feels that he scarcely succeeds at all—but such successes as he has are what make the thing worth doing.

34 There is no book of rules for this game. One progresses through everlasting experiment on the basis of ever-widening experience. There are few useful generalizations that one can make about words as words, but there are perhaps a few.

35 Some words are what we call "colorful." By this we mean that they are calculated to produce a picture or induce an emotion. They are dressy instead of plain, specific instead of general, loud instead of soft. Thus, in place of "Her heart beat," we may write "Her heart *pounded, throbbed, fluttered, danced.*" Instead of "He sat in his chair," we may say, "He *lounged, sprawled, coiled.*" Instead of "It was hot," we may say, "It was *blistering, sultry, muggy, suffocating, steamy, wilting.*"

36 However, it should not be supposed that the fancy word is always better. Often it is as well to write "Her heart beat" or "It was hot" if that is all it did or all it was. Ages differ in how they like their prose. The nineteenth century liked it rich and smoky. The twentieth has usually preferred it lean and cool. The twentieth century writer, like all writers, is forever seeking the exact word, but he is wary of sounding feverish. He tends to pitch it low, to understate it, to throw it away. He knows that if he gets too colorful, the audience is likely to giggle.

37 See how this strikes you: "As the rich, golden glow of the sunset died away along the eternal western hills, Angela's limpid blue eyes looked softly and trustingly into Montague's flashing brown ones, and her heart pounded like a drum in time with the joyous song surging in her soul." Some people like that sort of thing, but most modern readers would say, "Good grief," and turn on the television.

Colored Words

38 Some words we would call not so much colorful as colored—that is, loaded with associations, good or bad. All words—except perhaps structure words—have associations of some sort. We have said that the meaning of a word is the sum of the contexts in which it occurs. When we hear a word, we hear with it an echo of all the situations in which we have heard it before.

In some words, these echoes are obvious and discussable. The word   39
mother, for example, has, for most people, agreeable associations.
When you hear *mother* you probably think of home, safety, love, food,
and various other pleasant things. If one writes, "She was like a
mother to me," he gets an effect which he would not get in "She was
like an aunt to me." The advertiser makes use of the associations of
mother by working it in when he talks about his product. The politician works it in when he talks about himself.

So also with such words as *home, liberty, fireside, contentment, patriot,*   40
tenderness, sacrifice, childlike, manly, bluff, limpid. All of these words are
loaded with favorable associations that would be rather hard to indicate in a straightforward definition. There is more than a literal difference between "They sat around the fireside" and "They sat around
the stove." They might have been equally warm and happy around
the stove, but *fireside* suggests leisure, grace, quiet tradition, congenial
company, and *stove* does not.

Conversely, some words have bad associations. *Mother* suggests   41
pleasant things, but *mother-in-law* does not. Many mothers-in-law are
heroically lovable and some mothers drink gin all day and beat their
children insensible, but these facts of life are beside the point. The
thing is that *mother* sounds good and *mother-in-law* does not.

Or consider the word *intellectual.* This would seem to be a compli-   42
mentary term, but in point of fact it is not, for it has picked up associations of impracticality and ineffectuality and general dopiness. So
also with such words as *liberal, reactionary, Communist, socialist, capitalist,*
radical, schoolteacher, truck driver, undertaker, operator, salesman, huckster,
speculator. These convey meanings on the literal level, but beyond
that—sometimes, in some places—they convey contempt on the part
of the speaker.

The question of whether to use loaded words or not depends on   43
what is being written. The scientist, the scholar, try to avoid them; for
the poet, the advertising writer, the public speaker, they are standard
equipment. But every writer should take care that they do not substitute for thought. If you write, "Anyone who thinks that is nothing but
a Socialist (or Communist or capitalist)" you have said nothing except
that you don't like people who think that, and such remarks are effective only with the most naïve readers. It is always a bad mistake to
think your readers more naïve than they really are.

Colorless Words

But probably most student writers come to grief not with words   44
that are colorful or those that are colored but with those that have no
color at all. A pet example is *nice*, a word we would find it hard to

dispense with in casual conversation but which is no longer capable of adding much to a description. Colorless words are those of such general meaning that in a particular sentence they mean nothing. Slang adjectives, like *cool* ("That's real cool") tend to explode all over the language. They are applied to everything, lose their original force, and quickly die.

45   Beware also of nouns of very general meaning, like *circumstances, cases, instances, aspects, factors, relationships, attitudes, eventualities,* etc. In most circumstances you will find that those cases of writing which contain too many instances of words like these will in this and other aspects have factors leading to unsatisfactory relationships with the reader resulting in unfavorable attitudes on his part and perhaps other eventualities, like a grade of "D." Notice also what "etc." means. It means "I'd like to make this list longer, but I can't think of any more examples."

Telling Truths

Ken Macrorie

Ken Macrorie, a past editor of College Composition and Communication, *is the author of a number of books on writing, including* Uptaught *(1970),* Telling Writing *(1970), and* Writing to Be Read *(revised second edition, 1976). The last book is the source for the following selection. It is made up of selections from Chapters 1 and 2, "The Language in You" and "Writing Freely." Our title, "Telling Truths," comes from one of the subtitles in Chapter 2.*

Thousands of persons in the United States believe they don't know 1 how to write well. But look at what children do. A third-grade girl writes:

> When mother fride my egg this morning it limbered out like corn surp. Then it got buggles. They went up, then went down, like breethen heavy.

The writer surprised the reader with an original use of the verb *limber*, meaning to become supple or flexible. She compared the movement of the egg to the slow spreading of corn syrup in a pan. She invented her own term, *buggles* (playing on *bubbles*), and showed she knew what she was talking about. She compactly described the movement of a frying egg. This passage is not only fresh and surprising but precise and true. It puts the reader there, watching the egg and feeling its action through his own experience, "like breethen heavy."

At times every young child makes memorable statements in writing 2 or speaking. But as he advances in school, his language turns ever duller and emptier. By the time he becomes a senior in high school, he is often submitting papers to his teacher which sound like this:

> I consider experience to be an important part in the process of learning. For example, in the case of an athlete, experience plays an important role. After each game, he tends to acquire more knowledge and proficiency, thereby

making him a better athlete. An athlete could also gain more knowledge by studying up on the sport, but it is doubtful if he could participate for the first time in sport with study alone and without experience and still do an adequate job.

The writer says nothing new—athletes learn by experience. And he does not put the reader there, watching a player bunt foul or tackle a halfback. A five-year-old boy at breakfast says, "The Rice Krispies are doing the dead man's float." He doesn't tell the reader anything new either, but he speaks originally. With the metaphor he puts the reader in the milk.

3   A second-grader told to quiet her feet in class said, "They're too Saturday to listen." She expected the listener to make the jump necessary to understand her metaphor. The boy writing about athletes expected nothing of his reader.

4   A sixth-grader wrote a letter to the custodian of a state park who had showed his class around:

Dear Mr. Lemmien,

I liked the trailer ride and the dips got my stomach. Thank you for everything.

Your Friend,
David Booth

David communicated a significant moment in five short words: "the dips got my stomach." The word *dips* gives the passage authority. The sentence is believable, unforgettable. None of the sentences in the writing about athletes carries as much meaning.

5   Young children do not always talk and write with such point and liveliness, but they do so often enough that their parents repeat their sayings and writings to other persons with delight. When these children grow up and become high school and college students, they seldom turn in writing that is memorable. Yet outside class, they often use language with power. A student poster for a dance reads:

35¢ Stag. 50¢ Drag.

Metaphor. Rhyme. Economy in words.

6   Entering the school cafeteria, a girl says that she can't see a clear table. Her friend answers:

I don't see one either. It's like looking for your best friend at the Rose Bowl on T.V.

At times you have spoken and written skillfully. You can rediscover your tongue—if you've lost it—and bring your writing to life. One way is to take the pressure off for a while. In schoolrooms where students have been asked to write freely, they have written like this:

I like to go fishing. But I don't like to touch the soft, elongated, repulsive nightcrawlers. They wiggle and contract themselves. Then I can't grab the one I want. Of all the other things in this world I can't stand, baiting the hook is the worst. It's like giving a shot. Sometimes the hook won't go through the worm's wrinkled, slimy body. Then I have to wiggle and force it. That's like stepping on a cockroach and hearing the bones crack, or piercing a stubborn earlobe.

Gertie Bax

The wooden bars on the chair look like prison bars as they reflect on the floor from the light. I was in trouble once and getting into trouble makes a person feel bad that it happened and that it never should have happened but it did and there is no way around. I had to sit in a room for three hours waiting, hoping that my brother would be all right and hoping the other boy was too, although from those minutes on, I knew I hated him. Only a chair, a desk, and a man saying, "I'll be back in about a half hour," which really became three. I had to sweat it out walking back and forth in the room with nothing to look at but four lousy walls, I wanted to get out. I wanted them to come and get me out of there. Thoughts passed through my mind as I sat there in the only chair. Chairs can be made to look like different things when their shadow is lying on the floor. The chair over there in the corner looks like part of a ladder. The chair in the police station was uncomfortable and I couldn't sit in it. It was a cheap looking chair in a cheap looking room meant for people who are wrong.

(Name withheld)

A girl once told her teacher that she couldn't write any kind of paper because she had been raised in a Polish-speaking home and couldn't compose sentences in idiomatic English. Encouraged to write freely of what she cared about, she wrote this of her father:

The only difference between him and a lion is that a lion does not laugh. Upon meeting up with him one most naturally will see the strict lines on his face and his mouth set just so. He may appear tough, but he also has the devil in him. His appearance is stirring. He looks like a foreign foreigner. His voice is low and scary. It really frightens my friends, even male ones. Sometime when I call to say I may be home later, he answers the phone with a deep, husky, and broken "Haaallooo" and I feel I should apologize for calling.

(Name withheld)

Outside of class, and in the years of childhood, you and every other person have at times expressed yourself forcefully, with art. It is nonsense to say you cannot do that again when you want to. And you can learn to write honestly and truthfully, too.

7   All good writers speak in honest voices and tell the truth. For example, here is Eudora Welty in her novel *Delta Wedding* writing about India, a girl of nine, watching her Uncle George make up with his wife after a quarrel:

> Just now they kissed, with India coming up close on her toes to see if she could tell yet what there was about a kiss.

Asked what makes students write badly, Eudora Welty once said:

> The trouble with bad student writing is the trouble with all bad writing. It is not serious, and it does not tell the truth.

This is the first requirement for good writing: truth; not *the* truth (whoever knows surely what that is?), but some kind of truth—a connection between the things written about, the words used in the writing, and the author's real experience in the world he knows well—whether in fact or dream or imagination.

8   Part of growing up is learning to tell lies, big and little, sophisticated and crude, conscious and unconscious. The good writer differs from the bad one in that he constantly tries to shake the habit. He holds himself to the highest standard of truth telling. Often he emulates children, who tell the truth so easily, partly because they do not sense how truth will shock their elders.

9   A seventh-grade boy once wrote:

> I'd like to be a car. You get to go all over and get to go through mud puddles without getting yelled at . . . that's what I'd like to be.

The style of this passage is not distinguished. *Get* is here not a key word and yet it is employed three times. The writer switches confusingly from *I* to *you*. The language of the passage is not exciting. No memorable pictures are projected. Yet the statement strikes with force because the boy speaks truly: his shoes and the tires of the car do become muddy. He gets yelled at by his parents and the car does not. The comparison surprises. Its candor draws a smile from the reader.

I never think I have hit it hard unless it rebounds.

Samuel Johnson

Any person trying to write honestly and accurately soon finds he   10
has already learned a hundred ways of writing falsely. As a child he
spoke and wrote honestly most of the time, but when he reaches fifteen, honesty and truth come harder. The pressures on his ego are
greater. He reaches for impressive language; often it is pretentious and
phony. He imitates the style of adults, who are often bad writers themselves. They ask questions. So he asks questions in his writing: "Did
you ever think what might have happened to South Africa if the Boer
War had not been fought?" A false question. The writer knows most—
if not all—of his readers have not thought of this possibility. However
well meant—a false question. In class this person is anxious to impress
the teacher, so he begins his paper by saying:

> The automobile is a mechanism fascinating to everyone in all its diverse
> manifestations and in every conceivable kind of situation or circumstance.

His first remark is simply untrue. Cars do not fascinate everyone.

In this paper the writer has placed his vocabulary on exhibit *(mech-*   11
anism, diverse, manifestations, conceivable, situation, circumstance) rather
than put it to work. An honest writer makes every word pull its
weight. In this writer's opening sentence, the words *kind of* are not
working at all. They could be dropped with no loss. What does he
mean by "all the diverse manifestations" of a car? Cars don't occur in
manifestations but in models. If the cars he is referring to are custom-
made and not strictly speaking "models," then he should say he is
writing about hybrid cars. At the opening of his paper, his reader has
no inkling that he is talking about home-made cars. And nothing
could be more untrue than the thought conveyed by the last phrase—
that everyone finds cars fascinating "in every conceivable kind of situation or circumstance." When the valves need regrinding at 17,000
miles at a cost of $125.00, even the car lover finds his loved one
repulsive.

Compare this writer's pretentious and untrue statement about cars   12
with this account:

> Thundering down a Northern Michigan highway at night I am separated
> from the rest of the world. The windows of the car are all rolled down and
> the wind makes a deep rumbling as the car rises and falls with the dips in
> the pavement. The white center lines come out of the darkness ahead into
> the beams of the headlights only to disappear again under the front edge
> of the hood. The lights also pick up trees, fenceposts, and an occasional deer

or raccoon standing by the roadside, but like the white lines they come into view only for a few seconds and then are lost in the blackness behind me. The only signs I have that any world exists outside the range of the headlights are the continuous cheerping and buzzing of the crickets and the smells from farms and sulphur pits I pass. But the rushing wind soon clears out these odors, leaving me by myself again to listen to the quickly passing crickets I will never see. The faint green lights and the red bar on the dashboard tell me I'm plunging ahead at 90 m.p.h.; I put more pressure on the pedal under my foot; the bar moves up to 100 . . . 110. The lines flash by faster and the roar of the wind drowns out the noise of the crickets and the night. I am flying through. I can feel the vibrations of the road through the steering wheel. I turn the wheel slightly for the gradual curve ahead and then back again for the long straightaway. I press the pedal to the floor and at the same time reach down to touch the buttons on my left that will roll up the windows for more speed; the bar reads 115 . . . 120, buried. With the windows up, the only sound is the high-pitched moan from the engine as it labors to keep the rest of the machine hurtling blindly ahead like a runaway express train. Only I have the power to control it. I flick on the brights to advance my scope of vision and the white lines come out of the black further up ahead, yet because of the speed, they're out of sight even faster than before. I am detached from the rest of the world as it blurs past. I am alone.

Henry Hall James

This boy may have been driving at an immorally high speed—even for a relatively uninhabited region—but he was writing morally, because he was staying true to the feel of his experience. Writing this way requires a quick jump in the car and a zooming away before one remembers all the driving habits he has picked up watching bad older drivers. Try writing for truth.

Never say that you feel a thing unless you feel it distinctly; and if you do not feel it distinctly, say at once that you do not as yet quite know your own mind.

Samuel Butler

CHAPTER TWO

Description

There is a common misconception that good writing is the result of either an exciting subject ("Last week I went skydiving . . .") or a strongly stated position ("I hate politicians . . .") or frenzied words and punctuation marks. ("Wow! Last week I read a book that was super!")

This is not the case at all. A trip to the dentist can be absorbing if the writer can help readers see it clearly enough—or can help them hear the whine and feel the heat of a high-speed drill as it burrows its way into a smoking nerve ending. On the other hand, something as potentially exciting as a crash landing in a Boeing 747 can be paralyzingly dull if the writer's powers of observation and descriptive skills are too feeble to turn that experience into graphic images.

Description is the lifeblood of all kinds of writing, from letters to mom to freshman themes and business reports. And it underlies most of the methods of development we discuss in this book, from narration to classification.

Image Making Through Description

Without precise and vivid description, prose is usually lifeless and unclear. Buddy Hackett, the well-known comedian, once said that the effectiveness of a joke usually depends on the comedian's ability to get the audience to visualize the joke's narrative details *before* the punch line arrives. In the same way, the effectiveness of a piece of prose usually rests on the writer's skill in getting readers to see (or hear, feel, smell, taste) what they are reading. Consider the following sentence:

She looked at the animal.

Now try to visualize that sentence. If you are having trouble, it's not surprising. The writer hasn't helped you form any images in your mind. Naturally, you have no idea what "she" looks like, and you can't possibly visualize "animal," because we can see only particular kinds of animals. Now let's make the sentence a bit more precise:

> She stared at the brown bear.

Now the image is beginning to come into focus because the writer has used the more specific verb "stared" instead of the vague "looked." And he has replaced the abstract noun "animal" with the more specific "brown bear." Let's continue to move toward more specificity:

> The tiny girl stared in horror at the charging bloody-mouthed grizzly bear.

As you can see (in your mind's eye), the image now snaps into focus because the writer has shaped the image you see through his use of specific words.

Types of Description

Description that gives the impression of being detached and impersonal is called objective description. All those who aspire to objectivity in their approach to problems—historians, scientists, sociologists, business executives—usually try to write a prose that matches their objective approach. The ideal, never reached of course, is to record with the objectivity of a camera. The following is a relatively objective description of a buffalo hunter's shooting technique, taken from John Madson's essay "On the Trail of the Curly Cows" (reprinted in this chapter):

> Since Frank's favorite Sharps weighed more than 16 pounds and had a 32-inch barrel, he always shot from crossed rest sticks in a kneeling or sitting position. For one thing, it was dead steady. For another, it put the rifle up over sagebrush and other obstructions. Frank also felt that the sound of a heavy rifle fired just above the ground carried much farther than it did if the muzzle was 30 inches higher.

The absence of colored words (words loaded with positive or negative associations) and Madson's hesitancy to describe his personal reactions to the scene show that he was more interested in describing exactly the way it was than in giving his reactions to the way it was.

By contrast, the writer of a subjective description doesn't attempt to be detached and impersonal. He records not only the scene "out there," but he lets his readers know his reactions to it. A subjective description is thus more like an impressionistic painting than a photograph.

In this subjective description from Edward Abbey's "The Spadefoot Toad" (reprinted in this chapter), the author not only describes reality but interprets it for us as well:

> . . . when the pool dries up they [toads] dig into the sediment as their parents did before, making burrows which they seal with mucus in order to preserve that moisture necessary to life. There they wait, day after day, week after week, in patient spadefoot torpor, perhaps listening—we can imagine—for the sound of raindrops pattering at last on the earthen crust above their heads.

A strictly objective description of the same scene, such as a biologist might write in a scientific journal, might look something like this:

> . . . when the pool dries up, the surviving spadefoot toads burrow into the sediment and seal the opening with mucus to preserve their bodies' moisture. If it rains within two months (the limit of their hibernation), they emerge.

Notice that in the second paragraph the phrases "day after day, week after week" have been removed; since they describe the slow passing of time from the point of view of the toads, they lack the kind of objectivity that a biologist needs. Notice too that the adjective "patient," used to describe the toads' response to their hibernation, is also missing; it conveys something of the author's attitude—sympathy in this case—toward the toads. Finally, notice that the phrase "perhaps listening" is also missing. An objective description does not imagine what might be happening; it describes what *is* happening.

Most prose, naturally, is a mix of objective and subjective description. But certain assignments—a report, a newspaper article, a research paper—demand objective description. Other assignments—a book review, a personal essay, a movie review—allow for more subjectivity in descriptive passages.

How to Write Vivid Descriptions

1. *Observe carefully the thing you are describing.*

2. *Search out telling details.* Don't dwell on the obvious, what the reader will probably see clearly for himself. Instead, describe the vivid and the peculiar detail. In describing a cat by the name of Fluffy, for

instance, pass over quickly those details that Fluffy shares with other cats; go on to those things that make Fluffy unique—the scar on his left ear, the hesitant way he sniffs his food every morning, the snarls he gets in his tummy fur, his bent tail.

3. *Avoid the general and the abstract by using concrete and specific words.* As the poet Ezra Pound once advised writers, "Go in fear of abstractions." Concrete details are those that make a special appeal to the senses. "The thick, gassy rotten-egg smell of an outhouse" is concrete language; "the bad-smelling outhouse" is not. Specific language points to particular things: Cokes, blue-tailed flies, elm trees, mackinaw coats, penny-loafers. "The bird died" is not specific language; "the sparrow tumbled backward off its perch, and a trickle of blood stained its white breast feathers" is. "Walk" is a general word; "stroll," "mince," "trudge," and "saunter" are specific words. (See Paul Roberts' discussion of colorful words in his essay, "How to Say Nothing in Five Hundred Words" in Chapter 1.)

4. *Use figurative language when what you're describing is particularly difficult to describe or when you want to make a special appeal to the senses.* How cold is it? It is colder than a _____. If you can fill in the blank with a fresh, vivid image that suggests how cold it is, you have aided readers by clarifying your concept of coldness.

A word of warning. Description is not used as heavily as it once was. Novelists and essayists in the 19th century didn't hesitate to stop their narratives or arguments to describe, in great detail, a verdant meadow. If you do that today you are apt to wear out your readers' ability or inclination to form images. Readers will likely find themselves saying, "OK, OK, let's get on with it, please!" So, use description sparingly, focus on the telling detail, and weave your descriptions into the points you are developing. You'll do fine.

MODEL DESCRIPTION PARAGRAPH

The '51 Merc

After a couple of years, The Kid has managed to pile on mountains of customizing goodies. The grille is out, replaced by a '53 Chevy bar with six added bumperettes. Duals are installed, with twin Belonds rapping off every time he lifts his foot from the Moon "barefoot" gas pedal. Frenched headlights and a flame job are there, along with a shaved deck, Porta walls and Cruiser Skirts with razor blades carefully positioned behind the release handles to maim any Midnight Auto Store shoppers.

He's also made inroads toward excellence in the engine compartment. A set of warped aluminum Edelbrock heads with chrome acorn head bolts now grace the flathead V-8. In addition, a draft notice to another Road Rebel has resulted in the bequeathal of an Offenhauser dual-pot manifold with twin Stromberg 97's. A Flame Thrower ignition, SW electric juice pump and burnished copper radiator crouch under the Blue-Coraled hood. The Merc is now a son-of-a-bitch to start and overheats every six miles which is okay since it's only getting seven miles to the gallon and is costing The Kid a fortune just to cruise the drive-ins.

By William Jeanes; reprinted from Car and Driver Magazine. *Copyright* © *1972 Ziff-Davis Publishing Co.*

ANALYSIS

One way of enhancing descriptive passages is to name specific things—bellybutton lint, Garfield the cat, the Shroud of Turin, and so forth. William Jeanes' paragraph on the custom work of The Kid's '51 Merc relies heavily, as you see, on specific brand names.

Even the unfamiliar brands in Jeanes' paragraph—those Edelbrock heads and Stromberg 97's—accomplish their purpose by reinforcing the dominant impression of the paragraph: that The Kid's Merc is chock-full of carefully chosen, terribly expensive "customizing goodies." Of course, when you can use brand names that your readers will recognize—Jensen car speakers, Casio digital watches, and Bubble Yum—they will see even more clearly what you are describing.

ASSIGNMENT

Write a paragraph in which you describe, through brand names and other specific and concrete words, a person you know. Select your details carefully so that you communicate a single, dominant idea about the person. Perhaps you want to leave the reader with the impression that your subject is brand-conscious or non-brand-conscious or sloppy or obsessively neat or preppy or hip or punkish or nerdish or what have you. A reminder: Don't try to force your adjectives into carrying the weight of your description.

The Spadefoot Toad

Edward Abbey

Edward Abbey, one of America's finest nature writers, usually has in mind more than lyrical descriptions of sand and bugs—as you will see from his description of the spadefoot toad in the following essay. This selection comes from Desert Solitaire, *a book of reminiscences of a season that Abbey spent as a park ranger in the Arches National Monument in Utah.*

1   After the storms pass and the flash floods have dumped their loads of silt into the Colorado, leaving the streambeds as arid as they were before, it is still possible to find rainwater in the desert. All over the slickrock country there are natural cisterns or potholes, tubs, tanks, and basins sculptured in the soft sandstone by the erosive force of weathering, wind and sand. Many of them serve as little catchment basins during rain and a few may contain water for days or even weeks after a storm, the length of time depending on the shape and depth of the hole and the consequent rate of evaporation.

2   Often far from any spring, these temporary pools attract doves, ravens and other birds, and deer and coyotes; you, too, if you know where to look or find one by luck, can slake your thirst and fill your water gourd. Such pools may be found in what seem like the most improbable places: out on the desolate White Rim below Grandview Point, for example, or on top of the elephant-back dome above the Double Arch. At Toroweap in Grand Canyon I found a deep tank of clear sweet water almost over my head, countersunk in the summit of a sandstone bluff which overhung my campsite by a hundred feet. A week after rain there was still enough water there to fill my needs; hard to reach, it was well worth the effort. The Bedouin know what I mean.

3   The rain-filled potholes, set in naked rock, are usually devoid of visible plant life but not of animal life. In addition to the inevitable microscopic creatures there may be certain amphibians like the spadefoot toad. This little animal lives through dry spells in a state of estivation under the dried-up sediment in the bottom of a hole. When the

rain comes, if it comes, he emerges from the mud singing madly in his fashion, mates with the handiest female and fills the pool with a swarm of tadpoles, most of them doomed to a most ephemeral existence. But a few survive, mature, become real toads, and when the pool dries up they dig into the sediment as their parents did before, making burrows which they seal with mucus in order to preserve that moisture necessary to life. There they wait, day after day, week after week, in patient spadefoot torpor, perhaps listening—we can imagine—for the sound of raindrops pattering at last on the earthen crust above their heads. If it comes in time the glorious cycle is repeated; if not, this particular colony of *Bufonidae* is reduced eventually to dust, a burden on the wind.

Rain and puddles bring out other amphibia, even in the desert. It's 4 a strange, stirring, but not uncommon thing to come on a pool at night, after an evening of thunder and lightning and a bit of rainfall, and see the frogs clinging to the edge of their impermanent pond, bodies immersed in water but heads out, all croaking away in tricky counterpoint. They are windbags: with each croak the pouch under the frog's chin swells like a bubble, then collapses.

Why do they sing? What do they have to sing about? Somewhat 5 apart from one another, separated by roughly equal distances, facing outward from the water, they clank and croak all through the night with tireless perseverance. To human ears their music has a bleak, dismal, tragic quality, dirgelike rather than jubilant. It may nevertheless be the case that these small beings are singing not only to claim their stake in the pond, not only to attract a mate, but also out of spontaneous love and joy, a contrapuntal choral celebration of the coolness and wetness after weeks of desert fire, for love of their own existence, however brief it may be, and for joy in the common life.

Has joy any survival value in the operations of evolution? I suspect 6 that it does; I suspect that the morose and fearful are doomed to quick extinction. Where there is no joy there can be no courage; and without courage all other virtues are useless. Therefore the frogs, the toads, keep on singing even though we know, if they don't, that the sound of their uproar must surely be luring all the snakes and ringtail cats and kit foxes and coyotes and great horned owls toward the scene of their happiness.

What then? A few of the little amphibians will continue their meta- 7 morphosis by way of the nerves and tissues of one of the higher animals, in which process the joy of one becomes the contentment of the second. Nothing is lost, except an individual consciousness here and there, a trivial perhaps even illusory phenomenon. The rest survive, mate, multiply, burrow, estivate, dream, and rise again. The rains will come, the potholes shall be filled. Again. And again. And again.

Questions About Meaning

1. Why does Abbey think the frogs and toads sing after a rain?
2. Why, from an individual frog's point of view, shouldn't he sing?
3. What emotion does Abbey believe enhances one's chances of survival?
4. What does Abbey mean in paragraph 2 when he says, "The Bedouin know what I mean"?

Matters of Technique

1. Abbey obviously had in mind an idea *about* the toads when he sat down to write his essay. What was that idea, or thesis? That is, sum up in your own words Abbey's thesis.
2. Writers usually place their thesis in their first paragraph. Why do you suppose Abbey begins with description and waits till later to discuss his thesis?
3. Locate a sentence in Abbey's essay that comes closest to summing up his essay.
4. Where does Abbey turn from precise description to philosophic speculation? What would Abbey have lost if he had begun with philosophic speculation?
5. Turn sentence 2 of paragraph 4 into a general statement. Now compare your general statement with Abbey's more specific one. Your sentence is probably shorter. Why do you suppose that Abbey sacrificed brevity for precise, though lengthy, description?
6. Poetic use of language occurs often in prose when there is a reason. Where does this occur in the last paragraph? What effect is Abbey trying for?
7. Reverse the sentence structure of the first sentence in paragraph 1. Begin your sentence with "It is still possible to find rainwater. . . ." What is the difference in effect between the two sentences?

Vocabulary

1. slake (2)
2. Bedouin (2)
3. inevitable (3)
4. estivation (3)
5. ephemeral (3)
6. counterpoint (4)
7. dirgelike (5)
8. morose (6)
9. metamorphosis (7)
10. phenomenon (7)

Suggestions for Writing

1. Write a descriptive essay on a special place of your own, and unobtrusively weave a thesis through your description.
2. Write a one-page subjective description of your dorm room; then write a one-page objective description of the same room. See the introduction to this chapter for an explanation of the two types of description.
3. In a paragraph, describe in detail an animal, bird, insect, or plant species you are familiar with.
4. Write a two-paragraph essay. In the first paragraph, describe a visit to the dentist in the blandest, most generalized terms you know. In the second paragraph, describe the same experience using specific and concrete verbs and precise adjectives and nouns. See "How to Write Vivid Descriptions" in the introduction to this chapter.
5. Write a descriptive essay about an event or a place or an experience that evoked (or that evokes) a certain mood in you. Make sure that you describe both the stimulus and the mood very clearly.

How It Feels to Be Shot

George Orwell

Although Orwell is largely known for his charming ard satiric fantasy, Animal Farm *(1945) and his dark and satiric science fiction novel,* 1984 *(1949), he is also one of England's finest 20th-century essayists. We have chosen a passage from a book on his experiences in the Spanish Civil War,* Homage to Catalonia *(1938).*

1 At nights we patrolled as usual—more dangerous than it used to be, because the Fascist trenches were better manned and they had grown more alert; they had scattered tin cans just outside their wire and used to open up with the machine-guns when they heard a clank. In the daytime we sniped from no man's land. By crawling a hundred yards you could get to a ditch, hidden by tall grasses, which commanded a gap in the Fascist parapet. We had set up a rifle-rest in the ditch. If you waited long enough you generally saw a khaki-clad figure slip hurriedly across the gap. I had several shots. I don't know whether I hit anyone—it is most unlikely; I am a very poor shot with a rifle. But it was rather fun, the Fascists did not know where the shots were coming from, and I made sure I would get one of them sooner or later. However, the dog it was that died—a Fascist sniper got me instead. I had been about ten days at the front when it happened. The whole experience of being hit by a bullet is very interesting and I think it is worth describing in detail.

2 It was at the corner of the parapet, at five o'clock in the morning. This was always a dangerous time, because we had the dawn at our backs, and if you stuck your head above the parapet it was clearly outlined against the sky. I was talking to the sentries preparatory to changing the guard. Suddenly, in the very middle of saying something, I felt—it is very hard to describe what I felt, though I remember it with the utmost vividness.

Roughly speaking it was the sensation of being *at the centre* of an 3
explosion. There seemed to be a loud bang and a blinding flash of
light all round me, and I felt a tremendous shock—no pain, only a
violent shock, such as you get from an electric terminal: with it a sense
of utter weakness, a feeling of being stricken and shrivelled up to
nothing. The sand-bags in front of me receded into immense distance.
I fancy you would feel much the same if you were struck by lightning.
I knew immediately that I was hit, but because of the seeming bang
and flash I thought it was a rifle nearby that had gone off accidentally
and shot me. All this happened in a space of time much less than a
second. The next moment my knees crumpled up and I was falling,
my head hitting the ground with a violent bang which, to my relief,
did not hurt. I had a numb, dazed feeling, a consciousness of being
very badly hurt, but no pain in the ordinary sense.

The American sentry I had been talking to had started forward. 4
"Gosh! Are you hit?" People gathered round. There was the usual
fuss—"Lift him up! Where's he hit? Get his shirt open!" etc., etc. The
American called for a knife to cut my shirt open. I knew that there
was one in my pocket and tried to get it out, but discovered that my
right arm was paralysed. Not being in pain, I felt a vague satisfaction.
This ought to please my wife, I thought; she had always wanted me
to be wounded, which would save me from being killed when the
great battle came. It was only now that it occurred to me to wonder
where I was hit, and how badly; I could feel nothing, but I was conscious that the bullet had struck me somewhere in the front of the
body. When I tried to speak I found that I had no voice, only a faint
squeak, but at the second attempt I managed to ask where I was hit.
In the throat, they said. Harry Webb, our stretcher-bearer, had brought
a bandage and one of the little bottles of alcohol they gave us for field-
dressings. As they lifted me up a lot of blood poured out of my mouth,
and I heard a Spaniard behind me say that the bullet had gone clean
through my neck. I felt the alcohol, which at ordinary times would
sting like the devil, splash on to the wound as a pleasant coolness.

They laid me down again while somebody fetched a stretcher. As 5
soon as I knew that the bullet had gone clean through my neck I took
it for granted that I was done for. I had never heard of a man or an
animal getting a bullet through the middle of the neck and surviving
it. The blood was dribbling out of the corner of my mouth. 'The arter-
y's gone,' I thought. I wondered how long you last when your carotid
artery is cut; not many minutes, presumably. Everything was very
blurry. There must have been about two minutes during which I
assumed that I was killed. And that too was interesting—I mean it is
interesting to know what your thoughts would be at such a time. My
first thought, conventionally enough, was for my wife. My second was

a violent resentment at having to leave this world which, when all is said and done, suits me so well. I had time to feel this very vividly. The stupid mischance infuriated me. The meaninglessness of it! To be bumped off, not even in battle, but in this stale corner of the trenches, thanks to a moment's carelessness! I thought, too, of the man who had shot me—wondered what he was like, whether he was a Spaniard or a foreigner, whether he knew he had got me, and so forth. I could not feel any resentment against him. I reflected that as he was a Fascist I would have killed him if I could, but that if he had been taken prisoner and brought before me at this moment I would merely have congratulated him on his good shooting. It may be, though, that if you were really dying your thoughts would be quite different.

6   They had just got me on to the stretcher when my paralysed right arm came to life and began hurting damnably. At the time I imagined that I must have broken it in falling; but the pain reassured me, for I knew that your sensations do not become more acute when you are dying. I began to feel more normal and to be sorry for the four poor devils who were sweating and slithering with the stretcher on their shoulders. It was a mile and a half to the ambulance, and vile going, over lumpy, slippery tracks. I knew what a sweat it was, having helped to carry a wounded man down a day or two earlier. The leaves of the silver poplars which, in places, fringed our trenches brushed against my face; I thought what a good thing it was to be alive in a world where silver poplars grow. But all the while the pain in my arm was diabolical, making me swear and then try not to swear, because every time I breathed too hard the blood bubbled out of my mouth.

7   The doctor re-bandaged the wound, gave me a shot of morphia, and sent me off to Sietamo.

Questions About Meaning

1. Why do you suppose Orwell found sniping at the enemy soldiers "rather fun"? (Imagine yourself in his place.)
2. What did Orwell think he would have said if he could have spoken to the man who shot him?
3. Most people would expect to feel terror and pain if they thought they were at the point of death. What was surprising about Orwell's reaction?
4. What infuriated Orwell about the experience?
5. What does Orwell say he felt for the stretcher bearers? What thought did he have about the silver poplars? Why did he regard these thoughts as important?

Matters of Technique

1. Orwell writes in a very contemporary style and thus tends to break paragraphs in two that once might have been left joined. Find a place where this occurs. What is the effect on the reader of short paragraphs? of long ones?
2. In paragraph 2 Orwell mixes the first person point of view with the impersonal second person. Where *exactly* does it happen? What could Orwell have done to rid the passage of the impersonal second person?
3. It is often said that Orwell writes in an informal style of English prose. What is there about the sentence length and diction in paragraph 5 that gives the passage the appearance of informality?
4. Does the author describe his sensations on being shot as clearly as he describes the external scene? How does he attempt to distinguish internal sensation from external reality? Why does he do so?

Vocabulary

1. Fascist (1)
2. parapet (1)
3. acute (6)
4. diabolical (6)

Suggestions for Writing

1. Describe in very specific and concrete terms a serious injury that you have had. Before you begin, read again Orwell's paragraph 3.
2. Describe a traumatic experience. Make your feelings vivid by using concrete and specific language, analogies, and metaphors.
3. Have you ever had an experience like the one Orwell describes, in which you seemed to be a spectator of your own body's sensations or of your own actions? If so, describe in detail, if possible within a narrative framework, this experience. Be sure to maintain consistently the objective point of view toward the experience.
4. Describe a terrifying or embarrassing experience that you have had. Present a very concrete description of the setting, characters, and circumstances, then be equally precise in your description of your emotional reaction.

The Abyss

Rachel Carson

Rachel Carson was a zoologist with special training in marine biology. The selection below is from Under the Sea-Wind *(1941), her first book. Later in her life, she was to become famous as the author of* Silent Spring *(1962), a well-documented attack on the indiscriminate use of pesticides. "The Abyss" is our title.*

1 Billions of young eels—billions of pairs of black, pinprick eyes peering into the strange sea world that overlay the abyss. Before the eyes of the eels, clouds of copepods vibrated in their ceaseless dance of life, their crystal bodies catching the light like dust motes when the blue gleam came down from above. Clear bells pulsated in the water, fragile jellyfish adjusted to life where five hundred pounds of water pressed on every square inch of surface. Fleeing before the descending light, shoals of pteropods, or winged snails, swept down from above before the eyes of the watching eels, their forms glistening with reflected light like a rain of strangely shaped hailstones—daggers and spirals and cones of glassy clearness. Shrimps loomed up—pale ghosts in the dim light. Sometimes the shrimps were pursued by pale fishes, round of mouth and flabby of flesh, with rows of light organs set like jewels on their gray flanks. Then the shrimps often expelled jets of luminous fluid that turned to a fiery cloud to blind and confuse their enemies. Most of the fishes seen by the eels wore silver armor, for silver is the prevailing color or badge of those waters that lie at the end of the sun's rays. Such were the small dragonfish, long and slender of form, with fangs glistening in their opened mouths as they roamed through the water in an endless pursuit of prey. Strangest of all were the fishes, half as long as a man's finger and clothed in a leathery skin, that shone with turquoise and amethyst lights and gleamed like quicksilver over their flanks. Their bodies were thin from side to side and tapered to sharp edges. When enemies looked down from above, they saw nothing, for the backs of the hatchetfish

were bluish black that was invisible in the black sea. When sea hunters looked up from below, they were confused and could not distinguish their prey with certainty, for the mirrorlike flanks of the hatchetfish reflected the blueness of the water and their outlines were lost
in a shimmer of light.

The young eels lived in one layer or tier of a whole series of hori- 2
zontal communities that lay one below the other, from the nereid
worms that spun their strands of silk from frond to frond of the brown
sargassum weed floating on the surface to the sea spiders and prawns
that crawled precariously over the deep and yielding oozes of the floor
of the abyss.

Above the eels was the sunlight world where plants grew, and 3
small fishes shone green and azure in the sun, and blue and crystal
jellyfish moved at the surface.

Then came the twilight zone where fishes were opalescent or silver, 4
and red prawns shed eggs of a bright orange color, and round-
mouthed fishes were pale, and the first light organs twinkled in the
gloom.

Then came the first black layer, where none wore silvery sheen or 5
opalescent luster, but all were as drab as the water in which they lived,
wearing monotones of reds and browns and blacks whereby they
might fade into the surrounding obscurity and defer the moment of
death in the jaws of an enemy. Here the red prawns shed deep-red
eggs, and the round-mouthed fishes were black, and many creatures
wore luminous torches or a multitude of small lights arranged in rows
or patterns that they might recognize friend or enemy.

Below them lay the abyss, the primeval bed of the sea, the deepest 6
of all the Atlantic. The abyss is a place where change comes slow,
where the passing of the years has no meaning, nor the swift succes-
sion of the seasons. The sun has no power in those depths, and so their
blackness is a blackness without end, or beginning, or degree. No
beating of tropical sun on the surface miles above can lessen the bleak
iciness of those abyssal waters that varies little through summer or
winter, through the years that melt into centuries, and the centuries
into ages of geologic time. Along the floor of the ocean basins, the
currents are a slow creep of frigid water, deliberate and inexorable as
the flow of time itself.

Down beneath mile after mile of water—more than four miles in 7
all—lay the sea bottom, covered with a soft, deep ooze that had been
accumulating there through eons upon eons of time. These greatest
depths of the Atlantic are carpeted with red clay, a pumicelike deposit
hurled out of the earth from time to time by submarine volcanoes.
Mingled with the pumice are spherules of iron and nickel that had
their origin on some far-off sun and once rushed millions of miles

through interstellar space, to perish in the earth's atmosphere and find their grave in the deep sea. Far up on the sides of the great bowl of the Atlantic the bottom oozes are thick with the skeletal remains of minute sea creatures of the surface waters—the shells of starry Foraminifera and the limy remains of algae and corals, the flintlike skeletons of Radiolaria and the frustules of diatoms. But long before such delicate structures reach this deepest bed of the abyss, they are dissolved and made one with the sea. Almost the only organic remains that have not passed into solution before they reach these cold and silent deeps are the ear bones of whales and the teeth of sharks. Here in the red clay, in the darkness and stillness, lies all that remains of ancient races of sharks that lived, perhaps, before there were whales in the sea; before the giant ferns flourished on the earth or ever the coal measures were laid down. All of the living flesh of these sharks was returned to the sea millions of years before, to be used over and over again in the fashioning of other creatures, but here and there a tooth still lies in the red-clay ooze of the deep sea, coated with a deposit of iron from a distant sun.

Questions About Meaning

1. What objects stand out in the ooze that covers the floor of the abyss?
2. What sentences in the last paragraph indicate that Carson's viewpoint is not merely earthbound, but encompasses the entire universe?
3. Carson's piece doesn't have a formal thesis, stated or unstated. However, if you had to sum up her major idea, what would it be?
4. What is Carson implying about the life system of the natural world when she writes that nature's camouflage helps the sea's creatures "defer the moment of death in the jaws of an enemy?" Why does she use the word "defer"?

Matters of Technique

1. The first paragraph is an awfully dense and detailed description that may require your full powers of concentration. As a matter of fact, it may take you a second or third reading to understand it fully. With this in mind, what are the advantages and disadvantages of long passages of pure description?
2. What animal does Carson use to focus her description in paragraph 1?
3. The selection opens with a sentence fragment. What advantage

does this device give the author? How would you change this structure into a standard sentence?
4. How does Carson make it easier for you to follow the first five paragraphs of pure description?

Vocabulary

1. luminous (1)
2. frond (2)
3. sheen (5)

4. opalescent (5)
5. primeval (6)
6. inexorable (6)

Suggestions for Writing

1. Describe a few layers of earth in your backyard. Begin by describing the covering vegetation (if your spot of earth has vegetation) and continue your description by digging down about a foot or two. Or describe the layers of the face of an earthen wall.
2. Describe a natural scene you have observed, attempting to limit the point of view to that of the animals (or to that of a single animal) inhabiting the area. Try to weave into your description your own conception of the natural world.
3. Using a detached viewpoint like that of a naturalist describing the behavior of an animal, describe in detail your ordinary habitat and the fellow creatures who inhabit it with you.

On the Trail of the Curly Cows

John Madson

The following selection is a condensation of an article that originally appeared in a 1981 issue of Outdoor Life. *That article was partly based on buffalo hunter Frank Mayer's own words, as recorded by Charles B. Roth and published in two articles in* The American Rifleman *in·the 1930s. Madson's essay, heavily descriptive, shows how a writer can put description to work in the service of another rhetorical type, in this case narration.*

1   For millions of us, shackled to stale jobs or dull schoolwork and dreaming of opening day, the old times on the Western buffalo plains and high elk ranges seem like heaven on earth. Game beyond reckoning, free for the taking!

2   Imagine being a professional rifleman and your own boss, hunting in virgin wilderness with ready markets for all the hides and meat you can bring in. High adventure in the uncurried West, roaming free! What could be better? Well, if you believe some of the men who lived that life, almost anything was better.

3   One of those men was Frank Mayer, an old-time buffalo hunter who lived to see jet trails over his Colorado mountains. His mind and memory stayed keen as a skinning knife, and the years never lessened his disgust with the old days of professional hunting. . . .

4   He "set his trigger on his first buffalo" on his 22nd birthday. It was an old bull that was coming out of a mud wallow near the Red River in what is now Oklahoma, and Frank shot him in the butt of the neck at 200 yards, dropping the bull in its tracks.

5   He hurried back to Waco with the hide, head, and meat. He pawned his watch for $30 to have the hide tanned and the head mounted as gifts for his father back home. Out of money, he had to eat "tough bull" for three weeks, and he never again ate buffalo meat unless driven by starvation. . . .

6   Disillusioned and disgusted with his first try at buffalo hunting,

Frank would have hung it up for good if he hadn't met Brazos Bob McRae, one of the most respected buffalo runners in the business.

Old Brazos laughed at Frank's tale of woe and invited him to go 7
along on a short hunt. They took 198 hides and sold them for $3 apiece. Brazos paid his young partner an equal share, though Frank had doubts that he'd really earned his cut. But now he was fired up with enthusiasm and even more determined to "run buff"....

As the basis of his first real hunting outfit, Frank Mayer ordered 8
two wagons from St. Joseph—a big one drawn by 12 mules for hauling hides to market, and a smaller six-mule one for camp gear. Each had iron wheels with treads nine inches wide and boxes made from one-eighth inch steel. The two cost about $1,000. Frank hired two French-Canadian skinners and a black cook and camp tender. He chose well. He was shrewd enough to know that his success (and probably his life) would depend on the skill and loyalty of his men....

One of the things Brazos McRae had impressed on Frank was the 9
importance of having a good rifle. Brazos himself used one of the big Remington single-shots, usually a .44-90-400 with a Malcolm 10X telescopic sight with plain crosswires. Frank soon learned to distrust bottleneck cases. He found they were inclined to stick in the chamber as the rifle heated up. Almost all of his buffalo shooting was done with various Sharps cartridges with straight cases.

The ideal was to kill one buffalo with one cartridge, and the good 10
hunters came mighty close to doing that. Brazos McRae once killed an entire herd of 54 buffalo with 54 rounds. Frank's best was 62 cartridges for a run of 59 buff....

Since Frank's favorite Sharps weighed more than 16 pounds and 11
had a 32-inch barrel, he always shot from crossed rest sticks in a kneeling or sitting position. For one thing, it was dead steady. For another, it put the rifle up over sagebrush and other obstructions. Frank also felt that the sound of a heavy rifle fired just above the ground carried much farther than it did if the muzzle was 30 inches higher. Buffalo runners took pains to disturb the animals as little as possible. Frank liked to shoot at 300 yards or more. He found that his efficiency fell off when he crawled too close, say to within 200 yards or less.

A buffalo herd, he said later, rarely numbered more than 200 and 12
usually consisted of a few head to 60. This was important. A runner could hunt small herds rather than just individuals. He could kill an entire bunch and move on to the next.

To "work a stand" a runner positioned himself several hundred 13
yards downwind, preferably on a slight rise, and tried to pick out the herd leader (usually an old cow) and take her with the first shot. This was not intended to be an immediate kill. If shot through the lungs, the buffalo would stay on her feet for a time while the others, scenting

blood, would lose their heads and begin milling helplessly. Then the runner really went to work. With cartridges spread out before him, he downed buffalo with neck and heart shots.

14   "It was about as adventurous and exciting as killing beeves in a slaughterhouse," Frank said.

15   There were times, though, when it was exciting, times when the hunter became the hunted. On the southern buffalo grounds, the deadliest dangers were the Apaches and Comanches, up north, the Sioux, Blackfeet, and Cheyenne. It was important to know what the different sounds of shots meant. If it was the heavy, distant thud of a buffalo gun, it meant that another runner was working a stand. No danger. But if the sound was the sharp crack of a small caliber, beware! It meant there were Injuns about.

16   Frank had several close calls, but his luck always held. Just the same, he carried insurance against capture: two empty Sharps cartridge cases, a .40 fitted inside a .45, containing a thin glass vial of deadly hydrocyanic acid. To be taken alive by some Indian tribes was such a terrible fate that many buffalo runners refused to trust in a suicide bullet. What if that last cartridge misfired? No—"biting the bite" was surer. Cyanide couldn't fail.

17   Frank never killed all the buffalo he might have. He shot only as many as his skinners could handle in a day, usually about 25. To kill more would have been wasteful—not of buffalo, which wasn't important, but of ammunition, which was. There were days, however, when Frank might kill 50 or 60 buffalo if his skinners were in fine fettle. As a hunter, of course, he never touched a skinning knife. Such work was beneath the hunter who was not only the outfit's owner, but the linchpin of the whole operation. When not actually killing, he was scouting, reloading, cleaning his rifles, or just sitting around looking wiser than a treeful of owls. Philosophical loafing, Frank called it.

18   There were many variables in this seemingly simple business. Everything was expensive on the frontier; it cost a bundle to put together a good working outfit. You had to hire good men. Then you had to find buffalo, which wasn't easy. There were millions of them, but often they were scattered in small herds through broken, rolling country that was larger than Europe. Once the buffs were located, the hunter had to kill them efficiently and within a small area so that the camp had to be moved as infrequently as possible. The skinners had to work fast and well, be able to keep up with the daily kill, and be capable of handling hides with a minimum of spoilage. Even so, Frank lost up to 20 percent of his hides. . . .

19   On paper, buffalo-running seemed to be a sure way to exploit a limitless resource free for the taking. But it didn't work exactly that way. Many years later, Frank explained why.

"It was one of those economic propositions that work out on scratch   20
paper but not on bank paper," he said. "The plain fact is that all any
runner ever got out of the game was a poverty wage. Though I was
counted one of the five best and most successful runners on the range,
my actual earnings over a nine-year period averaged a little less than
$100 a month net.

"During my first year I didn't make anything to speak of. In my   21
second year I learned the game a little better and grossed around
$5,000. My third year was my big one—1874. By that time I had gone
into the meat, smoked-tongue, and specimen-bull-head business as a
sideline. I kept careful figures of all my dealings with the buffalo, and
my 1874 income sheet looked like this:

Hides	$3,020
Meat	1,260
Tongues	905
Heads	250
Total	$5,435

"These figures, mind you, are gross. By the time overhead and fixed   22
charges and other expenses came out, I had $3,124 left. When I finally
sold out I had less than $5,000 on deposit for nearly nine years' work.
I have talked to dozens of other runners about their earnings, and
each one has said, 'Well, you got a heap more out of it than any feller
I know of.' A good high average of all persons engaged was less than
$1,000 a year net.". . .

He shot his last buffalo on the Musselshell in Wyoming in 1881—   23
an old bull surrounded by wolves.

"It seemed an act of mercy to put him down," Frank, then 31 years   24
old, said. "I set the trigger on my old .40-90 and held on his neck. Not
far away was a herd of a dozen cows. I could easily have killed them
all, but my buffalo days were over. The whole business disgusted me.
I wanted to get out."

Frank Mayer continued shooting long after most men would have   25
hung up their rifles. At 84 he was still firing 1,000-yard targets accurately with his old Sharps. He died in Fairplay, Colorado, in 1954 at
the age of 104, the last of the old-time buffalo runners.

Oh, it's now we've crossed Pease River, and homeward we are bound.
No more in that hell-fired country shall e'er we be found.
Go home to our wives and sweethearts, tell others not to go.
For God's forsaken the buffalo range and the darned old buffalo!

Questions About Meaning

1. What is the generalization that serves as the thesis of this piece? How does Madson make a more specific restatement of this generalization?
2. How did Frank Mayer learn to dislike buffalo meat?
3. Give three reasons why Mayer shot from crossed rest sticks.
4. Why did Mayer fear the sound of a small caliber rifle?
5. What was wasteful about killing more buffalo than his skinners could handle in a day? (See paragraph 17 for the surprising answer.)
6. Why did some buffalo hunters carry a vial of hydrocyanic acid with them?

Matters of Technique

1. Madson uses an unusual method to lead up to his thesis statement. Point out how he does this.
2. How does Madson tell us, in the third paragraph, that Mayer lived into the 1950s?
3. Examine paragraph 19 to see what it takes to get into the quotation in the following paragraph. Pay particular attention to the third sentence in the paragraph, which acts as a transition between Madson's idea and the quotation from Mayer.
4. Point out the figurative language in paragraph 3. Refer back to number 4 in "How to Write Vivid Descriptions" in the introduction to this chapter.
5. Although this piece is heavily descriptive, the descriptive details are presented in the context of a narrative. What are the advantages of presenting a descriptive essay within a narrative framework?

Vocabulary

1. uncurried (2)
2. keen (3)
3. disillusioned (6)
4. fine fettle (17)
5. linchpin (17)
6. variables (18)
7. exploit (19)
8. net (*economics*; 22)

Suggestions for Writing

1. Describe the first animal you remember killing. Try to let the reader know how you felt without moralizing too much.
2. In a single paragraph describe a small natural object (such as a rock,

twig, insect, or flower). Either do this assignment out of class or bring the object to class to describe.

3. Discuss the morality of buffalo hunting. Refer to Madson's essay in your essay. Be sure to produce a reasoned discussion.

4. You have probably looked forward eagerly to an experience or an adventure, only to find that experience disappointing. Describe such an experience, placing it within a narrative framework.

5. Do the same thing called for in the previous suggestion, but focus on an experience that lived up to your dreams, or on one that surprised you by not being as bad as you had feared.

CHAPTER THREE

Narration

After the atomic war, he was the only survivor of the human race. Then one dark, rainy night he heard a knock on the door.

Who can resist a good story, true or not? Perhaps that's a good enough reason to use short narratives (called anecdotes) in expository prose. Storytelling is too good to leave to the novelists.

Naturally, we are not concerned with narration for its own sake, the way a novelist is. Our concern is with narration for the sake of exposition—to clarify a concept, to support a point, perhaps even to enliven an otherwise long and dreary explanation.

Narration is not as rare in expository prose as one might think. The history student who writes a paper on the causes of World War I will no doubt have to relate the incidents that led to the outbreak of war. The business student asked to write a case study of the bankruptcy of a department store is also writing narration. Actually, any time a writer describes related events in chronological order, he is writing narration.

How to Use Narration in Exposition

Although narration begs for a more thorough treatment, our description of its principles and the ways it can be used in your essays is necessarily brief. If you have a deeper interest in narration, you may wish to take a course in it later in college. For the time being, here are some ways it can be used in an essay.

You can use a narrative to catch your readers' attention at the beginning of an essay. Then you can go on to explain the connection between your narrative and your thesis. For instance, if you began an essay by telling the story of Goldilocks and the Three Bears, you might begin the second paragraph with a transitional sentence similar to this one: "Unlike the patient Bear family, who saw their porridge eaten and their baby's chair broken into pieces, we can no longer tolerate housebreakers."

You can also insert an anecdote into the middle of your essay. Let's say you are discussing the negative effects of poor communication between employees and employers. You might be able to make your point more forcefully by inventing a narrative. It might begin, "Now let's imagine an office in which a surly boss arrives at 10 A.M. and silently stalks into . . ."

A more subtle way is to use an anecdote as your conclusion. If you have done your job well, it won't even be necessary to explain the connection between the anecdote and your thesis. Let's say you have just finished the body of your essay. Each paragraph in your essay has developed your thesis that poets should make their poetry bitter and melancholy so that readers will become inured to the bitterness of life. You might (as the poet A. E. Housman did in "Terence, This Is Stupid Stuff") begin your concluding paragraph with "There was a king reigned in the East," and then go on to tell the story of Mithridates, who drank small daily doses of poison in order to make himself immune to fatal larger doses.

Finally, as long as you are using it for an expository purpose, you can use a narrative as the entire framework of your essay. For instance, if you were showing that college is often a liberating experience, you might want to reveal that thesis through your own experiences, put in narrative form. You might want to begin by suggesting that your experiences are typical.

Principles of Narration

1. Move your plot forward through action and dialogue rather than through explanation and description. Instead of saying that a man has a limp, show him in action: "He limped toward the crowd." Instead of writing, "They talked angrily about cars," write "Damn, you don't know a Packard from a Hupmobile!"

2. *Show* characters in action instead of merely telling about them. Instead of writing that a man was very angry, write, "As his forehead turned blood-red, he shut his eyes and his hands began to shake."

3. Be sparing but telling in your details. Instead of trying to describe everything about a character, capture her essence by choosing those details that make her unique—her blue-tinted hair, perhaps, or the roll of fat under her arms, or the varicose veins in her chubby legs.

4. In writing dialogue, don't be afraid to use the conventional introductory clause, "He said." The repetition of this clause may seem obtrusive to you, but readers accept it easily. Of course when your character whispers, introduce his speech with "He whispered." But don't overdo this. If you try too hard to begin your quotes with a concrete verb or a verb plus an adverb, your prose will begin to sound like the Tom Swifties of a few years back: "'Don't see that play,' she said dramatically." Or you will start to get redundant: "'You pig!' he said insultingly."

5. Select incidents and details judiciously and pare away, in second drafts, fanatically. No doubt you've listened to a dull storyteller who has no sense of proportion. In telling the story of his trip out West, he describes every Stuckey's he passed, every gas fill-up, every state decal he bought for his car window, and every conversation he had with strangers. ("Then I said . . .") Always remember that your story is twice as interesting to you as it is to your reader.

6. Keep the purpose of your narrative in mind as you write it so that each of your words will match the tone and purpose of your thesis.

MODEL NARRATIVE PARAGRAPH

The Meeting

There are moments in one's life that are so acutely embarrassing that they can only be seen in perspective through the mist of time. It is only in the last year that I have been able to look back with detached amusement at one of those moments. At the time, I was travelling in Russia as an exchange student. After a bumpy three hour flight from Moscow to Ufa, a provincial capital in Siberia, natural urges compelled me to seek out the lavatory in the airport. On entering, I was shocked to see that the "toilets" not only had no dividers between them, but they were also so low to the ground that a fat, furry cat could have stepped over them without brushing his tummy. I wanted to back out, but nature's call was too strong to resist. Besides, I noticed that a plump Russian lady was going about her business with little fuss. So I smiled weakly at her, squatted down (still a good two feet from the toilet) and emptied my intestines. It was then that I discovered, to my horror, that the place had no toilet paper. I looked again at my neighbor. She smiled. I smiled back. I began to pantomime my lack of toilet paper. Slowly a look of enlightenment came over her face. After shuffling through her worn satchel, she triumphantly pulled a sheet of newspaper from its depths. She then shook it in the air to straighten the creases (a nice gesture, I thought), ceremoniously tore it in two, and gave me exactly half (a generous gesture, I thought). We nodded to each other and smiled. Then we laughed out loud. Thank God for détente.

Marilyn Ganger, 1974. Used by permission of the author.

ANALYSIS

As you know from listening to a good joke by a bad joke teller, the way a person tells a story makes all the difference. It is true that the bones of Ganger's story were promising to begin with, but her story would have emerged flat and unfunny if she hadn't told it well.

She told it well by being sparing in her use of adjectives, by using strongly visual verbs ("squatted," "shuffling through"), and by communicating one of her central points—the height of the toilets—by inventing a highly visual image of a furry cat.

ASSIGNMENT

Write a narrative paragraph with the same basic thesis that Ganger uses (the real thesis of the first sentence, not the facetious thesis of the last sentence). Keep the climax of your story firmly in mind so that you select only those details that will build toward that climax. Use strong verbs and try to create a highly visual image.

The Bird and the Snake

Loren Eiseley

Eiseley is an anthropologist who has a marvelous knack of making the natural world come alive. He shows us that there are indeed sermons in the stones. His books include The Immense Journey *(1957) and* The Unexpected Universe *(1969). "The Bird and the Snake" (our title) comes from* The Firmament of Time *(1960).*

1   "The special value of science," a perceptive philosopher once wrote, "lies not in what it makes of the world, but in what it makes of the knower." Some years ago, while camping in a vast eroded area in the West, I came upon one of those unlikely sights which illuminate such truths.

2   I suppose that nothing living had moved among those great stones for centuries. They lay toppled against each other like fallen dolmens. The huge stones were beasts, I used to think, of a kind man ordinarily lived too fast to understand. They seemed inanimate because the tempo of the life in them was slow. They lived ages in one place and moved only when man was not looking. Sometimes at night I would hear a low rumble as one drew itself into a new position and subsided again. Sometimes I found their tracks ground deeply into the hillsides.

3   It was with considerable surprise that while traversing this barren valley I came, one afternoon, upon what I can only describe as a very remarkable sight. Some distance away, so far that for a little space I could make nothing of the spectacle, my eyes were attracted by a dun-colored object about the size of a football, which periodically bounded up from the desert floor. Wonderingly, I drew closer and observed that something ropelike which glittered in the sun appeared to be dangling from the ball-shaped object. Whatever the object was, it appeared to be bouncing faster and more desperately as I approached. My surroundings were such that this hysterical dance of what at first glance appeared to be a common stone was quite unnerving, as though suddenly all the natural objects in the valley were about to break into a jig. Going closer, I penetrated the mystery.

The sun was sparkling on the scales of a huge blacksnake which   4
was partially looped about the body of a hen pheasant. Desperately
the bird tried to rise, and just as desperately the big snake coiled and
clung, though each time the bird, falling several feet, was pounding
the snake's body in the gravel. I gazed at the scene in astonishment.
Here in this silent waste, like an emanation from nowhere, two bitter
and desperate vapors, two little whirlwinds of contending energy,
were beating each other to death because their plans—something, I
suspected, about whether a clutch of eggs was to turn into a thing with
wings or scales—this problem, I say, of the onrushing nonexistent
future, had catapulted serpent against bird.

The bird was too big for the snake to have had it in mind as prey.   5
Most probably, he had been intent on stealing the pheasant's eggs and
had been set upon and pecked. Somehow in the ensuing scuffle he
had flung a loop over the bird's back and partially blocked her wings.
She could not take off, and the snake would not let go. The snake was
taking a heavy battering among the stones, but the high-speed metabolism and tremendous flight exertion of the mother bird were rapidly
exhausting her. I stood a moment and saw the bloodshot glaze deepen
in her eyes. I suppose I could have waited there to see what would
happen when she could not fly; I suppose it might have been worth
scientifically recording. But I could not stand that ceaseless, bloody
pounding in the gravel. I thought of the eggs somewhere about, and
whether they were to elongate and writhe into an armor of scales, or
eventually to go whistling into the wind with their wild mother.

So I, the mammal, in my way supple, and less bound by instinct,   6
arbitrated the matter. I unwound the serpent from the bird and let him
hiss and wrap his battered coils around my arm. The bird, her wings
flung out, rocked on her legs and gasped repeatedly. I moved away in
order not to drive her further from her nest. Thus the serpent and I,
two terrible and feared beings, passed quickly out of view.

Over the next ridge, where he could do no more damage, I let the   7
snake, whose anger had subsided, slowly uncoil and slither from my
arm. He flowed away into a little patch of bunch grass—aloof, forget-
ting, unaware of the journey he had made upon my wrist, which
throbbed from his expert constriction. The bird had contended for
birds against the oncoming future; the serpent writhing into the
bunch grass had contended just as desperately for serpents. And I, the
apparition in that valley—for what had I contended?—I who contained the serpent and the bird and who read the past long written in
their bodies.

Slowly, as I sauntered dwarfed among overhanging pinnacles, as   8
the great slabs which were the visible remnants of past ages laid their
enormous shadows rhythmically as life and death across my face, the

answer came to me. Man could contain more than himself. Among these many appearances that flew, or swam in the waters, or wavered momentarily into being, man alone possessed that unique ability.

9   The Renaissance thinkers were right when they said that man, the Microcosm, contains the Macrocosm. I had touched the lives of creatures other than myself and had seen their shapes waver and blow like smoke through the corridors of time. I had watched, with sudden concentrated attention, myself, this brain, unrolling from the seed like a genie from a bottle, and casting my eyes forward, I had seen it vanish again into the formless alchemies of the earth.

10   For what then had I contended, weighing the serpent with the bird in that wild valley? I had struggled, I am now convinced, for a greater, more comprehensive version of myself.

Questions About Meaning

1. What brought about the struggle Eiseley observes?
2. When Eiseley first sees the combatants, what does he think they are?
3. Which animal appears to be winning when the author arrives on the scene?
4. According to Eiseley, what is the difference between humans and animals?
5. In his conclusion, Eiseley comes back to the idea that he began with. What is that idea?

Matters of Technique

1. What sentence in paragraph 1 indicates that Eiseley is going to put his essay in the form of a narrative?
2. At what point in the essay does Eiseley begin his narrative in earnest?
3. Rewrite the first sentence in paragraph 3. Make it shorter without losing any meaning.
4. In paragraphs 4 and 5 Eiseley wonders about the fate of the waiting eggs. Find a sentence in paragraph 5 that describes concretely the two possible outcomes of the struggle. (How can a bird's egg become a snake?)
5. Point out the shift in descriptive precision as Eiseley moves closer to the scene of the combat.

Vocabulary

1. dolmen (2)
2. unnerving (3)
3. emanation (4)
4. metabolism (5)
5. sauntered (8)

6. remnants (8)
7. Microcosm (9)
8. Macrocosm (9)
9. alchemies (9)

Suggestions for Writing

1. Write a narrative that demonstrates how a confrontation with the natural world changed, in some small way, the way you look at the world.
2. In a narrative essay, describe your reaction when you came unexpectedly upon something surprising in nature. Make sure that the essay illustrates a clearly stated thesis.
3. Develop a narration about the behavior of a pet that taught you something about the intelligence of animals.

Cross-Reference

Both Eiseley and Bronowski conclude that humans differ from the rest of nature. Write a paper that contrasts their conclusions.

Once More to the Lake

E. B. White

Although E. B. White excels as a storyteller in books like Charlotte's Web *(1952), a delightful children's story, he is primarily known as an essayist for* The New Yorker *and* Harper's. *"Once More to the Lake," an often-reprinted piece, is from his collection of essays,* One Man's Meat *(1944).*

1   One summer, along about 1904, my father rented a camp on a lake in Maine and took us all there for the month of August. We all got ring-worm from some kittens and had to rub Pond's Extract on our arms and legs night and morning, and my father rolled over in a canoe with all his clothes on; but outside of that the vacation was a success and from then on none of us ever thought there was any place in the world like that lake in Maine. We returned summer after summer—always on August 1st for one month. I have since become a salt-water man, but sometimes in summer there are days when the restlessness of the tides and the fearful cold of the sea water and the incessant wind which blows across the afternoon and into the evening make me wish for the placidity of a lake in the woods. A few weeks ago this feeling got so strong I bought myself a couple of bass hooks and a spinner and returned to the lake where we used to go, for a week's fishing and to revisit old haunts.

2   I took along my son, who had never had any fresh water up his nose and who had seen lily pads only from train windows. On the journey over to the lake I began to wonder what it would be like. I wondered how time would have marred this unique, this holy spot—the coves and streams, the hills that the sun set behind, the camps and the paths behind the camps. I was sure that the tarred road would have found it out and I wondered in what other ways it would be desolated. It is strange how much you can remember about places like that once you allow your mind to return into the grooves which lead back. You remember one thing, and that suddenly reminds you of another thing. I guess I remembered clearest of all the early mornings, when the lake was cool and motionless, remembered how the bed-

room smelled of the lumber it was made of and of the wet woods whose scent entered through the screen. The partitions in the camp were thin and did not extend clear to the top of the rooms, and as I was always the first up I would dress softly so as not to wake the others, and sneak out into the sweet outdoors and start out in the canoe, keeping close along the shore in the long shadows of the pines. I remembered being very careful never to rub my paddle against the gunwale for fear of disturbing the stillness of the cathedral.

The lake had never been what you would call a wild lake. There 3
were cottages sprinkled around the shores, and it was in farming country although the shores of the lake were quite heavily wooded. Some of the cottages were owned by nearby farmers, and you would live at the shore and eat your meals at the farmhouse. That's what our family did. But although it wasn't wild, it was a fairly large and undisturbed lake and there were places in it which, to a child at least, seemed infinitely remote and primeval.

I was right about the tar: it led to within half a mile of the shore. 4
But when I got back there, with my boy, and we settled into a camp near a farmhouse and into the kind of summertime I had known, I could tell that it was going to be pretty much the same as it had been before—I knew it, lying in bed the first morning, smelling the bedroom, and hearing the boy sneak quietly out and go off along the shore in a boat. I began to sustain the illusion that he was I, and therefore, by simple transposition, that I was my father. This sensation persisted, kept cropping up all the time we were there. It was not an entirely new feeling, but in this setting it grew much stronger. I seemed to be living a dual existence. I would be in the middle of some simple act, I would be picking up a bait box or laying down a table fork, or I would be saying something, and suddenly it would be not I but my father who was saying the words or making the gesture. It gave me a creepy sensation.

We went fishing the first morning. I felt the same damp moss cov- 5
ering the worms in the bait can, and saw the dragonfly alight on the tip of my rod as it hovered a few inches from the surface of the water. It was the arrival of this fly that convinced me beyond any doubt that everything was as it always had been, that the years were a mirage and there had been no years. The small waves were the same, chucking the rowboat under the chin as we fished at anchor, and the boat was the same boat, the same color green and the ribs broken in the same places, and under the floor-boards the same fresh-water leavings and débris—the dead helgramite, the wisps of moss, the rusty discarded fishhook, the dried blood from yesterday's catch. We stared silently at the tips of our rods, at the dragonflies that came and went. I lowered the tip of mine into the water, tentatively, pensively dis-

lodging the fly, which darted two feet away, poised, darted two feet
back, and came to rest again a little farther up the rod. There had been
no years between the ducking of this dragonfly and the other one—
the one that was part of memory. I looked at the boy, who was silently
watching his fly, and it was my hands that held his rod, my eyes
watching. I felt dizzy and didn't know which rod I was at the end of.

6   We caught two bass, hauling them in briskly as though they were
mackerel, pulling them over the side of the boat in a businesslike
manner without any landing net, and stunning them with a blow on
the back of the head. When we got back for a swim before lunch, the
lake was exactly where we had left it, the same number of inches from
the dock, and there was only the merest suggestion of a breeze. This
seemed an utterly enchanted sea, this lake you could leave to its own
devices for a few hours and come back to, and find that it had not
stirred, this constant and trustworthy body of water. In the shallows,
the dark, water-soaked sticks and twigs, smooth and old, were undu-
lating in clusters on the bottom against the clean ribbed sand, and the
track of the mussel was plain. A school of minnows swam by, each
minnow with its small individual shadow, doubling the attendance,
so clear and sharp in the sunlight. Some of the other campers were in
swimming, along the shore, one of them with a cake of soap, and the
water felt thin and clear and unsubstantial. Over the years there had
been this person with the cake of soap, this cultist, and here he was.
There had been no years.

7   Up to the farmhouse to dinner through the teeming, dusty field,
the road under our sneakers was only a two-track road. The middle
track was missing, the one with the marks of the hooves and the
splotches of dried, flaky manure. There had always been three tracks
to choose from in choosing which track to walk in; now the choice
was narrowed down to two. For a moment I missed terribly the middle
alternative. But the way led past the tennis court, and something about
the way it lay there in the sun reassured me; the tape had loosened
along the backline, the alleys were green with plantains and other
weeds, and the net (installed in June and removed in September)
sagged in the dry noon, and the whole place steamed with midday
heat and hunger and emptiness. There was a choice of pie for dessert,
and one was blueberry and one was apple, and the waitresses were
the same country girls, there having been no passage of time, only the
illusion of it as in a dropped curtain—the waitresses were still fifteen;
their hair had been washed, that was the only difference—they had
been to the movies and seen the pretty girls with the clean hair.

8   Summertime, oh summertime, pattern of life indelible, the fade-
proof lake, the woods unshatterable, the pasture with the sweetfern
and the juniper forever and ever, summer without end; this was the

background, and the life along the shore was the design, the cottages with their innocent and tranquil design, their tiny docks with the flag-pole and the American flag floating against the white clouds in the blue sky, the little paths over the roots of the trees leading from camp to camp and the paths leading back to the outhouses and the can of lime for sprinkling, and at the souvenir counters at the store the min-iature birch-bark canoes and the post cards that showed things look-ing a little better than they looked. This was the American family at play, escaping the city heat, wondering whether the newcomers in the camp at the head of the cove were "common" or "nice," wondering whether it was true that the people who drove up for Sunday dinner at the farmhouse were turned away because there wasn't enough chicken.

It seemed to me, as I kept remembering all this, that those times 9 and those summers had been infinitely precious and worth saving. There had been jollity and peace and goodness. The arriving (at the beginning of August) had been so big a business in itself, at the rail-way station the farm wagon drawn up, the first smell of the pine-laden air, the first glimpse of the smiling farmer, and the great importance of the trunks and your father's enormous authority in such matters, and the feel of the wagon under you for the long ten-mile haul, and at the top of the last long hill catching the first view of the lake after eleven months of not seeing this cherished body of water. The shouts and cries of the other campers when they saw you, and the trunks to be unpacked, to give up their rich burden. (Arriving was less exciting nowadays, when you sneaked up in your car and parked it under a tree near the camp and took out the bags and in five minutes it was all over, no fuss, no loud wonderful fuss about trunks.)

Peace and goodness and jollity. The only thing that was wrong 10 now, really, was the sound of the place, an unfamiliar nervous sound of the outboard motors. This was the note that jarred, the one thing that would sometimes break the illusion and set the years moving. In those other summertimes all motors were inboard; and when they were at a little distance, the noise they made was a sedative, an ingre-dient of summer sleep. They were one-cylinder and two-cylinder engines, and some were make-and-break and some were jump-spark, but they all made a sleepy sound across the lake. The one-lungers throbbed and fluttered, and the twin-cylinder ones purred and purred, and that was a quiet sound too. But now the campers all had outboards. In the daytime, in the hot mornings, these motors made a petulant, irritable sound; at night, in the still evening when the after-glow lit the water, they whined about one's ears like mosquitoes. My boy loved our rented outboard, and his great desire was to achieve singlehanded mastery over it, and authority, and he soon learned the trick of choking it a little (but not too much), and the adjustment of the needle valve. Watching him I would remember the things you could do with the old one-cylinder engine with the heavy flywheel, how you could have it eating out of your hand if you got really close to it spiritually. Motor boats in those days didn't have clutches, and you would make a landing by shutting off the motor at the proper time and coasting in with a dead rudder. But there was a way of reversing them, if you learned the trick, by cutting the switch and putting it on again exactly on the final dying revolution of the fly-wheel, so that it would kick back against compression and begin reversing. Approaching a dock in a strong following breeze, it was difficult to slow up sufficiently by the ordinary coasting method, and if a boy felt he had complete mastery over his motor, he was tempted to keep it running beyond its time and then reverse it a few feet from the dock. It took a cool nerve, because if you threw the switch a twen-tieth of a second too soon you would catch the flywheel when it still had speed enough to go up past center, and the boat would leap ahead, charging bull-fashion at the dock.

11   We had a good week at the camp. The bass were biting well and the sun shone endlessly, day after day. We would be tired at night and lie down in the accumulated heat of the little bedrooms after the long hot day and the breeze would stir almost imperceptibly outside and the smell of the swamp drift in through the rusty screens. Sleep would come easily and in the morning the red squirrel would be on the roof, tapping out his gay routine. I kept remembering everything, lying in bed in the mornings—the small steamboat that had a long rounded stern like the lip of a Ubangi, and how quietly she ran on the moon-light sails, when the older boys played their mandolins and the girls sang and we ate doughnuts dipped in sugar, and how sweet the music was on the water in the shining night, and what it had felt like to think about girls then. After breakfast we would go up to the store and the things were in the same place—the minnows in a bottle, the plugs and spinners disarranged and pawed over by the youngsters from the boys' camp, the fig newtons and the Beeman's gum. Outside, the road was tarred and cars stood in front of the store. Inside, all was just as it had always been, except there was more Coca Cola and not so much Moxie and root beer and birch beer and sarsaparilla. We would walk out with a bottle of pop apiece and sometimes the pop would backfire up our noses and hurt. We explored the streams, qui-etly, where the turtles slid off the sunny logs and dug their way into the soft bottom; and we lay on the town wharf and fed worms to the tame bass. Everywhere we went I had trouble making out which was I, the one walking at my side, the one walking in my pants.

12   One afternoon while we were there at the lake a thunderstorm

came up. It was like the revival of an old melodrama that I had seen long ago with childish awe. The second-act climax of the drama of the electrical disturbance over a lake in America had not changed in any important respect. This was the big scene, still the big scene. The whole thing was so familiar, the first feeling of oppression and heat and a general air around camp of not wanting to go very far away. In midafternoon (it was all the same) a curious darkening of the sky, and a lull in everything that had made life tick; and then the way the boats suddenly swung the other way at their moorings with the coming of a breeze out of the new quarter, and the premonitory rumble. Then the kettle drum, then the snare, then the bass drum and cymbals, then crackling light against the dark, and the gods grinning and licking their chops in the hills. Afterward the calm, the rain steadily rustling in the calm lake, the return of light and hope and spirits, and the campers running out in joy and relief to go swimming in the rain, their bright cries perpetuating the deathless joke about how they were getting simply drenched, and the children screaming with delight at the new sensation of bathing in the rain, and the joke about getting drenched linking the generations in a strong indestructible chain. And the comedian who waded in carrying an umbrella.

When the others went swimming my son said he was going in too. 13
He pulled his dripping trunks from the line where they had hung all through the shower, and wrung them out. Languidly, and with no thought of going in, I watched him, his hard little body, skinny and bare, saw him wince slightly as he pulled up around his vitals the small, soggy, icy garment. As he buckled the swollen belt suddenly my groin felt the chill of death.

Questions About Meaning

1. The major thesis of "Once More to the Lake" is never stated. However, what most readers will think to be the thesis of the piece—at least before they arrive at the last paragraph—is stated a number of times. What is that "preliminary" thesis?
2. What caused White to want to return to the lake as an adult? What does the sea probably represent to him?
3. What did he fear he would find when he returned?
4. What "illusion" did White begin to experience on this revisit to the lake with his son? What does this indicate about his reason for revisiting the vacation scene of his boyhood?
5. Why does White say *he* "suddenly . . . felt the chill of death" as he watched his son put on his wet, cold bathing trunks?
6. What is the ultimate thesis of the essay?

Matters of Technique

1. What is the author's attitude toward the narrative he recounts in paragraph 1?
2. What words in the second paragraph suggest that White's attitude toward the lake approaches religious veneration?
3. What does White set up in paragraph 6 as a contrast to the restless sea he describes in paragraph 1?
4. Without looking at the essay, write down five details you remember from it. Compare yours to those listed by the rest of the class. Now reread the five most commonly remembered details to analyze *why* they were remembered.
5. Write a descriptive paragraph in which you describe a concrete situation with the kind of vividness White achieves in paragraphs 5, 6, or 7.
6. At several points—for example, in paragraphs 9 and 12—White uses sentence fragments. What advantages do they give him? How would you convert these into standard sentences?

Vocabulary

1. incessant (1)
2. placidity (1)
3. unique (2)
4. primeval (3)
5. tentatively (5)
6. pensively (5)
7. cultist (6)
8. indelible (8)
9. petulant (10)
10. premonitory (12)
11. languidly (13)

Suggestions for Writing

1. Write about a special place that you knew when you were younger. Describe it as vividly as possible so that you get across to readers what it meant to you without your having to belabor the thesis of your essay. Present your description in the context of a narrative.
2. Describe a moment when you felt the chill of death. Place the moment within a narrative framework.
3. Have you revisited a place you knew as a child—such as a city, neighborhood, farm, or vacation spot—after the passage of a number of years? If so, compare and contrast your early perception of the place with your later perspective. Do this in order to demonstrate your sense of change and the lapse of time.

Linking "A" to "Aleph"

Faye Moskowitz

When Faye Moskowitz wrote "Linking 'A' to 'Aleph'" in 1975, she was work-ing on a Ph.D. in American literature at George Washington University and was the director of the middle school at Edmund Burke School in Washington.

My mother wrote me one letter in her life. She was in California, then,   1
seeking treatment for the disease whose name she denied until the
day it defeated her. I have the letter in front of me now. Sorting
through a box of old papers today, I found it, written in the round
hand of Americanization school on tissue-thin paper that still retains
a narrow red edge of gum rubber where it was once attached to a
tablet.

March 7 1947

> Dear Faye chaim and Roger.
>
> How are you kids? I am filling little better. My beck still hurts. Today I was
> at doctors for a tritement & Saturday I am going again for a tritement. I
> hope to god I shut fill better. Please write to me. How is evrething in the
> house? How is Zada and how does daddy fill? The weather is here won-
> dufull and hot. I was sitting outside today. Well I have to say goodnight. I
> have to be in bed early for my health. Take care of daddy.
>
> your mother
>
> regart from evrewone.

On the back flap of the envelope she had written her name, Sophie   2
Stollman, and the street address of a sister with whom she was staying
in California. For the rest of the address, she had lettered in "Detroit,
Michigan," her home. Even today, more than 25 years later, I can't
look at that confused address without weeping. Spilling out of her fear
and loneliness and homesickness, that handful of laboriously penciled
words with its poignant error that was not really a mistake, speaks to
me still.

3   I think I will tell my students about my mother's letter sometime. Perhaps on the first day of school when classes begin and I am confronted by the passive faces and listless bodies so fashionable now, I will read them my mother's note; tell them the story of the envelope. I will say that my mother's words were so many fading letters on a crumbling page until I reread them and invested them with my own memories and connections. When I sense that someone is about to ask what this all has to do with an English course, I will explain that I want them to study literature and composition actively, constantly adding dimension to all that they read and write by drawing on their individual rich stores of memory and experience.

4   Some of the new students will fidget in their seats a bit, wondering whether to take this down in their notes, whether they will be responsible for it on a test. But what I want to say to them about teaching and learning is just the opposite of that kind of measuring-cup sifting-out of life. I have in mind an education that has no beginning, middle, or end; an education that raises more questions than it answers. I realize that as a teacher, I set goals and requirements, and I know that my students have deadlines and grades to consider.

5   Nevertheless, I dream that even within those constrictions, a different understanding of the nature of a liberal-arts education will insinuate itself into the corners of the time-boxes we must deal with. To see learning and life as ever ongoing connection, is to bevel the rough edges, miter the corners so those containers of time will stack, pile, form a line, a chain, a row of always accessible segments, not fragments, of knowledge and experience.

6   This will be a day of stories. I will tell my students about my father's father who was a Chasid. Each year at Passover, as Jews in exile have always done, we turned to each other and said, "Next year in Jerusalem." I was acting out a ritual; my grandfather believed it. When he died, he was wrapped in a winding sheet and placed on the front-room floor of his two-family flat in Detroit, a candle at his head, his feet pointed east, toward Israel.

7   As the slow-moving chain of automobiles wound its way to the cemetery the day after he died, it coiled past his house for one last time. The "two-families" on Hazelwood were set on narrow lots, each with a few square feet of ground in front. Monopolizing my grandparent's microscopic front yard was a strange lumpy tree whose name I didn't know. Each fall, Zada cut back all the branches, and early in spring I was certain it was dead until it leapt into leaf. That was over 30 years ago. Last year on my first trip to Europe, I went to France and everywhere I saw plane trees, pruned mercilessly, lining the avenues like endless rows of clenched arthritic fists. Instantly I flew in memory back to Hazelwood, back to the plane tree knobbily dominating the

diminutive patch of desperate grass and back to my grandfather reaching with stiff yellow toes to a Holy Land he had only known through his prayer book.

It has become a cliché to speak of 20th-century man as fragmented, disoriented, displaced. Why speak in the abstract? We all know students and non-students, too, who see the educational years as finite, as a time to get through so the real business of living can begin. They never see that life and education are seamless, a unified creative act. We must be open to all experience, be willing to suspend the habit of parceling out time into carefully labeled fragments. If life is to be a unity (and it must, to have any meaning), then all of thinking and learning must be a continuous process of connections.

I will explain to my pupils the real germ of all this storytelling. Some time ago, a student gave me a book to read called *Stranger in a Strange Land*. The book lay around on my desk for a while and I was intrigued by a chain I began to feel silverly slipping, loop by loop, back into my consciousness. Where had I heard that title before? I asked my students and they told me about a record by Leon Russell with the same title, "Stranger in a Strange Land." I said, no, wait, it is Camus I am thinking of, but still I felt a clawing at the edges of my memory.

One day, when I was not even thinking about it, I tripped over the phrase in a book I was reading. Yes, I said, there's more, surely, and there was. I took down my Bible and searched through *Ruth* and it wasn't there and in *Exodus* I rediscovered it and I was content for the moment and then the chain began to slip again.

When I was four we moved from Detroit to Jackson, a little Michigan town of 40,000 inhabitants. The nation was in the depths of the Great Depression and someone thought my father might find work in a smaller town. I remember the Depression in Detroit as a time when men sat around all day on front porches playing poker for toothpicks. At night, the women complained that burning porch lights ran up the electric bills, so then we all sat in the dark and talked until the mosquitoes drove us inside.

There were few Jews in Jackson and my parents spoke little English. My father had no one to play cards with. We often talked together inside the house, sitting at a red-and-white, porcelain-topped kitchen table, drinking tea from tall glasses.

My father did not own any books, but *The Jewish Daily Forward* came in the mail each morning. I learned to read Yiddish from it. English came on cereal boxes and Bon Ami cans. I did not crack the cipher "Reg. U.S. Pat. Off." until I had become quite sophisticated. I slowly began to make my language connections with *The Forward's* Sunday supplement, a rotogravure section printed in rich brown ink. Under the photographs of President Roosevelt, Franco, Mussolini, and Eddy Cantor, were captions in both Yiddish and English.

14   One night, when I was about seven, a salesman came to our door. I recall a stiff new briefcase from which he slipped a large book bound in a pebbly blue material. On the book's cover, stamped in gold, was a representation of the globe. "Here, sister," the salesman said to me, "Read this." And so I stumbled through a paragraph, sliding my right index finger under each word as I had been taught in school, my cheeks burning, the sound of my own voice bouncing in my ears.

15   Of course my parents couldn't afford that set of encyclopedias, but, convinced by the salesman that such a clever little girl deserved the best, they bought it, and for the next 36 months Elmer became a regular visitor, collecting the painfully put-together dollar a week.

16   It wasn't until I read James Joyce and learned his concept of "epiphany" that I found a name for what happened to me when I opened Volume 1 of *The World Book* and puzzled out the first entry, "Aa." I can visualize the page yet with its crude drawing to illustrate that the Roman letter "A" came from the Phoenician letter, "Aleph," the word for ox. There, at last, was a way to link the "A" of my Americanness to the "Aleph" of my Jewishness, and the land slowly began to be more familiar, and the stranger began to feel less strange. By the time Elmer marked "paid in full" in our receipt book, I had worked my way through the entire 19 volumes of the encyclopedia.

17   Shape your own absolutely personal combinations, I will say to my students as the hour draws to a close and the notebooks remain blank, but remember that this shaping must be a conscious thing, a reaching out and back and forward for those details which create pattern and form motif in a life. I dream of a life that is a continuous education, fusing all disciplines, making use of every atom of experience. I see a process of education that doesn't stop when a class is over (as if it ever began there) but spins off forever.

18   I want my students to be able to move from Bob Dylan to T. S. Eliot to Dante to the *Roman de la Rose* and back again. I dream of an education in which Dreiser and F. Scott Fitzgerald are read with *The Autobiography of Benjamin Franklin* in mind, in which literary realism is viewed in combination with Dutch painting of interiors, in which a student learns to understand the nature of autobiography, not only by reading some but by attempting to write his own. I want to teach point of view by having my students imagine "A Rose for Emily" written in Emily's voice. If they read *Soledad Brother*, I hope they will do it by trying to conceive of those other letters, the ones George Jackson's parents wrote to *him*.

19   And so we are back to letters again, and a kind of circuit is complete. Do you see what I mean about teaching and learning as connection, of the power of a subconscious slip to move me to tears 25 years

later, of the power of a knobby plane tree to carry me back to the Holy Land, of the power of a book title to write an essay, and of the power of "A" joined with "Aleph" to make me—in some sense at least—no longer a sojourner, but a native, firmly bound, here, then, now, and for all time in those connecting chains that are the bonds of freedom?

Questions About Meaning

1. Why does Moskowitz want to read her mother's letter to her English class?
2. What does Moskowitz mean when she speaks of studying literature and composition "actively"?
3. What does one's own "memory and experience" have to do with one's reading?
4. What changed Moskowitz's mother's words from "so many fading letters on a crumbling page" to a real communication with the past?
5. What is the difference between "reading" and "understanding"?
6. What does Moskowitz mean by objecting to the idea that "the educational years" are "finite" and insisting instead that "all of thinking and learning must be a continuous process of connections"? How does she illustrate this idea?

Matters of Technique

1. Essays usually aren't as personal as Moskowitz's. Does the personal nature make her essay more effective, or less?
2. Moskowitz begins by describing, then quoting, a letter her mother once wrote to her. Why is this an effective way for her to introduce her subject?
3. What does the title refer to? What does it have to do with the essay's thesis?
4. Moskowitz's style is characterized by relatively simple sentences full of visualized details. Point out examples of this in paragraph 1. Point out other examples in paragraphs 6, 7, 11, and 12.
5. Who is the author's audience? What details in her essay suggest that she was writing with that particular audience in mind?

Vocabulary

1. passive (3)
2. listless (3)
3. insinuate (5)

4. bevel (5)
5. Chasid (6)
6. finite (8)

7. Yiddish (13)
8. epiphany (16)

9. aleph (16)
10. motif (17)

Suggestions for Writing

1. Write an essay in which you make a connection between *your* "rich stores of memory and experience" and something you learned in a literature or history class. Perhaps the title of a book, an incident in the Civil War, or a quotation from Shakespeare brings to mind something similar that your grandparents or parents said or did.
2. Write an essay based on an epiphany (see paragraph 16) of your own.
3. Write an essay in which you describe an incident that taught you that things are often not what they appear to be. Put this into a narrative framework.
4. Write a narrative illustrating an occasion when you felt like a stranger, though in familiar surroundings. Make clear the reasons for your feeling.

A Watery Grave and the Stars

Bruce Catton

"A Watery Grave and the Stars" is a selection from Bruce Catton's autobiographical Waiting for the Morning Train *(1972). Catton is best known for his Pulitzer Prize work,* A Stillness at Appomattox *(1953), the third volume of a historical trilogy on the Army of the Potomac.*

We lived then in a time of great expectations. We believed in ourselves 1
and in the future, and we welcomed all of the omens that were good.
We were not, to be sure, altogether half-witted. It is good to know that
the world is not exactly what it seems to be, but to know this is to be
dimly aware that it may be worse instead of better. These voices that
spoke to us out of spring sunlight and the dawn of life could be lying,
and a well-read person had to keep an ear open for confused echoes
from the darkling plain. However, bookish knowledge did not necessarily mean much. We lived by our emotions rather than by our
brains, and although we did not know where we were going we
trusted the future. We lived for it, confident that when it came it
would rub out all of the mistakes of the past. It was the one thing we
really believed in. Mercifully, we could not know that when it finally
came it would frighten us more than anything else on earth. We were
at halfway house; the quarters were good, the grounds were pleasant,
and there was a fine view of the surrounding country. What more
could we want? . . .

Yet there was something about our north country (or maybe it was 2
something about me) that issued disquieting warnings now and then.
There was the emptiness off to the north, thousands of miles of it, with
the cold tang of the ice age in the air; to the south was the land of the
mound builders, whose best efforts produced nothing more than
unobtrusive scars on the earth; and all about us were the bleak acres
of stumps, the dying towns and the desolate farms that were being
given up, discards in a game where most of the players had lost. Now
and again these things demanded thought.

3   There was for instance one January morning that winter when Lewis Stoneman and I went sailing on skates. I do not know whether anyone does that nowadays, but it was quite a thing at the time and we had read about it in some magazine. You took thin strips of wood and made an oblong frame, about four feet long by three feet wide, added a couple of cross braces for stiffening and for handholds, and covered the frame with a piece of discarded bed sheet cut to size. Then you went to the ice, put on your skates, held the frame in front of you, and let the wind take charge. I talked about this with Lewis, who was a student at the academy and was for some reason known as Yutch, and it sounded like fun. We built the frames in the basement of Father's house, talked Mother into giving us a frayed old sheet, tacked pieces of it to the wood, got our skates, and one Saturday went down to Crystal Lake to see about it.

4   We were in luck. The lake had frozen late, that winter, and although the countryside was covered with snow there was little or none on the ice, which was smooth and clear as plate glass. Skating conditions were perfect, the sun was bright, the bare ice was like polished steel, and there was a brisk wind from the east—which was fine, because we were at the eastern end of the lake and the open ice stretched away to the west for more than eight miles. We put on our skating shoes, knotted the laces of our regular shoes together and hung them about our necks, got out on the frozen lake, held the sails in front of us, and took off.

5   The wind was strong, blowing steadily and without gusts, and it filled our sails and took us down the lake at what seemed a fabulous speed. We had never moved so fast on skates before—had not imagined that it was possible to move so fast—and it was all completely effortless. All we had to do was stand erect, hold on to our sails, and glide away; it was like being a hawk, soaring above the length of a ridge on an updraft of air, and it felt more like flying than anything that ever happened to me, later on in life, in an airplane.

6   Neither one of us knew anything at all about sailing. To tack, or even to go on a broad reach, was entirely beyond us; we had to go where the wind blew us, and that was that, and now and then I was uneasily aware that skating back against the wind, by sheer leg power, was going to be hard. However, there would be time enough to worry about that later. For the moment it was enough to be carried by the wind. The whole world had been made for our enjoyment. The sky was unstained blue, with white clouds dropping shadows now and then to race along with us, the hills that rimmed the lake were white with snow, gray and blue with bare tree trunks, clear gold in places where the wind had blown the snow away from sandy bluffs, the sun was a friendly weight on our shoulders, the wind was blowing harder and we were going faster than ever, and there was hardly a sound

anywhere. I do not believe I have ever felt more completely in tune with the universe than I felt that morning on Crystal Lake. It was friendly. All of its secrets were good.

Then, suddenly, came awakening. We had ridden the wind for six miles or more, and we were within about two miles of the western end of the lake; and we realized that not far ahead of us there was a broad stretch of sparkling, dazzling blue running from shore to shore, flecked with picturesque whitecaps—open water. It was beautiful, but it carried the threat of sudden death. The lake had not been entirely frozen, after all. Its west end was clear, and at the rate we were going we would reach the end of ice in a short time. The lake was a good hundred feet deep there, the water was about one degree warmer than the ice itself, and the nearest land—wholly uninhabited, in the dead of winter—was a mile away. Two boys dropped into that would never get out alive. 7

There was also a change in the ice beneath us. It was transparent, and the water below was black as a starless midnight; the ice had become thin, it was flexible, sagging a little under our weight, giving out ominous creakings and crackling sounds, and only the fact that we kept moving saved us from breaking through. It was high time, in short, for us to get off of that lake. 8

Yutch saw it at the same moment I did. We both pointed, and yelled, and then we made a ninety-degree turn to the left and headed for the southern shore. If we had known how to use our sails properly the wind would have taken us there, but we knew nothing about that. All we could think of was to skate for the shore with all speed, and those sails were just in the way. We dropped them incontinently, and we never saw them again, and we made a grotesque race for safety, half-skating and half-running. We came at last to the packed floe ice over the shallows, galloped clumsily across it, reached the snow-covered beach, and collapsed on a log to catch our breath and to talk in awed tones about our narrow escape.... 9

Actually, we had not so much as got our feet wet, and our escape had not been quite as narrow as we believed, but we had had an authentic glimpse over the rim and we did not like what we had seen; although, now that it was all over, it was fun to talk about it. 10

Yet the whole business cut a hard groove in my mind. I found after a while that I did not want to talk about it. I did not even want to think about it, but I could not help myself. What I had seen through the transparent bending ice seemed to be nothing less than the heart of darkness. It was not just my own death that had been down there; it was the ultimate horror, lying below all life, kept away by something so fragile that it could break at any moment. Everything we did or dreamed or hoped for had this just beneath it ... One gets knotty thoughts, sometimes, at halfway house. 11

12   This seemed especially hard to digest because it came so soon after Christmas.

13   Christmas, without any question, was the greatest day of the year. It was not just that it was a time for receiving gifts, although Heaven knows that was enough in itself; the suspense of the last few days before Christmas was almost too much to bear, and the culminating moment when we walked into the living room on Christmas morning and saw the lighted tree with the packages underneath it was undiluted ecstasy. But aside from all of this—taking color from it, but springing from something deeper—was the implicit assurance that everything was going to be all right. This was a religious holiday and we never lost sight of the fact. The most sacred of all legends revealed itself then as the almost incredible truth, and all but literally we went about on tiptoe. On starry evenings during Christmas week groups of young people would go about town, stopping before various houses to sing Christmas carols, and as their harmonies floated off across the night we could see the town of Bethlehem not far away, and our snowy Michigan hills became one with the tawny slopes of Palestine. . . .

14   By the time I was sixteen the old excitement of Christmas gifts had of course worn somewhat thin, and I was ready to admit that the intense emotion centering about the tree in the living room was primarily something for small children, whose ranks I had left. Yet in some ways Christmas that year had an impact it had never had before. It seemed to come out of what I had always considered a routine observance: the Christmas Eve celebration in the village church.

15   Every year, on the night before Christmas, or sometimes on the last Sunday night before Christmas, the tallest balsam that could be got into the church was erected on the raised platform where the choir ordinarily sat, and it was covered with homemade decorations: looped chains made of colored paper, white popcorn threaded on long strings, tinsel stars, metal clips holding lighted candles, and so on. We had no electric lights for Christmas trees in those days; we simply used candles with open flames, burning within inches of drying evergreen needles, and the fire hazard must have been considerable. I should think a few houses would have burned down every year, but it never seemed to happen. Anyway, the church was filled with people. It was imperfectly lighted, and its interior seemed immense, larger than life, dominated by the great tree that reached up to the shadows just beneath the rafters, its tiny flames all twinkling. Just to be in the place was to partake of a mystery. The services were extremely simple. There were carols, prayers, readings of the gospel story of the first Christmas, a few quiet remarks by the minister, distribution of candy canes and molasses-and-popcorn balls to the small children, and a final hymn: and when the wheezy organ (pumped vigorously by a

sweating young man behind a screen) sounded off with "Joy to the World," and the doors opened to let us out into the winter night, it was as if we heard the sound of far-off trumpets.

Walking home afterward was what did it. It was cold and there was plenty of snow, which creaked under our feet as we went along the road, and the silent air seemed to be echoing with the carols we had sung; and overhead, infinitely remote yet for all of that very near and comforting, there was the endless host of golden stars whose clear flames denied the darkness. The message was unmistakable. Life was leading us—somewhere, somehow, miraculously—to a transfiguration. **16**

It stayed with me. I felt that I had had a glimpse behind the veil. I had seen the ultimate truth, and that truth was good; or so, at any rate, it seemed to me at the time. But while this remembered vision still lingered I had gone on that wind-borne cruise along the Crystal Lake ice, and at the far end of it I had seen something altogether different. Under the ice lay a flat denial of everything I had seen beyond the stars on Christmas Eve. I had had two visions, of the horror and of the transfiguration, and they seemed equally authentic. What did I do now? ... **17**

I realized, finally, that these contrasting visions were not actually at war with each other; they were simply the two sides of the same coin. Life's dimensions are infinite. It reaches from the abyss to the heights, and it touches the truth at each extreme. It stretches between terror and hope, and given the terms on which it is lived it cannot do anything else. The worst and the best visions are true, and the ultimate truth that embraces both is fantastically beyond comprehension. Life is a flame burning in water, shining on a sea that has no shore, and far overhead there are other flames which we call stars. **18**

Questions About Meaning

1. What does Catton say was the attitude toward life and the future held by the people around him in his youth?
2. What were the factors in the environment that hinted to them of another side to reality?
3. What does he mean by saying that what he "had seen through the transparent bending ice ... [was] the heart of darkness"?
4. What was the "ultimate truth" Catton says he thought he had glimpsed earlier, after the community Christmas Eve celebration?
5. What does Catton believe is the whole truth about life? What, then, is the analogy in this essay? (You may have to look up the term "analogy" in a good dictionary.)

Matters of Technique

1. Why do you suppose that Catton begins with the skating episode, which occurred after the Christmas Eve celebration? That is, why did he revise the normal chronology?
2. Paragraph 11 begins with, "The whole business cut a hard groove in my mind." Rewrite that sentence to make it more abstract. Now compare the two to note the superiority of concrete expressions to abstract ones.
3. Other concrete expressions occur in the same paragraph. Point them out.
4. What is the function of paragraph 12?
5. Rewrite Catton's final sentence to make it an abstract statement.

Vocabulary

1. omens (1)
2. disquieting (2)
3. ominous (8)
4. incontinently (9)
5. transfiguration (16)

Suggestions for Writing

1. Write about an experience that cut a "hard groove" in your mind.
2. Write about a moment when you, like Catton, "felt . . . completely in tune with the universe. . . ." Try to avoid simply telling readers how you felt. Instead, use the details of your experience to convey your feeling.
3. Write an essay based on your own experiences of life's glory and terror.
4. Write an essay based on your own experiences of the positive and negative aspects of your own personality.

CHAPTER FOUR

Illustration

Nothing smothers a subject more thoroughly than a long, dusty sequence of abstractions unrelieved by lively illustrations.

If you have an eccentric grandmother, illustrate her eccentricity with examples. Show us how she dyes her hair blonde, reads *Cosmopolitan*, and wears sweatshirts with "If It Feels Good, Do It" lettered across the front. If you think that humans are splendid creatures, illustrate how splendid they are with examples. Point out that they occasionally write a *Hamlet*, paint a *Night Watch*, compose a *Fifth Symphony*. We will then know, at the very least, what you are talking about, and you might even persuade us that humans are as splendid as you say they are.

Clarifying and Persuading Through Examples

Let's begin with how examples clarify. In a passage reprinted in this chapter, Joseph Campbell tells us that the "innate releasing mechanism" is the "inherited structure in the nervous system that enables an animal to respond ... to a circumstance never experienced before. . . ." For most of us, Campbell's generalization, left on its own, would be vague and unsatisfying. We desperately need an example to tell us what this "innate releasing mechanism" is. Happily for us, Campbell provides us one by showing that the newborn chicken, just out of its shell, runs from the "situation never experienced before," the chicken hawk. Now we know.

Examples also persuade. P. S. Wood's "Female Athletes: They've Come a Long Way, Baby" (reprinted in Chapter 6) contains such a sim-

73

ple idea—that female athletes are quickly catching up with male athletes—that it was unnecessary for the author to use examples to
merely clarify the idea. However, because his idea was so controversial, so arguable, he had a great need for examples to persuade. Wood
thus used a great number of examples, from many areas of sport—
from tennis, swimming, marathon running and racquetball, among
others—to persuade us of the truth of his generalization. When *you*
want to persuade through examples, multiply your examples past the
need for clarification.

Naturally, most examples clarify *and* persuade. In "On Natural
Death" (reprinted in this chapter), Lewis Thomas makes the comforting generalization that when death is near, when it is "end game"
time, there is something in the animal's system that turns off pain.
Thomas illustrates this idea with three marvelous examples: the languid mouse being chewed on by a cat, the painless death of two soldiers who lie crushed in a jeep, and Montaigne's feeling of detachment as he lies seriously injured after a fall from a horse. We now
know more clearly under what circumstances pain is turned off, and
we are probably now closer to believing that it *is* turned off.

How to Introduce Examples

1. When you can't think of a stylish or elegant way of moving from a
general statement to an example that supports that statement, merely
write "for example" or "for instance" or "to illustrate." And don't
worry about repeating these phrases. They are as invisible to readers
as a "he said" is.

2. Vary the structure of your introductory sentences occasionally.
After beginning with a phrase like "for example" a few times, begin
your next sentence with the word that normally follows the "for
example," and then insert the phrase:

He drinks, *for example*, like a fish.

3. Avoid placing a phrase like "for example" last in a sentence. This
placement usually weakens a sentence because readers expect a sentence to follow a natural climactic order.

4. Most examples are not introduced with a phrase like "for example." Usually the relationship between a general statement and the
example that serves to illustrate that statement is too obvious to need
a "for example." Consider the following sentences:

A. Female dogs are especially annoying when they are in heat. *For example*,
they scratch the door, moan in their sleep, and stink up the house.

Illustration **75**

B. Female dogs are especially annoying when they are in heat. They scratch the door, moan in their sleep, and stink up the house.

It is easy to see that *A* is a bit "mechanical" because the function the examples serve is so obvious.

5. When in doubt, use an introductory phrase like "for example" or "for instance." When there is a choice between elegance and clarity, take clarity every time.

MODEL ILLUSTRATION PARAGRAPH

Leftovers

There is always the miracle of the by-products. Plane a board, the shavings accumulate around your toes ready to be chucked into the stove to kindle your fires (to warm your toes so that you can plane a board). Draw some milk from a creature to relieve her fullness, the milk goes to the little pig to relieve his emptiness. Drain some oil from a crankcase, and you smear it on the roosts to control the mites. The worm fattens on the apple, the young goose fattens on the wormy fruit, the man fattens on the young goose, the worm awaits the man. Clean up the barnyard, the pulverized dung from the sheep goes to improve the lawn (before a rain in autumn); mow the lawn next spring, the clippings go to the compost pile, with a few thrown to the baby chickens on the way; spread the compost on the garden and in the fall the original dung, after many vicissitudes, returns to the sheep in the form of an old squash. From the fireplace, at the end of a November afternoon, the ashes are carried to the feet of the lilac bush, guaranteeing the excellence of a June morning.

From the essay "Cold Weather" in One Man's Meat *by E. B. White. Copyright 1943 by E. B. White. Reprinted by permission of Harper & Row, Publishers, Inc.*

ANALYSIS

Naturally, readers expect from illustration paragraphs *enough* examples to clarify the topic sentence, but they also expect sharply visualized examples. E. B. White's paragraph on by-products fulfills both of those expectations.

ASSIGNMENT

Illustrate a point about something by using at least five very specific and concrete examples.

On Natural Death

Lewis Thomas

Lewis Thomas, physician and biologist, is also a published poet and one of the finest essayists in the United States. He received the National Book Award for his first collection of essays, The Lives of a Cell *(1974). The selection we have printed comes from* The Medusa and the Snail *(1979).*

1   There are so many new books about dying that there are now special shelves set aside for them in bookshops, along with the health-diet and home-repair paperbacks and the sex manuals. Some of them are so packed with detailed information and step-by-step instructions for performing the function that you'd think this was a new sort of skill which all of us are now required to learn. The strongest impression the casual reader gets, leafing through, is that proper dying has become an extraordinary, even an exotic experience, something only the specially trained get to do.

2   Also, you could be led to believe that we are the only creatures capable of the awareness of death, that when all the rest of nature is being cycled through dying, one generation after another, it is a different kind of process, done automatically and trivially, more "natural," as we say.

3   An elm in our backyard caught the blight this summer and dropped stone dead, leafless, almost overnight. One weekend it was a normal-looking elm, maybe a little bare in spots but nothing alarming, and the next weekend it was gone, passed over, departed, taken. Taken is right, for the tree surgeon came by yesterday with his crew of young helpers and their cherry picker, and took it down branch by branch and carted it off in the back of a red truck, everyone singing.

4   The dying of a field mouse, at the jaws of an amiable household cat, is a spectacle I have beheld many times. It used to make me wince. Early in life I gave up throwing sticks at the cat to make him drop the mouse, because the dropped mouse regularly went ahead and died anyway, but I always shouted unaffections at the cat to let him know

the sort of animal he had become. Nature, I thought, was an abomination.

Recently I've done some thinking about that mouse, and I wonder 5
if his dying is necessarily all that different from the passing of our elm. The main difference, if there is one, would be in the matter of pain. I do not believe that an elm tree has pain receptors, and even so, the blight seems to me a relatively painless way to go even if there were nerve endings in a tree, which there are not. But the mouse dangling tail-down from the teeth of a gray cat is something else again, with pain beyond bearing, you'd think, all over his small body.

There are now some plausible reasons for thinking it is not like that 6
at all, and you can make up an entirely different story about the mouse and his dying if you like. At the instant of being trapped and penetrated by teeth, peptide hormones are released by cells in the hypothalamus and the pituitary gland; instantly these substances, called endorphins, are attached to the surfaces of other cells responsible for pain perception; the hormones have the pharmacologic properties of opium; there is no pain. Thus it is that the mouse seems always to dangle so languidly from the jaws, lies there so quietly when dropped, dies of his injuries without a struggle. If a mouse could shrug, he'd shrug.

I do not know if this is true or not, nor do I know how to prove it 7
if it is true. Maybe if you could get in there quickly enough and administer naloxone, a specific morphine antagonist, you could turn off the endorphins and observe the restoration of pain, but this is not something I would care to do or see. I think I will leave it there, as a good guess about the dying of a cat-chewed mouse, perhaps about dying in general.

Montaigne had a hunch about dying, based on his own close call 8
in a riding accident. He was so badly injured as to be believed dead by his companions, and was carried home with lamentations, "all bloody, stained all over with the blood I had thrown up." He remembers the entire episode, despite having been "dead, for two full hours," with wonderment:

It seemed to me that my life was hanging only by the tip of my lips. I closed my eyes in order, it seemed to me, to help push it out, and took pleasure in growing languid and letting myself go. It was an idea that was only floating on the surface of my soul, as delicate and feeble as all the rest, but in truth not only free from distress but mingled with that sweet feeling that people have who have let themselves slide into sleep. I believe that this is the same state in which people find themselves whom we see fainting in the agony of death, and I maintain that we pity them without cause. . . . In order to get used to the idea of death, I find there is nothing like coming close to it.

Later, in another essay, Montaigne returns to it:

If you know not how to die, never trouble yourself; Nature will in a moment fully and sufficiently instruct you; she will exactly do that business for you; take you no care for it.

9   The worst accident I've ever seen was on Okinawa, in the early days of the invasion, when a jeep ran into a troop carrier and was crushed nearly flat. Inside were two young MPs, trapped in bent steel, both mortally hurt, with only their heads and shoulders visible. We had a conversation while people with the right tools were prying them free. Sorry about the accident, they said. No, they said, they felt fine. Is everyone else okay, one of them said. Well, the other one said, no hurry now. And then they died.

10   Pain is useful for avoidance, for getting away when there's time to get away, but when it is end game, and no way back, pain is likely to be turned off, and the mechanisms for this are wonderfully precise and quick. If I had to design an ecosystem in which creatures had to live off each other and in which dying was an indispensable part of living, I could not think of a better way to manage.

Questions About Meaning

1. What is the initial thesis? How is this thesis expanded in paragraph 2? How is the thesis qualified in paragraphs 6, 8, and 9?
2. What examples does Thomas use to illustrate his points?
3. What idea connects the stories of the mouse, Montaigne, and the dying soldiers?
4. What is Thomas's theory about the body's reaction to pain at the point of death?
5. What game is the expression "end game" (paragraph 10) taken from?
6. Where does Thomas suggest his view that the natural order of things shows design and purpose?

Matters of Technique

1. What contrast does Thomas set up in paragraphs 3 and 4? What does he do in paragraphs 5 and 6 to introduce a new perspective?
2. Good writers vary the length of their sentences. Notice the effective

variation in the sentences in paragraph 4. Count the words in each sentence in that paragraph to discover how widely the sentence lengths vary.
3. Why does Thomas save the example of the dying boys in the jeep for last?
4. What relationship does the second Montaigne quotation have to the last sentence in Thomas's first paragraph?
5. A very short sentence will sometimes conclude a paragraph for the sake of emphasis. Find three paragraphs in Thomas's essay that are concluded by short sentences.
6. Change the colons that precede the Montaigne quotations into commas. (Naturally, you will have to restructure the sentences to make this possible.)
7. Write a topic sentence for the elm tree example in paragraph 3. Where in paragraph 5 does the author suggest a topic sentence for paragraph 3?

Vocabulary

1. amiable (4)
2. abomination (4)
3. pharmacologic (6)
4. plausible (6)
5. languidly (6)
6. lamentations (8)

Suggestions for Writing

1. Using several examples, describe *your* view of the most mysterious things about life.
2. Discuss the thesis that Nature is an "abomination." (See paragraph 4.)
3. Discuss the most important lesson (or lessons) you have learned about life, or about human nature—including your own. Use examples to illustrate your thesis.

Cross-Reference

Bertrand Russell says in "Do We Survive Death?" that if life "is the outcome of deliberate purpose, the purpose must have been that of a fiend." Contrast Thomas's view with Russell's.

The Witch in the Nervous System

Joseph Campbell

The following illustration of the "innate releasing mechanism" comes from the first volume, The Masks of God: Primitive Mythology *(1959), of a three-volume study in which Campbell brings to bear the insights of psychology, ethnology, philology, folklore, and other disciplines on the study of comparative mythology.*

1   A number of popular moving-picture films have shown the amazing phenomenon of the laying and hatching of the eggs of the sea turtle. The female leaves the water and crawls to a point on the beach safely above the tide line, where she digs a hole, deposits hundreds of eggs, covers the nest, and turns back to the sea. After eighteen days a multitude of tiny turtles come flipping up through the sand and, like a field of sprinters at the crack of the gun, make for the heavily crashing waves as fast as they can, while gulls drop screaming from overhead to pick them off.

2   No more vivid representation could be desired of spontaneity and the quest for the not-yet-seen. There is no question here of learning, trial-and-error; nor are the tiny things afraid of the great waves. They know that they must hurry, know how to do it, and know precisely where they are going. And finally, when they enter the sea, they know immediately both how to swim and that swim they must.

3   Students of animal behavior have coined the term "innate releasing mechanism" (IRM) to designate the inherited structure in the nervous system that enables an animal to respond thus to a circumstance never experienced before, and the factor triggering the response they term a "sign stimulus" or "releaser." It is obvious that the living entity responding to such a sign cannot be said to be the individual, since the individual has had no previous knowledge of the object to which it is reacting. The recognizing and responding subject is, rather, some sort of trans- or super-individual, inhabiting and moving the living creature. Let us not speculate here about the metaphysics of this mystery; for, as Schopenhauer sagely remarks in his paper on *The Will in*

Nature, "we are sunk in a sea of riddles and inscrutables, knowing and understanding neither what is around us nor ourselves."

Chicks with their eggshells still adhering to their tails dart for cover 4 when a hawk flies overhead, but not when the bird is a gull or duck, heron or pigeon. Furthermore, if the wooden model of a hawk is drawn over their coop on a wire, they react as though it were alive—unless it be drawn backward, when there is no response.

Here we have an extremely precise image—never seen before, yet 5 recognized with reference not merely to its form but to its form in motion, and linked, furthermore, to an immediate, unplanned, unlearned, and even unintended system of appropriate action: flight, to cover. The image of the inherited enemy is already sleeping in the nervous system, and along with it the well-proven reaction. Furthermore, even if all the hawks in the world were to vanish, their image would still sleep in the soul of the chick—never to be roused, however, unless by some accident of art; for example, a repetition of the clever experiment of the wooden hawk on a wire. With that (for a certain number of generations, at any rate) the obsolete reaction of the flight to cover would recur: and, unless we knew about the earlier danger of hawks to chicks, we should find the sudden eruption difficult to explain. "Whence," we might ask, "this abrupt seizure by an image to which there is no counterpart in the chicken's world? Living gulls and ducks, herons and pigeons, leave it cold; but the work of art strikes some very deep chord!"

Have we here a clue to the problem of the image of the witch in 6 the nervous system of the child? Some psychologists would say so. C. G. Jung, for example, identifies two fundamentally different systems of unconsciously motivated response in the human being. One he terms the personal unconscious. It is based on a context of forgotten, neglected, or suppressed memory images derived from personal experience (infantile impressions, shocks, frustrations, satisfactions, etc.), such as Sigmund Freud recognized and analyzed in his therapy. The other he names the collective unconscious. Its contents—which he calls archetypes—are just such images as that of the hawk in the nervous system of the chick. No one has yet been able to tell us how it got there; but there it is!

Questions About Meaning

1. What two animals does Campbell use to illustrate the operation of the "innate releasing mechanism"?
2. How do the chicks react when the wooden model of the hawk is pulled backwards?

3. What does Campbell's use of Schopenhauer's statement indicate about his point of view toward his subject?
4. What new application does Campbell make of the IRM concept in paragraph 6?
5. What does Jung call the stimulus that triggers the "innate releasing mechanism" for the human being?

Matters of Technique

1. Campbell begins with an example. Where is the sentence that that example serves?
2. Rewrite the first sentence in paragraph 2 to make it shorter (by at least a word) and clearer.
3. What does the second example (the baby chickens) have that the first example (the baby turtles) lacks?
4. What is a key transition word in paragraphs 4 and 5?
5. Campbell cites several authorities to illustrate the meaning of his examples. Why is this an effective technique?

Vocabulary

1. sagely (3)
2. inscrutables (3)

3. archetypes (6)

Suggestions for Writing

1. Relate an experience from your childhood that illustrates what Campbell means by "the witch in the nervous system." (See paragraph 6.)
2. Illustrate a principle of behavior that is common to both animals and humans. If possible, cite an authority or two to help clarify the meaning of your examples.
3. Discuss a spontaneous reaction you have observed in yourself to certain circumstances, situations, or people. Use at least three examples.

California Dreaming

Joan Didion

Joan Didion is a novelist (Play It as It Lays, *1970;* A Book of Common Prayer, *1976) and one of the finest contemporary essayists in the United States. "California Dreaming," from a critically acclaimed collection of essays,* Slouching Towards Bethlehem *(1968), shows how examples can be put in the service of a satire.*

Every weekday morning at eleven o'clock, just about the time the sun 1
burns the last haze off the Santa Barbara hills, fifteen or twenty men gather in what was once the dining room of a shirt manufacturer's mansion overlooking the Pacific Ocean and begin another session of what they like to call "clarifying the basic issues." The place is the Center for the Study of Democratic Institutions, the current mutation of the Fund for the Republic, and since 1959, when the Fund paid $250,000 for the marble villa and forty-one acres of eucalyptus, a favored retreat for people whom the Center's president, Robert M. Hutchins, deems controversial, stimulating, and, perhaps above all, cooperative, or *our kind.* "If they just want to work on their own stuff," Hutchins has said, "then they ought not to come here. Unless they're willing to come in and work with the group as a group, then this place is not for them."

Those invited to spend time at the Center get an office (there are 2
no living quarters at the Center) and a salary, the size of which is reportedly based on the University of California pay scale. The selection process is usually described as "mysterious," but it always involves "people we know." Paul Hoffman, who was at one time president of the Ford Foundation and then director of the Fund for the Republic, is now the Center's honorary chairman, and his son is there quite a bit, and Robert Hutchins's son-in-law. Rexford Tugwell, one of the New Deal "brain trust," is there ("Why not?" he asked me. "If I weren't here I'd be in a rest home"), and Harvey Wheeler, the co-author of *Fail-Safe.* Occasionally someone might be asked to the Center

because he has built-in celebrity value, *e.g.*, Bishop James Pike. "What we are is a group of highly skilled public-relations experts," Harry Ashmore says. Harry Ashmore is a fixture at the Center, and he regards Hutchins—or, as the president of the Center is inflexibly referred to in the presence of outsiders, Dr. Hutchins—as "a natural intellectual resource." What these highly skilled public-relations experts do, besides clarifying the basic issues and giving a lift to Bennett Cerf ("My talk with Paul Hoffman on the Coast gave me a lift I won't forget," Bennett Cerf observed some time ago), is to gather every weekday for a few hours of discussion, usually about one of several broad areas that the Center is concentrating upon at any given time—The City, say, or The Emerging Constitution. Papers are prepared, read, revised, reread, and sometimes finally published. This process is variously described by those who participate in it as "pointing the direction for all of us toward a greater understanding" and "applying human reason to the complex problems of our brand-new world."

3   I have long been interested in the Center's rhetoric, which has about it the kind of ectoplasmic generality that always makes me sense I am on the track of the real soufflé, the genuine American *kitsch*, and so not long ago I arranged to attend a few sessions in Santa Barbara. It was in no sense time wasted. The Center is the most perfectly indigenous cultural phenomenon since the Encyclopaedia Britannica's *Syntopicon*, which sets forth "The 102 Great Ideas of Western Man" and which we also owe to Robert, or Dr., Hutchins. "Don't make the mistake of taking a chair at the big table," I was warned *sotto voce* on my first visit to the Center. "The talk there is pretty high-powered."

4   "Is there any evidence that living in a violent age encourages violence?" someone was asking at the big table.

5   "That's hard to measure."

6   "I think it's the Westerns on television."

7   "I tend [*pause*] to agree."

8   Every word uttered at the Center is preserved on tape, and not only colleges and libraries but thousands of individuals receive Center tapes and pamphlets. Among the best-selling pamphlets have been A. A. Berle, Jr.'s *Economic Power and the Free Society*, Clark Kerr's *Unions and Union Leaders of Their Own Choosing*, Donald Michael's *Cybernation: The Silent Conquest*, and Harrison Brown's *Community of Fear*. Seventy-five thousand people a year then write fan letters to the Center, confirming the staff in its conviction that everything said around the place mystically improves the national, and in fact the international, weal. From a Colorado country-day-school teacher: "I use the Center's various papers in my U.S. history-current events course. It seems to me that there is no institution in the U.S. today engaged in more val-

uable and first-rate work than the Center." From a California mother: "Now my fifteen-year-old daughter has discovered your publications. This delights me as she is one of those regular teenagers. But when she curls up to read, it is with your booklets."

The notion that providing useful papers for eighth-grade current-events classes and reading for regular teenagers might not be at all times compatible with establishing "a true intellectual community" (another Hutchins aim) would be considered, at the Center, a downbeat and undemocratic cavil. "People are entitled to learn what we're thinking," someone there told me. The place is in fact avidly anti-intellectual, the deprecatory use of words like "egghead" and "ivory tower" reaching heights matched only in a country-club locker room. Hutchins takes pains to explain that by "an intellectual community" he does not mean a community "whose members regard themselves as 'intellectuals.'" Harry Ashmore frets particularly that "men of affairs" may fail to perceive the Center's "practical utility." Hutchins likes to quote Adlai Stevenson on this point: "The Center can be thought of as a kind of national insurance plan, a way of making certain that we will deserve better and better."

Although one suspects that this pragmatic Couéism as a mode of thought comes pretty naturally to most of the staff at the Center, it is also vital to the place's survival. In 1959 the Fund for the Republic bequeathed to the Center the $4 million left of its original $15 million Ford Foundation grant, but that is long gone, and because there was never any question of more Ford money, the Center must pay its own way. Its own way costs about a million dollars a year. Some twelve thousand contributors provide the million a year, and it helps if they can think of a gift to the Center not as a gift to support some visionaries who never met a payroll but "as an investment [tax-exempt] in the preservation of our free way of life." It helps, too, to present the donor with a fairly broadstroke picture of how the Center is besieged by the forces of darkness, and in this effort the Center has had an invaluable, if unintentional, ally in the Santa Barbara John Birch Society. "You can't let the fascists drive them out of town," I was advised by an admirer of the Center.

Actually, even without the Birch Society as a foil, Hutchins has evolved the $E = mc^2$ of all fund-raising formulae. The Center is supported on the same principle as a vanity press. People who are in a position to contribute large sums of money are encouraged to participate in clarifying the basic issues. Dinah Shore, a founding member, is invited up to discuss civil rights with Bayard Rustin. Steve Allen talks over "Ideology and Intervention" with Senator Fulbright and Arnold Toynbee, and Kirk Douglas, a founding member, speaks his piece on "The Arts in a Democratic Society." Paul Newman, in the role of "concerned citizen," is on hand to discuss "The University in America" with Dr. Hutchins, Supreme Court Justice William O. Douglas, Arnold Grant, Rosemary Park, and another concerned citizen, Jack Lemmon. "Apropos of absolutely nothing," Mr. Lemmon says, pulling on a pipe, "just for my own amazement—I don't *know*, but I *want* to know—" At this juncture he wants to know about student unrest, and, at another, he worries that government contracts will corrupt "pure research."

12   "You mean maybe they get a grant to develop some new kind of *plastic*," Mr. Newman muses, and Mr. Lemmon picks up the cue: "What happens then to the humanities?"

13   Everyone goes home flattered, and the Center prevails. Well, why not? One morning I was talking with the wife of a big contributor as we waited on the terrace for one of the Center's ready-mixed martinis and a few moments' chat with Dr. Hutchins. "These sessions are way over my head," she confided, "but I go out floating on air."

Questions About Meaning

1. State Didion's unstated thesis. (It is hinted at in the title.)
2. How did the Center support itself in the beginning? What three methods does the Center use to support itself now?
3. To what does Didion compare the Center in paragraph 3?

Matters of Technique

1. Which of the sentences in paragraph 2 sums up these examples: Paul Hoffman, Paul Hoffman's son, and Robert Hutchins's son-in-law?
2. How do the examples of dialogue in paragraphs 4, 5, 6, and 7 undercut the last sentence in paragraph 3: "The talk there is pretty high-powered"?
3. What purpose do the examples in paragraph 11 serve? What is the topic sentence for those examples?
4. What is the connection between Didion's final example (in paragraph 13) and the title of her essay?

Vocabulary

1. ectoplasmic (3)
2. kitsch (3)

3. indigenous (3)
4. *sotto voce* (3)

5. cavil (9)
6. deprecatory (9)
7. pragmatic (10)

8. Couéism (10)
9. muses (*verb*; 12)

Suggestions for Writing

1. Write an essay in which you analyze the techniques of Didion's satire. Begin by looking in a literary handbook for an extended definition or discussion of satire.
2. Write a satire of your own in which you use some of the techniques of satire that Didion uses in her essay. Try to be as subtle as Didion; that is, don't state too blatantly what points you are making.

Conundrum

Nora Ephron

Nora Ephron, one of America's finest satirists, is a freelance writer for a variety of magazines, including Esquire, The New Yorker, *and* Rolling Stone. *Her essays are collected in* Wallflower at the Orgy *(1970),* Scribble, Scribble *(1978), and the book from which our selection comes,* Crazy Salad *(1975). Ephron's writings, almost always wryly humorous, are often on changes in men's and women's roles.*

1   As I suppose everyone knows by now, James Morris was four years old and sitting under the piano listening to his mother play Sibelius when he was seized with the irreversible conviction that he ought to have been born a girl. By the age of nine, he was praying nightly for the miracle. "Let me be a girl. Amen." He went on to the army, became a journalist, climbed Mount Everest with Sir Edmund Hillary, won awards for his books, and had four children with a wife who knew that all he really wanted was a sex change. Almost two years ago, he went off to a clinic in Casablanca that had dirty floors, shaved off his pubic hair, "and went to say goodbye to myself in the mirror. We would never meet again, and I wanted to give that other self a long last look in the eye and a wink of luck." The wink of luck did that other self no good at all: the next morning, it was lopped off, and James Morris woke up to find himself as much a woman as hormones and surgery could make him. He promptly sold his dinner jacket and changed his name.

2   This entire mess could doubtless have been avoided had James Morris been born an Orthodox Jew (in which case he could have adopted the standard Jewish prayer thanking God for *not* making him a woman) or had he gone to see a good Freudian analyst, who might have realized that any young boy sitting under a piano was probably looking up his mother's skirt. But no such luck. James Morris has become Jan Morris, an Englishwoman who wears sweater sets and pearls, blushes frequently, bursts into tears at the littlest things, and loves having a gossip with someone named Mrs. Weatherby. Mrs.

Weatherby, Morris writes, "really is concerned . . . about my migraine yesterday; and when I examine myself I find that I am no less genuinely distressed to hear that Amanda missed the school outing because of her ankle."

Conundrum is Jan Morris's book about her experience, and I read it 3 with a great deal of interest, largely because I always wanted to be a girl, too. I, too, felt that I was born into the wrong body, a body that refused, in spite of every imprecation and exercise I could manage, to become anything but the boyish, lean thing it was. I, too, grew up wishing for protectors, strangers to carry my bags, truck drivers to whistle out windows. I wanted more than anything to be something I will never be—feminine, and feminine in the worst way. Submissive. Dependent. Soft-spoken. Coquettish. I was no good at all at any of it, no good at being a girl; on the other hand, I am not half-bad at being a woman. In contrast, Jan Morris is perfectly awful at being a woman; what she has become instead is exactly what James Morris wanted to become those many years ago. A girl. And worse, a forty-seven-year-old girl. And worst of all, a forty-seven-year-old *Cosmopolitan* girl. To wit:

"So I well understand what Kipling had in mind, about sisters 4 under the skin. Over coffee a lady from Montreal effuses about Bath— 'I don't know if you've done any traveling yourself' (not too much, I demurely lie) 'but I do feel it's important, don't you, to see how other people really live.' I bump into Jane W——— in the street, and she tells me about Archie's latest excess—'Honestly, Jan, you don't know how lucky you are.' I buy some typing paper—'How lovely to be able to write, you make me feel a proper dunce'—and walking home again to start work on a new chapter, find that workmen are in the flat, taking down a picture-rail. One of them has knocked my little red horse off the mantelpiece, chipping its enameled rump. I restrain my annoyance, summon a fairly frosty smile, and make them all cups of tea, but I am thinking to myself, as they sheepishly help themselves to sugar, a harsh feminist thought. It would be a man, I think. Well it would, wouldn't it?"

It is a truism of the women's movement that the exaggerated con- 5 cepts of femininity and masculinity have done their fair share to make a great many people unhappy, but nowhere is this more evident than in Jan Morris's mawkish and embarrassing book. I first read of Morris in a Sunday *New York Times Magazine* article that brought dignity and real sensitivity to Morris's obsession. But Morris's own sensibility is so giddy and relentlessly cheerful that her book has almost no dignity at all. What she has done in it is to retrace his/her life (I am going to go crazy from the pronouns and adjectives here) by applying sentimental gender judgments to everything. Oxford is wonderful because it is feminine. Venice is sublime because it is feminine. Statesmen are dreadful because they are masculine. "Even more than now," Morris writes of his years as a foreign correspondent, "the world of affairs was dominated by men. It was like stepping from cheap theater into reality, to pass from the ludicrous goings-on of minister's office or ambassador's study into the private house behind, where women were to be found doing real things, like bringing up children, painting pictures, or writing home."

6   And as for sex—but let Morris tell you about men and women and sex. "You are doubtless wondering, especially if you are male, what about sex? . . . One of the genuine and recurrent surprises of my life concerns the importance to men of physical sex. . . . For me the actual performance of the sexual act seemed of secondary importance and interest. I suspect this is true for most women. . . . In the ordinary course of events [the sex act] struck me as slightly distasteful, and I could imagine it only as part of some grand act, a declaration of absolute interdependence, or even a sacrifice."

7   Over the years, Morris saw a number of doctors, several of whom suggested he try homosexuality. (He had tried it several times before, but found it aesthetically unpleasant.) A meeting was arranged with the owner of a London art gallery. "We had a difficult lunch together," Morris writes, "and he made eyes at the wine waiter over the fruit salad." The remark is interesting, not just because of its hostility toward homosexuals but also because Jan Morris now makes exactly those same sorts of eyes at wine waiters—on page 150 of her book, in fact.

8   As James turns into a hermaphrodite and then into Jan, the prose in the book, which is cloying enough to begin with, turns into a kind of overembellished, simile-laden verbiage that makes the style of Victorian women novelists seem spare. Exclamation points and italicized words appear with increasing frequency. Everything blushes. James Morris blushes. His "small breasts blossomed like blushes." He starts talking to the flowers and wishing them a Happy Easter. He becomes even more devoted to animals. He is able for the first time ("the scales dropped from my eyes") to look out a plane window and see things on the ground below not as cars and homes seen at a distance but "Lo! . . . as dolls' houses and dinky toys." Shortly before the operation, he and his wife, Elizabeth, whose understanding defies understanding, take a trip, both as women, through Oregon. "How merrily we traveled!" Morris writes. "What fun the Oregonians gave us! How cheerfully we swapped badinage with boatmen and lumberjacks, flirtatious garage hands and hospitable trappers! I never felt so liberated, or more myself, nor was I ever more fond of Elizabeth. 'Come on in, girls,' the motel men would say, and childish though I expect it sounds to you,

silly in itself, perhaps a little pathetic, possibly grotesque, still if they had touched me with an accolade of nobility, or clad me ceremonially in crimson, I could not have been more flattered." The only thing Morris neglects to write into this passage is a little face with a smile on it.

Morris is infuriatingly vague about the reactions of her children 9 (she blandly insists they adjusted perfectly) and of Elizabeth (she says they are still the closest of friends). "I am not the first," Morris writes, "to discover that one recipe for an idyllic marriage is a blend of affection, physical potency and sexual incongruity." (Idyllic marriage? Where your husband becomes a lady? I suppose we owe this to creeping Harold-and-Vitaism; still, it is one of the more ridiculous trends of recent years to confuse great friendships with great marriages; great marriages are when you have it all.) As for her new sex life, Jan Morris lyrically trills that her sexuality is now unbounded. But how?

Unfortunately, she is a good deal more explicit about the details of 10 what she refers to as "truly the symptoms of womanhood." "The more I was treated as a woman, the more woman I became," she writes. "I adapted willy-nilly. If I was assumed to be incompetent at reversing cars, or opening bottles, oddly, incompetent I found myself becoming. If a case was thought too heavy for me, inexplicably I found it so myself.... I discovered that even now men prefer women to be less informed, less able, less talkative, and certainly less self-centered than they are themselves; so I generally obliged them.... I did not particularly want to be good at reversing cars, and did not in the least mind being patronized by illiterate garage-men, if it meant they were going to give me some extra trading stamps.... And when the news agent seems to look at me with approval, or the man in the milk-cart smiles, I feel absurdly elated, as though I have been given a good review in the Sunday *Times*. I know it is nonsense, but I cannot help it."

The truth, of course, is that Jan Morris does not know it is nonsense. 11 She thinks that is what it is about. And I wonder about all this, wonder how anyone in this day and age can think that this is what being a woman is about. And as I wonder, I find myself thinking a harsh feminist thought. It would be a man, I think. Well, it would, wouldn't it?

Questions About Meaning

1. How would Judaism and Freudian analysis have helped James Morris adjust?
2. What is a "*Cosmopolitan* girl"? (See paragraph 3.)
3. What happened to James/Jan's prose when he/she became a woman?

4. How does Morris describe the male view of women?
5. Ephron, like Morris, indulges in a "harsh feminist thought." What is it?

Matters of Technique

1. Ephron's opening paragraph virtually assures that her readers will continue on. What is there about that opening that makes it so good?
2. Where exactly does Ephron first state her thesis?
3. Which sentence in paragraph 2 is a fragment? Do you see any advantages to it in that particular paragraph?
4. Notice the rather heavy use Ephron makes of quotations in this essay, which is a review of Morris's book. These illustrations from Morris's book are especially heavy in paragraph 8. Why?

Vocabulary

1. conundrum (*title*)
2. imprecation (3)
3. coquettish (3)
4. demurely (4)
5. mawkish (5)

6. aesthetically (7)
7. verbiage (8)
8. accolade (8)
9. idyllic (9)
10. incongruity (9)

Suggestions for Writing

1. Write a two-paragraph "girlish" description of a brief social encounter you had yesterday. Then write about the same encounter the way a "man" would describe it.
2. Write a paper about what you consider exaggerated concepts of femininity or masculinity. Use several clear examples to illustrate your meaning.

CHAPTER FIVE

Process

1. Remove receiver.
2. Deposit coins.
3. Listen for dial tone.
4. Call number.

These simple instructions, written by an anonymous telephone company employee years ago and enshrined in thousands of pay telephones, are an example of what is known as process writing.

Process writing is no more than an explanation of how something works or how something is done. It is used in everything from a recipe for beef goulash to plans for how to build a nuclear submarine. ("First, get hold of a pound of enriched U-235 . . .")

Point of View

When you are explaining how something is done, you have a variety of points of view to use, and each produces a subtly different effect:

1. *the formal:* "One grasps the widget in one's left hand." The formal "one" point of view elevates the tone of the writing slightly. Because of this elevated effect and the increasingly informal tone of modern prose, the "one" point of view is not used as much as it once was. It is generally reserved nowadays for only the most formal writing situations.
2. *the personal:* "I grasp the widget in my left hand." Naturally, the "I" point of view cannot be used unless you have personally

experienced the process. But when you can use it, it does add vividness and immediacy to your process themes.

3. *the impersonal:* "She (he, it, they) grasps the widget in her left hand." The third person point of view is probably the most common viewpoint when a writer wants to explain a process without really expecting the reader to duplicate it. In level of formality, it lies somewhere between the formal "one" and the personal "I."

4. *the imperative:* "You grasp the widget with your left hand." The "you" point of view is reserved for those occasions when the writer is giving directions and expects the reader to be able to duplicate the process described.

The Instructional Process Essay

The first matter to think about before writing a process theme is which of the two basic types of process themes you will be writing. That decision will influence the shape, the tone, and the details you use—so you need to know before you start.

If, for instance, you are writing an informational process theme (an explanation of the make-up of something, not how to do something), you will need to work hard to develop reader interest through the use of the various rhetorical techniques we discuss in this book.

However, if you are writing an instructional process theme (directions on how to do something), you will need to fill your essay with the kinds of clear, precise details that will allow your readers to follow your instructions. (The ultimate instructional process essays are lab experiment reports, which are worthless unless the experiments described can be duplicated exactly.) But you needn't be overly concerned about developing reader interest.

The most direct and simple point of view for giving instructions is the imperative "you." Here are simple instructions on how to split firewood:

1. You will need a six- to eight-pound ax, preferably one with a fiberglass handle. Wood handles are handsome and rustic, but they also break much more easily.
2. Cut your wood into splittable lengths of no more than two feet. Longer lengths are difficult to split.
3. Stand the wood on its end, with the most knotted and gnarled end down.
4. Strike the wood in its center with a sharp blow. If you are splitting an easily splittable wood like walnut, hickory, or oak, you

should be able to split the wood with one blow. But if the wood is elm, or gnarled wood of any kind, you will probably have to hit the wood a number of times—or set it aside for later splitting by maul and wedge.

Notice that the imperative "you" uses the "you" only infrequently. When it isn't used, however, it is still clearly understood by readers. ("[You] use an eight-pound ax.")

All four points of view could have been used for the wood-splitting instructions, though the "one" point of view, the most formal of the four, would have been the most inappropriate because of the homey nature of the subject.

The Informational Process Essay

Not all process writing, of course, is instructional. When your intention is merely to explain how something is done, not how to do it, you are writing an *informational* process essay. For instance, if you were writing an explanation of how your state legislature works, you would not be expecting your readers to organize a legislature; you would be merely imparting information. Likewise, in "How Dictionaries Are Made" (reprinted in this chapter), S. I. Hayakawa doesn't expect his readers to write a dictionary.

Quite naturally, since the writer doesn't expect readers to duplicate the process described in the informational process essay, the "you" point of view is never used.

The informational process essay doesn't have the natural reader interest that the instructional process essay does. After all, anyone who reads an instructional process essay does so in order to find out how to do something, and usually is only concerned with clarity. The informational process essay, however, doesn't have that built-in reader interest. You might say that the need for developing reader interest increases as the need for precise instructions that can be followed decreases. As a result, the writer must work harder to make an informational essay interesting through the use of vivid examples, lively description, and other rhetorical devices.

Suggestions for the Process Essay

1. If the steps in your process are long and complicated, break the process up into stages. If, for instance, you were describing how a bill becomes a law, you would need to divide your essay into "How a Bill

Is Generated," "Its Journey Through the House," "Its Journey Through the Senate," and "Final White House Decision." Within these four major divisions you would explain the smaller steps.

2. You will sometimes want to give reasons for steps. In the directions above for splitting wood, for instance, readers are told in the second step that the wood is cut into lengths of two feet or less because longer lengths are difficult to split.

3. Try not to shift tense or point of view unless it is absolutely necessary. If you begin with the present tense imperative, finish with it.

4. Since you can't possibly explain everything, nor would you want to, you will need to estimate how much your readers already know and omit that in your theme. Don't irritate them by telling them too much. In the wood-splitting instructions, for instance, the writer doesn't explain what a knot or a gnarl is, nor does he explain what an ax is.

5. You may need to tell readers what *not* to do. If you were giving directions for turning wood on a lathe, you would certainly want to tell readers not to turn wood while wearing loose clothing or a tie.

MODEL PROCESS PARAGRAPH

Building a Fire with Buffalo Chips

... the camp has found a good substitute for wood in the dried buffalo dung which lies on the ground here in great plenty, and makes a good fire when properly managed. Kimball invented a new way of building a fire to cook on ... which is well adapted to the use of this kind of fuel. He dug a hole in the ground about eight inches deep, fifteen inches long, and eight inches wide. Then at each end of this hole he dug another about the same dimensions as the first, leaving about three inches of earth standing between the middle and two end holes. At the end of these partitions he made a hole through about three inches in diameter to serve as a draft. In the bottom of the middle hole the fire and fuel were placed, and across the top two wagon hammers to set the pots and pans on, so that the fire could have free circulation underneath. By this method much cooking was done with very little fuel.

William Clayton, 1847

ANALYSIS

A process description should be very clear and specific so that the details can be readily visualized. All you would need in order to duplicate the process Clayton describes is something to dig with, something to set your cooking utensils on, and a small stack of buffalo dung.

ASSIGNMENT

Write a paragraph in which you describe a simple process as clearly as Clayton does. But instead of using the third person point of view, which he uses, put your process description into the imperative "you" point of view. (Reread the introduction to this chapter if you need help with this.) Naturally, the "you" point of view will force you to write an instructional process paragraph (how to do something) rather than an informational process paragraph.

How Dictionaries Are Made

S. I. Hayakawa

Although S. I. Hayakawa began his career as a semanticist (a linguist who specializes in the science of meaning), he is now better known for his public roles: as the one-time president (1968–1973) of San Francisco State College during the tumultuous years of student unrest and as a U.S. Senator from California. "How Dictionaries Are Made" is from the fourth edition of Language in Thought and Action *(1978), one of a number of books on language that Hayakawa has written.*

1   It is widely believed that every word has a correct meaning, that we learn these meanings principally from teachers and grammarians (except that most of the time we don't bother to, so that we ordinarily speak "sloppy English"), and that dictionaries and grammars are the supreme authority in matters of meaning and usage. Few people ask by what authority the writers of dictionaries and grammars say what they say. I once got into a dispute with an Englishwoman over the pronunciation of a word and offered to look it up in the dictionary. The Englishwoman said firmly "What for? I am English. I was born and brought up in England. The way I speak *is* English." Such self-assurance about one's own language is not uncommon among the English. In the United States, however, anyone who is willing to quarrel with the dictionary is regarded as either eccentric or mad.

2   Let us see how dictionaries are made and how the editors arrive at definitions. What follows applies, incidentally, only to those dictionary offices where first-hand, original research goes on—not those in which editors simply copy existing dictionaries. The task of writing a dictionary begins with reading vast amounts of the literature of the period or subject that the dictionary is to cover. As the editors read, they copy on cards every interesting or rare word, every unusual or peculiar occurrence of a common word, a large number of common words in their ordinary uses, and also the sentences in which each of these words appears, thus

> pail
> The dairy *pails* bring home increase of milk
> KEATS, *Endymion*
> I, 44–45

That is to say, the context of each word is collected, along with the word itself. For a really big job of dictionary-writing, such as the *Oxford English Dictionary* (usually bound in about twenty-five volumes), millions of such cards are collected, and the task of editing occupies decades. As the cards are collected, they are alphabetized and sorted. When the sorting is completed, there will be for each word anywhere from two or three to several hundred illustrative quotations, each on its card.

To define a word, then, the dictionary-editor places before him the stack of cards illustrating that word; each of the cards represents an actual use of the word by a writer of some literary or historical importance. He reads the cards carefully, discards some, rereads the rest, and divides up the stack according to what he thinks are the several senses of the word. Finally, he writes his definitions, following the hard-and-fast rule that each definition *must* be based on what the quotations in front of him reveal about the meaning of the word. The editor cannot be influenced by what *he* thinks a given word *ought* to mean. He must work according to the cards or not at all.

The writing of a dictionary, therefore, is not a task of setting up authoritative statements about the "true meanings" of words, but a task of *recording*, to the best of one's ability, what various words have *meant* to authors in the distant or immediate past. *The writer of a dictionary is a historian, not a lawgiver.* If, for example, we had been writing a dictionary in 1890, or even as late as 1919, we could have said that the word "broadcast" means "to scatter" (seed, for example), but we could not have decreed that from 1921 on, the most common meaning of the word should become "to disseminate audible messages, etc., by radio transmission." To regard the dictionary as an "authority," therefore, is to credit the dictionary-writer with gifts of prophecy which neither he nor anyone else possesses. In choosing our words when we speak or write, we can be *guided* by the historical record afforded us by the dictionary, but we cannot be *bound* by it, because new situations, new experiences, new inventions, new feelings are always compelling us to give new uses to old words. Looking under a "hood," we should ordinarily have found, five hundred years ago, a monk; today, we find a motorcar engine.

Questions About Meaning

1. What widespread belief does Hayakawa describe in paragraph 1?
2. What does Hayakawa mean by saying that "The writer of a dictionary is a historian, not a lawgiver"?

Matters of Technique

1. What is the first paragraph doing in an essay that describes a process?
2. What three transitional words or phrases are used in the first sentences of paragraphs 3, 4, and 5?

Vocabulary

1. eccentric (1)
2. context (3)

3. disseminate (5)

Suggestions for Writing

1. Write a paper in which you describe, entirely in the third person, how something is made. If you have worked at a job where something simple is put together, describe the process. If you can't do that, describe a process for something done around your home or farm.
2. Give directions, using the "you" point of view ("First, you have to gather your tools"), on how to perform some simple task (such as how to paddle a canoe, arrange flowers, or change a diaper).
3. Describe in detail, and step by step, the process by which *you* learn the meaning of unfamiliar words.

An Exercise in Levitation

Hana Umlauf and Barry Youngerman

"An Exercise in Levitation" appeared in The World Almanac Book of the Strange *(1977), an objective reference guide to all kinds of weird things.*

A simple experiment in levitation can be easily performed by a group 1
of five people and one experimenter, using one small straight-backed
chair, preferably without arms.

The largest and heaviest person sits on the chair. Two others stand 2
behind him, and two stand on either side, near his knees. Throughout
the experiment the seated person remains seated. He should not do
anything; he should not cooperate, resist, or become active in any way.
The four other participants perform a specific set of movements in a
rhythm that they establish. The movements are simple and divided
into two parts. Person 1, at the seated person's right, places his right
hand on top of the seated person's head. Person 2, standing at the
right rear, then places his right hand on top of Person 1's right hand.
Person 3, standing at the left rear, places his right hand on top of Person 2's right hand, and Person 4 standing at the left front, places his
right hand on top of all the other hands. There are now four right
hands one on top of the other. Then Person 4 places his left hand on
top of his own right hand. Person 3 places his left hand on the top of
the pile of hands, and Person 2 and Person 1 do the same respectively.
These movements should be practiced until they can be performed
easily in a rhythmic manner.

Once a rhythm has been established another set of movements is 3
performed. When the experimenter, after the performance of the first
of the movements, calls out "Lift," persons 1, 2, 3, and 4 quickly move
their hands from the seated person's head, extend the forefingers of
each hand palm downward, and place them as follows: Person 1 places
his index and middle fingers under the seated person's right knee,
Person 2 places his fingers under the right armpit, Person 3 places his
fingers under the left armpit, and Person 4 places his fingers under
the left knee. These motions should also be practiced until they can

be done smoothly. Then, when the experimenter calls out "Lift," the four persons can easily lift the seated person into the air.

4   Before the experiment the experimenters should have the four persons place their fingers in the designated spots and attempt to lift the person seated in the chair. It will be obvious that it takes an enormous effort to lift the seated person even an inch in the air without the use of the technique described above. A simple physical explanation for this phenomenon might be the better coordination of effort that results from a well-established rhythm.

Questions About Meaning

1. What explanation does the author offer for the phenomenon he describes?
2. Does levitation actually occur? (See the definition of "levitation" in the dictionary.) Devise an alternate title.

Matters of Technique

1. Point out how the author manages to "place" the five persons without confusing readers. How does he manage to keep a separate, distinct focus on the movements of each?
2. Why does the author use the third person point of view (he, they) instead of the imperative "you"?
3. In paragraph 2, why does the author use the impersonal "he" to refer to a group that would probably include both males and females?

Vocabulary

1. levitation (1)
2. phenomenon (4)

Suggestions for Writing

1. Try the experiment described in the essay. Now, without rereading the essay, write instructions about how to perform the same experiment. Compare your instructions with the original.
2. Give instructions for performing a stage magic trick.
3. Give instructions for performing a task that requires the coordination and cooperation of two workers.

The Preying Tree

Joseph Wheelwright

Joseph Wheelwright is a woodworker from Massachusetts. The article below appeared originally in Fine Woodworking *(1981), a magazine aimed at an audience of experienced woodworkers.*

It is not for me to say whether certain objects of Nature are imbued 1
with a power beyond their physical being. Perhaps the human mind simply confers a special power on them. Whichever is the case, I am often halted on my walks through the forest or along the shore by the heartbeat of some casual offering of Nature. These found objects have become the basis for my recent works of art.

It is no accident, I suppose, that the fanned tail of the ruffed grouse 2
mirrors the shape and color of certain fungi found in its habitat, or that the shape of some trees is akin to the form of our own species. We all have a common ancestor back there somewhere.

In the woods of Vermont in 1978, I met up with a dying beech tree 3
of strikingly human character. Most beech trees have a taut, leather-like skin stretched over their musculature, but this one had the form of a human figure as well. The tree met the ground on two massive legs, each 10 ft. long. The space between the legs, left by years of rot, was large enough to walk through. At the hip the body bent backward, narrowing at the waist and broadening to the shoulder twenty feet up. The shoulder appeared to be a more recent growth, probably having arisen out of the wound of a broken predecessor. From the shoulder sprang an even newer growth, a powerful, perfectly vertical young arm straining for the light and reaching thirty feet up before branching. The poor tree had been hemmed in by great hemlocks at the crown and by hornbeams at the trunk. I set about clearing the area immediately, to give him air and to get a better look at this one-armed, headless giant. I removed some of the dirt around the feet to help him stand up smartly.

Later in the summer, in another beech tree I spotted a near-perfect 4

Originally appeared in *Fine Woodworking*, November/December 1981. Reprinted by permission of the author.

hand, the wrist of which appeared to be of similar diameter to the end of the giant's arm. I decided to join the two.

5   With the aid of a long ladder and ropes I hoisted a couple of 16-ft. 2x8s up to where the joint would be. These were nailed to the arm on one end and to nearby trees on the other in order to serve as floor joists for a small, triangular platform. Once this work deck was secure, I cut off the crown of the tree where the wrist was to be. I then built a wooden crane to support the chain hoist which would raise the 300-lb. hand.

6   The next Sunday morning several neighbors helped me gently remove the hand from its tree, and we lugged it up the hill to meet the giant. Our chain hoist was not long enough to bring the hand up to the deck in one pull, but by chaining it halfway up and rehooking, we made it on the second lift.

7   Next came the question of joinery. I decided to use the dovetail. With a bowsaw and chisels I cut the tail socket into the arm first, a single, centered, 10-in. by 8-in. cavity at the bottom, 6 in. deep. Then I cut the tail in the hand to match. Using the wooden crane, I upended the hand and bapped it home with my beetle. I used cement as glue, thinking the grey would be a fine match. This was a silly mistake; the cement would not take to the sappy wood, and besides, the joint was so snug that most of it squeezed out messily.

8   All that remained to be done was some final carving around the fingertips, and then I dismantled the platform. The effect was startling; whereas originally the tree had been in a posture of supplication, its arm reaching longingly to the sky as if to take a gift, it now scratched menacingly at the heavens. I had wanted to call it the "Praying Tree," but it chose the name "Preying Tree."

Questions About Meaning

1. What is there about *all* beech trees that reminds the author of humans?
2. Why, according to the author, is it no accident that some tree shapes resemble humans?
3. Why did the author change the name of his tree construction?
4. Why was it a mistake to use cement as glue?

Matters of Technique

1. What are the advantages of using the first person ("I") point of view in a process paper? What are the disadvantages?
2. What indications are there that "The Preying Tree" appeared orig-

inally in a magazine for experienced woodworkers? (See in particular paragraph 7.) Rewrite paragraph 7 to make it appropriate for a general-interest magazine like *Reader's Digest*.
3. What is there about the essay that indicates that the specific instructions for joining two trees was probably a secondary concern in the author's mind?
4. Why do you think Wheelwright personifies the beech tree by referring to it as "him" in paragraph 3?

Vocabulary

1. imbued (1)
2. taut (3)
3. predecessor (3)
4. dovetail (7)
5. tail socket (7)
6. tail (7)
7. bapped (7)
8. beetle (7)
9. preying (8)

What is there about Wheelwright's name that indicates that he had another woodworker in his family in the distant past?

Suggestions for Writing

1. Write an essay giving directions on how to make some simple object. Imitate Wheelwright by making the process only a part of your essay. That is, give your essay significance beyond the mere instructions by weaving a thesis into your instructions.
2. Write a process paper in which you begin with a brief and casual philosophical discussion that introduces your process. Close your essay by coming back to the philosophical idea you began with. Use the "I" point of view that Wheelwright uses.

The Maker's Eye: Revising Your Own Manuscripts

Donald M. Murray

Donald Murray, who won a Pulitzer Prize for editorial writing, is a teacher, poet, novelist, and essayist. The following essay first appeared in The Writer *in 1973.*

1   When students complete a first draft, they consider the job of writing done—and their teachers too often agree. When professional writers complete a first draft, they usually feel that they are at the start of the writing process. When a draft is completed, the job of writing can begin.

2   That difference in attitude is the difference between amateur and professional, inexperience and experience, journeyman and craftsman. Peter F. Drucker, the prolific business writer, calls his first draft "the zero draft"—after that he can start counting. Most writers share the feeling that the first draft, and all of those which follow, are opportunities to discover what they have to say and how best they can say it.

3   To produce a progression of drafts, each of which says more and says it more clearly, the writer has to develop a special kind of reading skill. In school we are taught to decode what appears on the page as finished writing. Writers, however, face a different category of possibility and responsibility when they read their own drafts. To them the words on the page are never finished. Each can be changed and rearranged, can set off a chain reaction of confusion or clarified meaning. This is a different kind of reading which is possibly more difficult and certainly more exciting.

4   Writers must learn to be their own best enemy. They must accept the criticism of others and be suspicious of it; they must accept the praise of others and be even more suspicious of it. Writers cannot depend on others. They must detach themselves from their own pages

so that they can apply both their caring and their craft to their own work.

Such detachment is not easy. Science fiction writer Ray Bradbury 5
supposedly puts each manuscript away for a year to the day and then rereads it as a stranger. Not many writers have the discipline or the time to do this. We must read when our judgment may be at its worst, when we are close to the euphoric moment of creation.

Then the writer, counsels novelist Nancy Hale, "should be critical 6
of everything that seems to him most delightful in his style. He should excise what he most admires, because he wouldn't thus admire it if he weren't . . . in a sense protecting it from criticism." John Ciardi, the poet, adds, "The last act of the writing must be to become one's own reader. It is, I suppose, a schizophrenic process, to begin passionately and to end critically, to begin hot and to end cold; and, more important, to be passion-hot and critic-cold at the same time."

Most people think that the principal problem is that writers are too 7
proud of what they have written. Actually, a greater problem for most professional writers is one shared by the majority of students. They are overly critical, think everything is dreadful, tear up page after page, never complete a draft, see the task as hopeless.

The writer must learn to read critically but constructively, to cut 8
what is bad, to reveal what is good. Eleanor Estes, the children's book author, explains: "The writer must survey his work critically, coolly, as though he were a stranger to it. He must be willing to prune, expertly and hard-heartedly. At the end of each revision, a manuscript may look . . . worked over, torn apart, pinned together, added to, deleted from, words changed and words changed back. Yet the book must maintain its original freshness and spontaneity."

Most readers underestimate the amount of rewriting it usually takes 9
to produce spontaneous reading. This is a great disadvantage to the student writer, who sees only a finished product and never watches the craftsman who takes the necessary step back, studies the work carefully, returns to the task, steps back, returns, steps back, again and again. Anthony Burgess, one of the most prolific writers in the English-speaking world, admits, "I might revise a page twenty times." Roald Dahl, the popular children's writer, states, "By the time I'm nearing the end of a story, the first part will have been reread and altered and corrected at least 150 times. . . . Good writing is essentially rewriting. I am positive of this."

Rewriting isn't virtuous. It isn't something that ought to be done. 10
It is simply something that most writers find they have to do to discover what they have to say and how to say it. It is a condition of the writer's life.

There are, however, a few writers who do little formal rewriting, 11 primarily because they have the capacity and experience to create and review a large number of invisible drafts in their minds before they approach the page. And some writers slowly produce finished pages, performing all the tasks of revision simultaneously, page by page, rather than draft by draft. But it is still possible to see the sequence followed by most writers most of the time in rereading their own work.

12   Most writers scan their drafts first, reading as quickly as possible to catch the larger problems of subject and form, then move in closer and closer as they read and write, reread and rewrite.

13   The first thing writers look for in their drafts is *information*. They know that a good piece of writing is built from specific, accurate, and interesting information. The writer must have an abundance of information from which to construct a readable piece of writing.

14   Next writers look for *meaning* in the information. The specifics must build to a pattern of significance. Each piece of specific information must carry the reader toward meaning.

15   Writers reading their own drafts are aware of *audience*. They put themselves in the reader's situation and make sure that they deliver information which a reader wants to know or needs to know in a manner which is easily digested. Writers try to be sure that they anticipate and answer the questions a critical reader will ask when reading the piece of writing.

16   Writers make sure that the *form* is appropriate to the subject and the audience. Form, or genre, is the vehicle which carries meaning to the reader, but form cannot be selected until the writer has adequate information to discover its significance and an audience which needs or wants that meaning.

17   Once writers are sure the form is appropriate, they must then look at the *structure*, the order of what they have written. Good writing is built on a solid framework of logic, argument, narrative, or motivation which runs through the entire piece of writing and holds it together. This is the time when many writers find it most effective to outline as a way of visualizing the hidden spine by which the piece of writing is supported.

18   The element on which writers may spend a majority of their time is *development*. Each section of a piece of writing must be adequately developed. It must give readers enough information so that they are satisfied. How much information is enough? That's as difficult as asking how much garlic belongs in a salad. It must be done to taste, but most beginning writers underdevelop, underestimating the reader's hunger for information.

19   As writers solve developmental problems, they often have to consider questions of *dimension*. There must be a pleasing and effective

proportion among all the parts of the piece of writing. There is a continual process of subtracting and adding to keep the piece of writing in balance.

Finally, writers have to listen to their own voices. *Voice* is the force   20
which drives a piece of writing forward. It is an expression of the writer's authority and concern. It is what is between the words on the page, what glues the piece of writing together. A good piece of writing is always marked by a consistent, individual voice.

As writers read and reread, write and rewrite, they move closer and   21
closer to the page until they are doing line-by-line editing. Writers read their own pages with infinite care. Each sentence, each line, each clause, each phrase, each word, each mark of punctuation, each section of white space between the type has to contribute to the clarification of meaning.

Slowly the writer moves from word to word, looking through lan-   22
guage to see the subject. As a word is changed, cut, or added, as a construction is rearranged, all the words used before that moment and all those that follow that moment must be considered and reconsidered.

Writers often read aloud at this stage of the editing process, mut-   23
tering or whispering to themselves, calling on the ear's experience with language. Does this sound right—or that? Writers edit, shifting back and forth from eye to page to ear to page. I find I must do this careful editing in short runs, no more than fifteen or twenty minutes at a stretch, or I become too kind with myself. I begin to see what I hope is on the page, not what actually is on the page.

This sounds tedious if you haven't done it, but actually it is fun.   24
Making something right is immensely satisfying, for writers begin to learn what they are writing about by writing. Language leads them to meaning, and there is the joy of discovery, of understanding, of making meaning clear as the writer employs the technical skills of language.

Words have double meanings, even triple and quadruple meanings.   25
Each word has its own potential for connotation and denotation. And when writers rub one word against the other, they are often rewarded with a sudden insight, an unexpected clarification.

The maker's eye moves back and forth from word to phrase to sen-   26
tence to paragraph to sentence to phrase to word. The maker's eye sees the need for variety and balance, for a firmer structure, for a more appropriate form. It peers into the interior of the paragraph, looking for coherence, unity, and emphasis, which make meaning clear.

I learned something about this process when my first bifocals were   27
prescribed. I had ordered a larger section of the reading portion of the glass because of my work, but even so, I could not contain my eyes within this new limit of vision. And I still find myself taking off my

glasses and bending my nose towards the page, for my eyes unconsciously flick back and forth across the page, back to another page, forward to still another, as I try to see each evolving line in relation to every other line.

28   When does this process end? Most writers agree with the great Russian writer Tolstoy, who said, "I scarcely ever reread my published writings; if by chance I come across a page, it always strikes me: all this must be rewritten; this is how I should have written it."

29   The maker's eye is never satisfied, for each word has the potential to ignite new meaning. This article has been twice written all the way through the writing process, and it was published four years ago. Now it is to be republished in a book. The editors made a few small suggestions, and then I read it with my maker's eye. Now it has been reedited, re-revised, re-read, re-re-edited, for each piece of writing to the writer is full of potential and alternatives.

30   A piece of writing is never finished. It is delivered to a deadline, torn out of the typewriter on demand, sent off with a sense of accomplishment and shame and pride and frustration. If only there were a couple more days, time for just another run at it, perhaps then . . .

Questions About Meaning

1. What contrast is made in the first paragraph between the professional writer and the student writer?
2. What does the author mean by this sentence: "The writer . . . must be his own best enemy"?
3. What does it mean to begin a piece of writing "hot" and end it "cold"?
4. What does Murray say most readers tend to underestimate about a piece of writing?
5. What are the eight things the writer must be conscious of in the process of revision?

Matters of Technique

1. At what point does Murray end his generalized comments about the significance of rewriting and begin his specific directions on what to look for when rewriting?
2. Examine the various techniques of quoting in paragraph 6. Now construct two sentences of your own based on the structures of the two sentences in which Murray uses quotations. For your examples, quote a couple of Murray's own statements.

3. What is the concrete image in paragraph 25?
4. What techniques does Murray use to advance his discussion in paragraph 28?

Vocabulary

1. prolific (2)
2. euphoric (5)
3. deleted (8)

4. connotation (25)
5. denotation (25)

Suggestions for Writing

1. Describe the process you go through to improve your first draft. Explain the difficulties you have with revision as you describe the process.
2. Clip out a letter to the editor from your local newspaper and revise it. Use Murray's suggestions.
3. Describe the process you go through to adjust to an unfamiliar situation—being away from home, for instance.

CHAPTER SIX

Comparison

Comparison thinking is probably the most important way we have of making sense of the swarm of facts that daily threaten to overwhelm us. The fire fighters in our town strike, and we compare their salaries with those of fire fighters in comparable cities. Ten police officers were killed by the IRA this year, and we compare this number with the number who were killed last year. In her old age our mother grows senile and crippled, and we compare her infirmities with the mental acuity and strength she enjoyed when she was younger. Comparisons give us a context so that we can see more clearly the significance of new information.

What to Compare?

Naturally, not all facts and ideas are worth comparing. A comparison between a rutabaga and a basketball, for instance, doesn't help to illuminate either the rutabaga or the basketball—or probably anything else. Their likeness—both are fairly round—isn't worth talking about; neither are their numerous differences. It's thus a good idea to stay within the same general class when making comparisons.

Even within the same class, not all pairs make worthwhile comparisons. It is meaningless, for instance, to compare a hardback book to a paperback book, despite the fact that they belong to the same class— books—and have significant differences, including price and size. The differences are not worth talking about because they are so obvious.

It is usually best to compare things that are outwardly similar but have significant inner differences, or things outwardly different but with significant inner similarities. Unless readers have thought hard about the two things before, they will thus learn something about the nature of one or both of the things being compared. For instance, a writer might show that two political philosophies—Communism and Fascism, let's say—that are outwardly different actually share significant similarities. In the same way, many things that appear to be similar (twin sisters, for instance) are different in subtle ways, and these are also worth talking about.

Often, a good comparison gives readers insights about one or both of the items that they couldn't have gotten by looking at each item separately. To look at Reggie Jackson's hitting statistics by themselves is interesting; to compare them with Lou Gehrig's illuminates each player's statistics in a way that couldn't have been done by looking at them separately.

The Preliminary List

The first step in writing a comparison essay is to list all the similarities and differences of the two items being compared. Let's say you are writing a comparison essay on the mass suicides at Masada in A.D. 72 and those at Jonestown, Guyana in 1978. Your list might look something like this:

Masada	*Jonestown*
960 dead	900 dead
men, women, children	men, women, children
religious/political motive	religious/political motive
charismatic leader (Eleazar Ben Yair)	charismatic leader (Jim Jones)
method: stabbing	method: poisoning
location: occupied homeland	location: foreign soil
state religion	religious cult
suicide occurred when hope of defense against Roman soldiers was gone	suicide occurred when residents were deluded into thinking that agents of the United States were about to destroy Jonestown

A list like this reveals not only what the important differences are, but also what the unimportant ones are. The fact that the Jonestown victims took poison while the Masada victims stabbed themselves is relatively unimportant (it has more to do with availability than anything else), and a writer would probably want to either ignore it or pass it over in a dependent clause. A list might also show which facts to play up, which to play down, which to begin with, which to conclude with—perhaps even which side, the differences or the similarities, you should focus your attention on.

Organizing the Comparison Essay

Once you have made a comparison list, the next step is to decide how you're going to organize that material. If your paper is short (two or three pages), you may want to fill the first half of your essay with the characteristics of one side (Jonestown, for instance), then use the second half to make the comparisons while describing the characteristics of the other side (Masada). In diagram form, this kind of organization looks like this:

```
xxxxxxxxxxxxxxxxxxxxxxxxxxxxx
xxxxxxxxxxxxxxxxxxxxxxxxxxxxx     Jonestown
xxxxxxxxxxxxxxxxxxxxxxxxxxxxx
ooooooooooooooooooooooooooooo
ooooooooooooooooooooooooooooo     Masada
ooooooooooooooooooooooooooooo
```

When using the half/half pattern of organization, be certain that you deal with the same characteristics in the second half that you deal with in the first half. If you are comparing two beauty contest winners, for instance, and you describe Barbara's talent in the first half, be certain to describe Susan's talent in the second half.

The half/half pattern requires many more transitional phrases and reminders than a normal essay. After all, readers are apt to forget, while they're reading the second half, what you said in the first half. Here are a few of the kinds of "reminder" phrases that the half/half paper uses:

> *Unlike the cultish religion at Jonestown*, the religion at Masada . . .
> *Although Jim Jones had some of the trappings of a religious leader*, Eleazar Ben Yair . . .
> Masada was *similar to Jonestown* in one respect . . .
> Naturally, Masada, *like Jonestown*, was . . .
> *Unlike Jonestown*, Masada was located in the victims' homeland.

These kinds of reminders are absolutely necessary in the second half of the half/half pattern. Without them, readers will be likely to forget what is being compared to what.

When your paper is rather long, you had better try another kind of organization, the alternating pattern, which in diagram form looks like this:

```
xxxxxxxxxxxxxxxxxxxxxxxxxxxx    Masada
oooooooooooooooooooooooooooo    Jonestown
xxxxxxxxxxxxxxxxxxxxxxxxxxxx
oooooooooooooooooooooooooooo
xxxxxxxxxxxxxxxxxxxxxxxxxxxx
oooooooooooooooooooooooooooo
```

Because the alternating pattern doesn't require readers to remember characteristics listed in the first half of the essay, it is almost always used in long comparison essays. The body of the alternating pattern essay looks something like this:

> Although Masada and Jonestown were alike in that over 900 in each group committed suicide for religious and political reasons, in most respects the two horrible events were vastly different. The people at Jonestown, for instance, were deluded into thinking that they were under attack; those at Masada actually were under siege by the world's most efficient and best organized soldiers, the Roman legions. And whereas the Jonestown residents belonged to a religious cult that rested almost entirely on the personality of Jim Jones, the Jews at Masada possessed a centuries-long religious tradition that rested on no single human leader. If Jones had died in San Francisco, the Jonestown tragedy would never have happened; if Eleazar Ben Yair had died in Jerusalem, Masada would still have taken place.

MODEL COMPARISON PARAGRAPH

Americans and Russians

The American struggles against the natural obstacles which oppose him; the adversaries of the Russian are men; the former combats the wilderness and savage life; the latter, civilization with all its weapons and its arts: the conquests of the one are therefore gained by the plowshare; those of the other by the sword. The Anglo-American relies upon personal interest to accomplish his ends, and gives free scope to the unguided exertions and common sense of the citizens; the Russian centers all the authority of society in a single arm: the principal instrument of the former is freedom; of the latter, servitude. Their starting-point is different, and their courses are not the same; yet each of them seems to be marked out by the will of Heaven to sway the destinies of half the globe.

Alexis de Tocqueville, 1835

ANALYSIS

De Tocqueville presents his discussion of the American and the Russian national character through the alternating method of comparison. What he says about the American is immediately balanced by a comment on the Russian. The author then extends the discussion by moving a step beyond character type and comparing the tendencies of the two social systems. From this more generalized point of view, he then makes a remarkable prophecy.

ASSIGNMENT

In a comparison paragraph of your own, imitate de Tocqueville's method. Do this in a discussion of two comparable but contrasting cities or communities, or two sections of the same one.

Man and the Grunion

Jacob Bronowski

The Ascent of Man *(1973), the book from which our selection was taken, was originally a BBC television series, written and narrated by Jacob Bronowski, the noted British physicist.*

Man is a singular creature. He has a set of gifts which make him unique among the animals: so that, unlike them, he is not a figure in the landscape—he is a shaper of the landscape. In body and in mind he is the explorer of nature, the ubiquitous animal, who did not find but has made his home in every continent. 1

It is reported that when the Spaniards arrived overland at the Pacific Ocean in 1769 the California Indians used to say that at full moon the fish came and danced on these beaches. And it is true that there is a local variety of fish, the grunion, that comes up out of the water and lays its eggs above the normal high-tide mark. The females bury themselves tail first in the sand and the males gyrate round them and fertilise the eggs as they are being laid. The full moon is important, because it gives the time needed for the eggs to incubate undisturbed in the sand, nine or ten days, between these very high tides and the next ones that will wash the hatched fish out to sea again. 2

Every landscape in the world is full of these exact and beautiful adaptations, by which an animal fits into its environment like one cogwheel into another. The sleeping hedgehog waits for the spring to burst its metabolism into life. The humming-bird beats the air and dips its needle-fine beak into hanging blossoms. Butterflies mimic leaves and even noxious creatures to deceive their predators. The mole plods through the ground as if he had been designed as a mechanical shuttle. 3

So millions of years of evolution have shaped the grunion to fit and sit exactly with the tides. But nature—that is, biological evolution—has not fitted man to any specific environment. On the contrary, by comparison with the grunion he has a rather crude survival kit; and yet—this is the paradox of the human condition—one that fits him to 4 all environments. Among the multitude of animals which scamper, fly, burrow and swim around us, man is the only one who is not locked into his environment. His imagination, his reason, his emotional subtlety and toughness, make it possible for him not to accept the environment but to change it.

Questions About Meaning

1. Why does the grunion lay its eggs during the full moon?
2. What point is Bronowski making when he compares the mole to a mechanical shuttle?
3. What is the basic difference between man and the animals, according to Bronowski?

Matters of Technique

1. Although "Man and the Grunion" is a comparison essay, paragraph 2 serves a subordinate purpose. What is that purpose?
2. Analyze the organization of the author's short comparison essay by describing the function of each of the four paragraphs.
3. At what point does Bronowski use a series of short action verbs to suggest different species of animals?

Vocabulary

1. singular (1)
2. ubiquitous (1)
3. metabolism (3)

4. noxious (3)
5. shuttle (*weaving;* 3)

Suggestions for Writing

1. Write a comparison essay in which you show what you see as the basic difference between human beings and animals. Illustrate your point about animals with a description of the actual behavior of a specific animal. (See Bronowski's paragraph 2.)
2. Compare the behavior of two animals (dogs and cats, horses and cows, chickens and turkeys). Or put two species of insect in a jar or two species of fish in a tank and observe them. Then compare their behavior.

3. Get a good reference book and look up some information on the social behavior of one of the following: bees, ants, crows, or wolves. Now write a paper in which you make comparisons between the behavior of the animal, bird, or insect selected and the behavior of humans.

Cross-Reference

In what way does Bronowski's view of animals differ from that of Edward Abbey in "The Spadefoot Toad"?

Voltaire and Frederick the Great

E. M. Forster

E. M. Forster, a British novelist, is the author of such works as Howards End *(1910) and* A Passage to India *(1924). He was also a tireless essayist. "Voltaire and Frederick the Great" (1941) is from a collection of essays,* Two Cheers for Democracy *(1951).*

There is an additional Forster essay in Chapter 9.

1   Two hundred years ago a Frenchman paid a visit to a German. It is a famous visit. The Frenchman was delighted to come to Germany, his German host delighted to welcome him. They were more than polite to one another, they were enthusiastic, and each thought, "I am sure we are going to be friends for ever." Yet the visit was a disaster. They still talk about it in Germany today, and they say it was the Frenchman's fault. And they still talk about it in France. And I'm going to talk about it now, partly because it makes such a good story, and partly because it contains a lesson for us all, even though it did happen two hundred years back.

2   The Frenchman was Voltaire. People today sometimes think of Voltaire as a person who sneered at everything, and made improper jokes. He was much more than that, he was the greatest man of his age, indeed he was one of the greatest men whom European civilisation has produced. If I had to name two people to speak for Europe at the Last Judgment I should choose Shakespeare and Voltaire—Shakespeare for his creative genius, Voltaire for his critical genius and humanity. Voltaire cared for the truth, he believed in tolerance, he pitied the oppressed, and since he was a forceful character he was able to drive his ideas home. They happen to be my own ideas, and like many other small people I am thankful when a great person comes along and says for me what I can't say properly for myself. Voltaire speaks for the thousands and thousands of us who hate injustice and work for a better world.

What did he do? He wrote enormously: plays (now forgotten); short stories, and some of them are still read—especially that masterpiece, *Candide*. He was a journalist, and a pamphleteer, he dabbled in science and philosophy, he was a good popular historian, he compiled a dictionary, and he wrote hundreds of letters to people all over Europe. He had correspondents everywhere, and he was so witty, so up-to-date, so on the spot that kings and emperors were proud to get a letter from Voltaire and hurried to answer it with their own hand. He is not a great creative artist. But he is a great man with a powerful intellect and a warm heart, enlisted in the service of humanity. That is why I rank him with Shakespeare as a spiritual spokesman for Europe. Two hundred years before the Nazis came, he was the complete anti-Nazi.

I am so fond of him that I should like to add he had a perfect character. Alas, he hadn't! He was a bundle of contradictions and nerves. Although he loved truth he often lied. Although he loved humanity he was often malicious. Though generous he was a money-maker. He was a born tease. He had no dignity. And he was no beauty to look at either—a gibbering monkey of a man, very small, very thin, with a long sharp nose, a bad complexion and beady black eyes. He overdressed, as little people sometimes do, and his wig was so large that it seemed to extinguish him.

That is the Frenchman who sets out for Berlin on June 13, 1751; the German whom he is about to visit is Frederick the Great, King of Prussia.

Frederick is one of the founders of modern Germany, and Hitler has made a careful study of him. He plunged Europe into wars to advance his ambitions. He believed in force and fraud and cruelty, and in doing everything himself. He had a genius for organising, he preferred to employ inferior men, and he despised the human race. That is the dividing line between him and Voltaire. Voltaire believed in humanity. Frederick did not. "You don't know this damned race of men," he once exclaimed. "You don't know them. I do." He was a cynic, and having had a very unhappy childhood he felt till the end of his life that he had not been properly appreciated; and we know how dangerous such men can be, and what miseries they can bring upon themselves and others.

But there was another side to Frederick. He was a cultivated, sensitive gentleman. He was a good musician, he had read widely, and he had made a careful study of French. He even composed a number of French poems—they are not good, still they serve to show that to him German wasn't everything. He was, in this way, more civilised than Hitler. There was no Nordic purity nonsense about him. He did not think that Germany was destined to rule the world: he knew that the world is a very complicated place, and that we have to live and let live in it; he even believed in freedom of speech. "People can say what they like as long as I do what I like" was the way he put it. One day, as he went through Berlin he saw a caricature of himself on a wall, and all he said was: "Oh—hang it down lower so that it can be seen better."

8   The visit began in a whirl of compliments. Voltaire called Frederick "The Solomon of the North," Frederick declared that of all his victorious titles the most precious was Possessor of Voltaire. He made his guest a court official, housed him royally, gave him a handsome salary, and promised an extra salary to his niece, Madame Denis, if she would come to keep house for him. (We shall hear more of poor Madame Denis in a minute.) Witty conversation, philosophic discussion, delicious food—Frederick liked good food, though he was careful to get it cheap. Everything seemed perfect—but! Not long after his arrival, Voltaire wrote a letter to a friend in France in which the ominous little word "But" keeps occurring.

9   "The supper parties are delicious. The King is the life of the company. But. I have operas and comedies, reviews and concerts, my studies and books. But, but. Berlin is fine, the princesses charming, the maids of honour handsome. But." We can interpret this But. It is the instinctive protest of the free man who finds himself in the power of a tyrant. Voltaire, for all his faults, was a free man. Frederick had charm and intelligence. But—he was a tyrant.

10   The visit went very slowly. Voltaire did several tiresome things. He got mixed up in a shady financial transaction, he quarrelled with another Frenchman who was in the king's service, he drank too much chocolate, and when the king rationed him he revenged himself by taking the wax candles out of the candlesticks and selling them. All very undignified. And—worst of all—he laughed at the king's French poems. Frederick, like Hitler, fancied himself as an artist, and he had often employed his guest to polish his verses up. Now he was told that the tiresome little monkey was poking fun at him and quoting him all over the place—a serious matter this, for some of the poems were imprudent, and intended for private circulation only. The Solomon of the North was vexed. He thought: "No doubt my visitor is a genius, but he is making more trouble than he's worth, and he's disloyal." And Voltaire thought: "No doubt my host is a mighty monarch, but I would rather worship him from a distance." He left Berlin, after a stay of two years, which had gradually become more and more uncomfortable for both parties.

11   But that is not the end. The real bust-up was yet to come. It occurred at Frankfurt, where Voltaire was waiting for Madame Denis to join him. Frankfurt did not belong to the King of Prussia. He had no legal authority there at all, but he had his "Gestapo" and he worked

through them to interfere with personal liberty. He discovered that Voltaire had taken away from Berlin (it seems by accident) a copy of the wretched French poems, flew into a passion and ordered Voltaire's luggage to be searched. As always, he employed second-rate people and they went too far. They not only searched Voltaire's luggage but they imprisoned him and bullied him night and day in the hope of extracting information which would please their royal master. It is an incredible affair, a real foretaste of Nazi methods. Voltaire tried to escape; he was stopped at the gates of Frankfurt and dragged back, and Madame Denis, who now arrived to join her uncle, was also arrested and ill-treated. Madame Denis was a stout, emotional lady, with some pretensions as an actress. She was not one to suffer in silence and she soon made Europe ring with her protests. Voltaire's health broke down and he feigned to be more ill than he really was: he ran from his tormentors into an inner room and gasped, "Will you not even allow me to be sick?" His secretary rushed up to assist him, and Voltaire, while making all the motions of vomiting, whispered in his ear, "I am pretending! I am pretending!" He loved fooling people; he could be mischievous even in his misery, and this is to me an endearing trait.

Frederick saw things had gone too far. Voltaire and his niece were released, and in later years the two great men corresponded almost as enthusiastically as before. But they were careful not to meet and Voltaire at all events had learnt a lesson. Berlin had taught him that if a man believes in liberty and variety and tolerance and sympathy he cannot breathe the air of the totalitarian state. It all may seem nice upon the surface—but! The tyrant may be charming and intelligent—but! The machinery may work perfectly—but! Something is missing: the human spirit is missing. Voltaire kept faith with the human spirit. He fought its battle against German dictatorship two hundred years before our time.

Questions About Meaning

1. What "lesson" does Forster's story of Voltaire and Frederick the Great teach us?
2. Why do you suppose Forster thinks that Voltaire can be considered a lover of truth and humanity even though "he often lied [and] he was often malicious"?
3. Why is Forster so forgiving of Voltaire's faults? What is he unable to forgive about Frederick the Great?
4. What trait in Voltaire does Forster find "endearing"?
5. What lesson did Voltaire learn by his two-year stay in Prussia?

Matters of Technique

1. Reduce the second sentence in paragraph 1 to a single word and insert that word into the first sentence. Why did Forster do it the other way?
2. Why would Forster withhold the name of Voltaire until paragraph 2 and the name of Frederick the Great until paragraph 5?
3. Forster says he is fond of Voltaire, yet he spends paragraph 4 deprecating him. Why does he do this?
4. There are a variety of sentence lengths in paragraph 4. Would it have been as effective for the writer to present the paragraph in sentences of the same length, either all long or all short? Try rewriting the paragraph in both these ways in order to compare the effectiveness of the result with Forster's paragraph.
5. Forster quotes both Frederick and Voltaire several times. What is the effect of this technique on the essay?
6. Describe the organization of Forster's comparison essay.

Vocabulary

1. humanity (2)
2. malicious (4)
3. gibbering (4)
4. cynic (6)

5. Nordic (7)
6. Gestapo (11)
7. totalitarian (12)

Suggestions for Writing

1. Write an essay in which you contrast two people you know well who seem to share many characteristics but who, underneath, are vastly different. Begin by showing how they are similar.
2. Write a "most unforgettable character" essay. Choose someone you know who is basically a good person, though with many negative characteristics. Study Forster's paragraph 4 on Voltaire.
3. After rereading paragraph 4 for an idea of how to proceed, write a single paragraph using a variety of sentence lengths. Begin your paragraph with the same sentence with which Forster begins his paragraph but substitute a friend of yours for Voltaire.
4. If you know people who lead others by cooperation and example, and others who attempt to lead by driving, by domination, write a paper in which you compare and contrast these two types of leaders. Use specific people as examples.

How to Tell Bad from Worse

Michael Levin

The author of the following essay is a philosophy professor at the City College of New York. He does what philosophers are trained to do: He makes distinctions when the rest of us insist on lumping things together. The essay originally appeared in Newsweek *in 1981.*

The distinction between authoritarianism and totalitarianism is much 1
in the news. Despite its clumsy defense by the Reagan Administration and the obfuscation of such critics as Amnesty International, the distinction is a clear and vital one. Nero was not Stalin, and it is important to understand why.

An authoritarian regime is the rule of a strongman or clique which 2
forbids all activities that threaten its position, such as a critical press or an opposition party. It punishes resistance ruthlessly. Authoritarian rulers are typically venal and capricious; their rule encourages corruption and disaffection. There is, however, an important limit to the excesses of authoritarian regimes: they are indifferent to behavior that does not threaten their security.

By contrast, a totalitarian regime wants to control *everything*— not 3
just political power, but all aspects of its subjects' lives. As its name suggests, a totalitarian state dictates values, art and personal and economic association. In addition to an official press, the totalitarian wants an official hour for calisthenics. The authoritarian does not care who becomes a doctor, so long as doctors remain apolitical; the totalitarian determines who becomes a doctor, where doctors practice, their remuneration and, so far as he can, their attitude toward doctoring. (Totalitarians want doctors to regard their skill as For The People.)

Where the authoritarian wants obedience, the totalitarian wants 4
worship—not for himself, but for his regime. He wants the hearts and minds of his subjects. The totalitarian attacks religious and moral traditions precisely because they are independent objects of devotion.

This difference in the degree of control should be obvious. It is, 5
however, relatively superficial. At a more fundamental level, what distinguishes totalitarians from authoritarians is the *kind of justification*

they claim. Only when this is appreciated does the greater menace of totalitarianism become apparent. Only then does it become clear why totalitarian states have given mankind a quite new idea of its own capacity for wickedness.

6   An authoritarian claims no legitimacy, properly speaking. He is where he is by being strong enough to get and stay there. He offers, at most, stability. But the totalitarian is a utopian who, intoxicated by some scheme for perfecting the world, regards his control as *justified* by the need to force his ideal on a shortsighted populace. Marxists, those paradigm utopians, see a workers' paradise emerging once the sin of ownership is extinguished, and they see this as entitling them to use whatever means are necessary to speed the process. A little duress is OK when there is a world to win.

7   Utopians always have a theory of Human Nature which implies that humanity as we know it is a stunted version of what it can be under their ministrations. Marxists, again, hold that people are all naturally creative, but have been "alienated" from their true selves by wage labor. As all past societies have thus deformed Human Nature, the utopian remedy is correspondingly sweeping; everything old—that is, everything—must go. The totalitarian sees his subjects as cripples, his measures as those of a dedicated surgeon. (Since what is being rectified is an abstraction—Human Nature—individuals get rather short shrift.)

8   A regime is totalitarian, then, if it justifies its full control as serving a higher good. In the China of the 1960s engineers were instructed to contemplate Mao's thoughts and courting couples to raise each other's revolutionary consciousness. Such policies were not instituted to prevent insurrection, but to speed the coming of the New Man. Even Nazi ideology was thought by its devotees to be a blueprint for a better world.

9   Totalitarian states are inevitably worse than authoritarian ones, first because the totalitarian sees nothing less than the human future at stake in his efforts. A Franco will execute (or imprison) all his rivals, but avoid further brutality as pointless. A Pol Pot will liquidate anyone with a European (hence "corrupt") education. If the disappearance of 8,000 Argentines is an outrage, what shall we make of the 20 million Russians that Beria eliminated?

10   Second, since *utopia will never arrive*, the totalitarian's "temporary" measures will become permanent. Worse, since the totalitarian must attribute failure to the insufficiency of his methods—the soundness of his overarching theory is a matter of faith—ever more surveillance and propaganda are inevitable. Disobedience is treated with special harshness. The authoritarian sees disobedience as a crime to be deterred; the totalitarian sees any deviation from the new order as persistent corruption in the human material he is out to mold. Indeed,

since he has shown the way to utopia, backsliding must be subversive. Deviation implies reaction, against which the totalitarian is always on guard. Lenin said it best: "A good communist is always at the same time a good Chekist." (The Cheka, or Committee against Counterrevolution, had unlimited powers of life and death.)

Worst of all, the totalitarian is driven by a reformer's zeal. Threaten a tyrant and you may dissuade him; threaten a zealot and you only stiffen his resolve. As George V. Higgins put it, "There is no one as dangerous as an idealist with a machine gun." **11**

Walter Mondale wants to know the difference between authoritarian and totalitarian torture. There is plenty. Totalitarian cruelty is worse than its authoritarian counterpart because of its scope, and because its rationale will always expand its scope. Murder is murder, but the scale of the murder counts. By this measure, totalitarianism easily outstrips all rival systems in evil. **12**

Totalitarianism is a new phenomenon. The idea of remaking man by remaking society is—Plato's anticipations aside—scarcely two centuries old, and only the technology of this century has permitted armed prophets to attempt it. The old vocabulary for assessing governments is too narrow, and current jargon too trivial, to encompass totalitarianism. If insisting that IRA gunmen wear prison uniforms is a serious issue of "human rights," we need some other words for the Gulag. **13**

Questions About Meaning

1. What, according to the author, "distinguishes totalitarians from authoritarians"?
2. Which regime sees itself as the agent of the "higher good"?
3. Which regime is indifferent to behavior that does not threaten its security?
4. Which regime wants worship?
5. Which regime is utopian?
6. Which regime is the "idealist with a machine gun"?
7. Who was Franco? Beria? Pol Pot? What is the Gulag?
8. What does the last sentence of the essay mean?

Matters of Technique

1. Levin writes that "Nero was not Stalin." Why, given the first two sentences of the essay, is Levin's sentence an effective lead-in to the subject?
2. Point out how Levin combines the techniques of definition and

contrast in the topic sentences of paragraphs 2 and 3 in order to organize and advance his discussion.
3. At what point does Levin virtually stop discussing authoritarian regimes to focus all his attention on totalitarian regimes? Given his thesis, is this technique justified? Is it effective?
4. Point out the method by which the author makes structurally balanced comparative statements in the fourth sentence of paragraph 10 and in the second sentence of paragraph 11.
5. Model a sentence of your own on the last sentence in paragraph 7. Do the same with the second sentence in paragraph 13.

Vocabulary

1. obfuscation (1)
2. venal (2)
3. capricious (2)
4. apolitical (3)
5. remuneration (3)
6. paradigm (6)
7. duress (6)
8. ideology (8)
9. deviation (10)
10. dissuade (11)

Suggestions for Writing

1. Contrast two words or ideas that people often lump together.
2. Contrast two people you know, or know of, who possess on a personal level the characteristics of authoritarian and totalitarian regimes.
3. Discuss, by means of comparison and contrast, your view of the differences between democracy and totalitarianism. (You will begin by showing how they are alike—both are systems of government.) Adopt a personal viewpoint to focus your discussion.

Female Athletes: They've Come a Long Way, Baby

P. S. Wood

P. S. Wood's fact-filled analysis of the comparative athletic prowess of men and women contains some surprising conclusions. The article is a Reader's Digest *condensation of an article that originally appeared in the* New York Times Magazine *in 1980.*

There has been an explosion in women's competitive sports. If women 1 have not yet achieved equal time on the playing fields of America, or equal space in the halls of fame, they have come a long way, and are moving up fast. For example:

- Thirty-three percent of all high-school athletes are female, a six- 2 fold increase since the early 1970s, according to figures supplied by the Women's Sports Foundation. In colleges, the figure is 30 percent, an increase in ten years of 250 percent.

- Since 1970, the number of women tennis players in the country 3 has jumped from about 3 million to 11 million, the number of golfers from less than a half million to more than 5 million. According to one survey, of the nation's 17.1 million joggers, well over one-third are women—in 1970, there were too few to count.

- In 1980, according to six sports federations (tennis, golf, bowling, 4 skiing, racquetball, basketball), financial rewards for female athletes topped more than $16 million, up from less than $1 million a decade ago.

As women rush into athletic competition, certain questions are 5 being raised: How good are women as athletes? How do they compare with men? Are women's bodies strong enough, tough enough, to take the battles?

New research on the physical and athletic differences between men 6 and women shows that in some respects women may be at least as tough as men. Some evidence suggests that women's endurance may be equal or perhaps even superior to men's. Women's bodies are constructed so that certain crucial organs are better guarded from injury; ovaries, for instance, lie inside the pelvic cavity, far better placed for protection than the testicles.

7   Furthermore, the folk wisdom that other elements of the female anatomy make women athletes more vulnerable seems incorrect. The suspicion that severe bruises cause breast cancer is not borne out; breasts are less susceptible to injury than knees or elbows, whether male or female. And the old idea that, at certain times of the month, women do not operate at peak performance is generally not true for athletes. World and Olympic records have been set by women in all stages of their menstrual cycles. Moreover, at certain intense levels of training, menstruation conveniently turns off for many women, a phenomenon that has been linked in some studies to a reduction in body fat, in other studies to physical and emotional stress.

8   The point is that, if concern for safety is a determining factor, women should have the same opportunities to participate in competitive athletics as men. And, by and large, they have the same reasons for wanting to do so. Says tennis star Billie Jean King: "Athletics are an essential part of education for both sexes. Girls and boys are going to grow up easier in each other's company."

9   No one suggests now that equal experience is going to lead to equal performance in all things athletic. Men are bigger and stronger, can run faster, throw and jump farther. But the fact that women are genetically ordained through most of life to compete with less powerful bodies, far from tarnishing their performance, makes it more worthy.

10   Actually, boys and girls start out with nearly identical equipment so far as fitness for sports goes. If anything, girls, because they mature faster, may have an edge, as youth soccer-league coaches, for example, are finding out.

11   At puberty, the situation abruptly changes. Estrogen levels begin to build in the female body. There is a growth spurt which peaks at about 12 years, then tapers off by 14 or 15. Most boys begin to mature sexually a year and a half to two years later than girls, and then keep on developing much longer, in some cases up to six years longer.

12   On the average, men end up ten percent bigger. They have longer bones, providing better leverage; wider shoulders—the foundation for a significant advantage in upper-body strength—and bigger hearts and lungs. In addition, while the body of the female adolescent is preparing for childbirth by storing up fat reserves, the male body is growing muscle. And this occurs quite apart from exercise. Exercise adds strength and endurance, and increases the size of the muscles. But on average, men have more muscle fibers than women; and they have an added advantage in the hormone testosterone, which adds bulk to those fibers.

When the Army first accepted women at West Point in 1976, it   13
found it necessary to quantify the strength differences of the incoming
plebes. The upshot of numerous tests indicated that women had
approximately one-third the strength of men in the upper body and
two-thirds the strength of men in the legs, and about the same amount
of strength as men in the abdomen. The implications are obvious for
those American games that have dominated the sports pages for years:
women are no match for men in football, baseball and basketball, all
of which place a high premium on upper-body strength. Tennis, too,
illustrates the female disadvantage. Tracy Austin has mastered the
basic strokes of the game every bit as well as most of the top male
players. But she simply cannot match them in the serve, which
demands upper-arm strength and happens to be the key stroke of the
game.

Sometimes the special combination of female traits works to wom-   14
en's advantage. Ever since Gertrude Ederle swam the English Channel
in 1926, two hours faster than any man had ever done it, women have
dominated the sport of long-distance swimming. Women generally
have ten percent more fat than men. This appears not only in the characteristic deposits on the thighs, buttocks and breasts, but in an overall
layer of subcutaneous fat. The result is that women are more buoyant
than men and better insulated against cold. An added edge is their
narrower shoulders, which offer less resistance through the water.

Another advantage long-distance swimmers may share with other   15
well-trained female athletes is the ability to call on reserves of energy
perhaps unavailable to men. Running the marathon, women get tired,
but few report "hitting the wall," an expression for the sudden pain
and debilitating weakness that strike many male runners after about
two hours, when most of the glycogen that fuels their muscles is gone.
The training necessary to run the marathon conditions the body to call
directly on fats after the glycogen is used up. One controversial theory
is that women, because of hormonal differences, utilize their fat more
efficiently than men. Another is that, since women have more stored
fat than men, their staying power is greater.

Beyond physical characteristics, past social attitudes have had a sub-   16
stantial influence on the sex factor in athletics. The old attitude was
epitomized in the expression "throwing like a girl." At first glance
there does appear to be a certain innate awkwardness in the way girls
throw a ball. But Prof. Jack Wilmore of the University of Arizona, in
researching female and male relative athletic ability, had a number of
right-handed men throw lefty: the men proved equally awkward. Wilmore said it seemed apparent from his studies that throwing is an
acquired trait. The broader shoulders and bigger muscles of men give
them an advantage in speed or distance, but not, innately, in grace.

17   The effect of such subtle forces on women's competitive athletics seems clear. A coach at an Ivy League university says, "Women have taken up athletics so recently that they don't understand what it takes to be good. They are greener and they lack competitive experience. Beyond that, and the greater strength and speed of men, there is no fundamental difference. Girls make the same mistakes boys do—and have the same youthful enthusiasm. It will just take time."

18   It already has taken time, but the first step may have been the hardest: shucking the encumbering skirts and petticoats in which Western women had been trapped. Another early milestone was the introduction around 1900 of the "safety bicycle," the basic two-wheeler used today. It is credited with getting women actively out on their own in large numbers for the first time. Then came World War II and the opportunity for Rosie the Riveter and her sisters to prove themselves.

19   Shortly thereafter, the communist world began to score propaganda points in the Olympics with the formidable showing of its female athletes. Eastern-bloc sports factories turned out such superior goods that when at Rome, in 1960, a hitherto unknown American sprinter named Wilma Rudolph ran off with three gold medals, she became an instant national hero. The vehicle that carried Rudolph to her fame was television—and from that year on, the upstart medium, with its voracious appetite for sporting events, would find ample fare in women's sports.

20   In the past decade, more milestones went by. In 1972, Congress passed Title IX of the Education Amendments of 1972, providing that "no person in the United States shall, on the basis of sex, be excluded from participation in any education program or activity receiving federal financial assistance." It took most of the remainder of the '70s for the Department of Health, Education and Welfare to define the law, and for schools across the country to begin to comply.

21   In 1973, New Jersey ruled that qualified girls must be allowed to play Little League baseball. Male coaches across the country screamed that the sky was falling. The following year, Little League changed its bylaws to include girls.

22   Even so, as the '80s begin, Donna Lopiano, director of women's athletics at the University of Texas at Austin, assesses women athletes as still ten years from realizing their potential. "The kids we think are super now," she says, "are going to be the rule, not the exception. We are just starting to get kids who are good already, who have received coaching from the age of 15."

23   Some believe the day is coming when women will compete head to head with men in more and more sports events, particularly in track and swimming events of longer distance. Australian scientist K. F. Dyer sees the difference between some men's and women's track and

swimming records closing so fast he expects it to disappear altogether in the not too distant future.

There are predictions, too, that women will eventually surpass men 24 in the super-marathons—those of 50 miles or more. Lyn Lemaire, a 29-year-old Harvard law student, proved that last year when she joined a field of 15 for the Iron Man Triathlon, a 140.6-mile non-stop race around the Hawaiian island of Oahu, combining swimming, cycling and a final, conventional 26-mile marathon. Of the 12 finishers, Lyn Lemaire placed fifth. The event may have to be renamed.

Questions About Meaning

1. What folk wisdom about the athletic disadvantages of female anatomy is proving to be false?
2. In 1976, the Army conducted tests to determine the relative strengths of men and women. What were the conclusions?
3. What is the female's disadvantage in tennis?
4. In what sport do women regularly beat men?
5. What does Donna Lopiano think will eventually make "super" athletic performances by women commonplace?
6. In what kinds of athletic contests might women hope to do at least as well as, if not better than, men?

Matters of Technique

1. The first three examples, in paragraphs 2, 3, and 4, are also comparisons. What is being compared to what in each case?
2. What is the other major comparison in the essay, beginning with paragraph 6?
3. The author chose to begin the essay with a series of specific examples illustrating the increasing importance of women's athletics. Is this an effective technique for getting into the subject? Why?
4. In paragraph 5, what technique does the author adopt for getting the principal categories of the discussion before the reader?

Vocabulary

1. vulnerable (7)
2. susceptible (7)
3. ordained (9)
4. estrogen (11)
5. quantify (13)
6. subcutaneous (14)
7. voracious (19)

Suggestions for Writing

1. Write a personal experience essay in which you describe an athletic confrontation between you and a member of the opposite sex. Develop a thesis as you describe that experience.
2. Write an essay in which you show that women athletes have "come a long way." Take your illustrations from personal experience.
3. Write a comparison essay on an outstanding male and an outstanding female athlete in your high school. Emphasize the importance of the contribution each made to his or her team.

CHAPTER SEVEN

Classification

Human beings are tireless classifiers. Dentists classify teeth as incisors, canines, bicuspids, and molars. Zoologists classify animals as carnivorous, herbivorous, or omnivorous. Composers group musical instruments into the categories of brass, woodwinds, strings, and percussion, while political theorists categorize political attitudes as radical, liberal, middle-of-the-road, conservative, and reactionary. Linguists group theories of the origin of language into categories called the Bow-Wow, the Pooh-Pooh, the Ding-Dong, and the Yo-He-Ho, and teachers classify the work of students into categories labeled A, B, C, D, or F. In the Middle Ages, doctors divided the fluids of the body into four "humours": blood, yellow bile, phlegm, and black bile. Today, astronomers group theories about the origin of the universe into two classes: the Big Bang and the Steady State.

Although the human infatuation with classification can cause mischief (as the division of mankind into races often causes mischief), classification is too good a tool to give up. It helps us make sense out of a world made up of billions of bits of random data. Until we sort out those bits, all is flux and chaos.

For one thing, classification imposes order on material that would otherwise be difficult to handle. A book called *The Movie Quote Book* contains over 2,500 quotations. Consider what it would be like to locate a particular quotation in that book if the author, Harry Haun, hadn't grouped the quotations according to subject. But because he did, we can look up the category "elephants" to find out if Groucho Marx, in the film *Animal Crackers*, really said, "One morning I shot an elephant in my pajamas. How he got into my pajamas I'll never know."

Consider what a trip to a department store would be like if the store were not divided into departments. It's hard enough now to find clothes for a Barbie doll in the toy section; they would be impossible to find if they were next to the cans of STP.

If classification serves the practical purpose of arranging quotations and Barbie doll clothing, it can also illuminate a subject in an essay. You see, classification reveals connections among seemingly disparate items. When the earliest editors of Shakespeare's plays divided them into three groups—comedies, tragedies, and histories—the editors were saying, in effect, that the plays were not simply random items— that in fact some of them shared significant characteristics. On a simple level, the article "Candy Man" by Alexander Theroux (reprinted in this section) divides candy into—among other categories—trash candies, pop candies, mumping candies, and chunkies. And we discover, through these categories, that there is indeed a connection between Milk Duds and Jujubes: Both have to be "mumped" rather than chewed. Not an outstanding insight, to be sure, but it does reveal what classification can do: It can bring into focus an item when it is placed with others that share certain of its significant characteristics.

In a 1974 *Time* Magazine essay, "Faces in the Crowd" (reprinted in this chapter), the author divides rock fans into five types: Heavy Metal, Listeners, Squeaky Cleans, Glitter Trippers, and Evening Outers. What he reveals when he breaks up the mass called "rock fans" is that rock audiences, which to the casual observer appear all the same, are actually separate entities, each with its own distinguishing characteristics.

Classification is also used to persuade. The classifier in this case sets out to show the superiority of one of the categories by contrasting it with the other categories. In "Three Ways of Responding to Oppression" (reprinted in this chapter), Martin Luther King was not so much interested in imposing order on chaos as he was in using classification as a method of revealing the moral and practical superiority of nonviolent resistance to the other two possible responses to oppression.

Naturally, classification is used as a principle of organizing material in courses outside of freshman composition. Let's say you were writing a paper for your sociology class on the negative responses to the publication, in 1948, of the Kinsey Report, *Sexual Behavior in the Human Male*. To organize and to thus help make sense out of those responses, you would need to arrange them into categories: perhaps one category for those who objected to the scientific methods used in the study, and another category for those who objected to the publication of the intimate details of male sexual behavior. By breaking up the mass of responses into categories, you would not only save time in the library by focusing your research, but you would also be organizing your paper.

Some teachers might even ask you to discuss the principles behind a particular classification system already in use. An art teacher, for instance, might ask you to discuss the principles that lie behind the traditional categories, or classes, that modern art works fall into.

Suggestions for Writing the Classification Essay

1. *Be certain that you write more than a mere list.* One of the most common errors is for a writer to feel that the fact that he has classified something should be enough, so he gives only the barest description of each of his categories. Actually, each category should be described thoroughly.

2. *Make sure that each item fits into only one category.* You wouldn't, for instance, divide English Channel swimmers into breast strokers, crawl strokers, and females. If you did that, Florence Chadwick would fit into two categories, crawl strokers and females. (Of course, you could break this rule if you were using classification to make a humorous point—for example, dividing people into Americans, foreigners, and Texans.)

3. *Every item should fit somewhere, and you shouldn't have to force any items into a slot.* Actually, the division of Shakespeare's plays into comedies, histories, and tragedies isn't one of the greatest schemes of classification. *Pericles*, for instance, was forced into the slot called "Comedies," which includes light, frothy things like *Love's Labor's Lost*, despite the fact that *Pericles* is vastly different in tone (it's often morbid and tragic) and action. (Deaths, reported and real, occur to admirable characters.)

4. *Use a single principle of classification.* If, for instance, you are going to classify books, don't divide them into fiction, baseball stories, and humor. If you begin by classifying a book as fiction, you will have to stick to a method of classification based on whether the incidents in the book actually took place or not. If you begin by classifying a book by its subject matter, you will have to classify other books by their subject matter.

5. *Try to discover a new way of classifying.* It is hardly worth writing a paper that divides humans into mesomorphs, endomorphs, and ectomorphs. That has already been done. But you might be able to make a humorous point by dividing people into cat haters and cat lovers.

6. *Try to make your essay do more than merely classify.* That is, try to formulate a thesis that underlies your classification scheme. In many

cases you can arrive at a conclusion about the relative worth of the categories you have devised.

7. *Classifications that consist of three or more groups usually make better essays.* The two-part classification is usually too large to handle ("There are basically two kinds of philosophies") or the humor is too stale ("Drivers come in two varieties: male and female").

Organization

The organization of a classification essay will sometimes be determined by your general method of classification. If you were classifying religions, for instance, you might wish to begin with the oldest and then arrange the others chronologically. Or you might wish to organize them from least common to most common.

Otherwise, your arrangement will depend upon your purpose. If you were classifying horror movies according to the menace, your groupings might be supernatural, animal, and human. If you were trying to show, through this classification, that the human menace is the scariest, you would want to save it for last. On the other hand, if you were using the three divisions merely as illustrations to support a thesis, you would want to arrange them according to their interest and appeal, and then save the most interesting and appealing till last. Always work toward a climax in your essays.

MODEL CLASSIFICATION PARAGRAPH

Of Pigeons, Fish, and Gulls

There are three ways of hustling pool games. In the Lemonade, the hustler disguises himself as, say, a successful-looking small-town salesman (purple double-knits, white belt, white tie). Then he walks into a strange poolroom and begins to knock the balls around until a greedy pigeon, emerging from the lineup of locals who are holding up the wall, challenges him to a game. Another type, the Hoorah hustle, works like this: The hustler struts into a poolroom, leather-cased two-piece cue in hand, and announces, "Hey, dis is da Ice Man, and I'll spot any fish here three balls in 9-ball and shoot one-handed." Few local sharks who are on the make can resist such a challenge, and the hustler soon has one hooked. Finally, there is the Needle, the rarest and most dangerous hustle of the three. In disguise again (penny loafers and house cue), the hustler gets into a friendly game with an unsuspecting gull and begins to needle him. Beginning slowly ("Hey man, my mama could have made that shot"), the hustler works his way up, a sneering notch at a time, until the gull, goaded beyond endurance, throws his money on the table and snarls, "Put up or shut up!" The "clever" gull doesn't realize that he has just been netted.

George Fern, 1982

ANALYSIS

As you can see, there are actually two things being classified in the above paragraph. The most obvious classification is the division of hustles into three types based on the hustlers' approaches to their victims. But the victims are also being classified; they are being divided into three groups on the basis of the motive that drives them into the hustler's snare.

Notice that Fern uses the same method of organization for each division. He begins by identifying the method of hustle, goes on to a brief description of the hustler, and then describes in dramatic terms the first contact between the hustler and his victim. A pattern makes it easier for readers to follow the development of a paragraph.

ASSIGNMENT

Write a classification paragraph in which you divide one of the following groups into three types: moviegoers, taxi drivers, card players, fishermen, salespeople, hitchhikers, dorm mates, sandlot athletes, joggers.

Faces in the Crowd

Time *Magazine's classification of rock audiences first appeared in 1974. It might be interesting to note if anything has changed in the rock scene since this essay was written.*

1   Who's playing at the local rock palace? One way to find out is to look at the marquee. Another, says California Promoter Steve Wolf, is to watch the crowd strolling—or floating, in the case of heavy grass consumers—through the door. "Audiences resemble the groups they come to see," says Wolf. Those words are reckless understatement.

2   No one who has ever mixed with a San Francisco psychedelic-style concert crowd is likely to forget the experience. Going to see the Boz Scaggs, Grace Slick or Hot Tuna? Better take ear muffs and a flak jacket. Psychedelic rock crowds can be hostile collections of spacy Viet-vets still suffering from post–Viet Nam syndrome, pimply feminists in granny glasses and young high school dropouts. Bottles and firecrackers spin through the air. At a Grateful Dead concert, usually a four- or five-hour affair, the typical freak is a blend of drug hunger, male lonerism and musical knowledgeability. He will attend somnolently to the music (perhaps taking downers), then suddenly (probably after swilling a bottle of wine) sway ecstatically forward toward the performers. In contrast, the audience for Balladeer James Taylor, or the country-rock group Poco, whose music has crisp patterns and infectious surfaces, has a well-scrubbed look and an enraptured response to the music.

3   Of course, when hallowed groups like the Rolling Stones, the Who, or Bob Dylan make one of their infrequent appearances, categories crumble; everybody comes, just like the World Series. Still, it is possible to define five general types of audiences on the basis of dress, manner, consumption, age and musical taste. The categories:

4   **Heavy Metal.** So named because of the massive banks of amplifiers, drums and loudspeakers employed by Grand Funk, Led Zeppelin, Black Sabbath and Blue Oyster Cult. The music is pure buzz—heavy, simplistic blues played at maximum volume and wallowed in mostly

140

by young teen-agers just experimenting with marijuana, the lingua franca of rock, and perhaps hard drugs too.

This audience can be trouble for concert-hall managers. Says Cleveland Promoter Jules Belkin, "They are up on the seats boogieing and running around the hall." Dress ranges from scruffy jeans to $200 velveteen jackets. The girls may come in couples to ogle, say, a topless Mark Farner of Grand Funk. Then there are the brassy groupies with their stevedore vocabularies who haughtily flaunt their backstage passes. The boys come in gangs and do what gangs do—fling lighted matches, fight the bouncers, sometimes toss empty wine bottles. Vomiting from too much beer or wine is a status symbol. If these kids do not have tickets, they break in. A heavy security force, sometimes including local police, is *de rigueur* at most rock concerts.

The Listeners. Performing groups that attract this crowd include the Moody Blues, Yes, Weather Report and The Eleventh House. The music is predominately classical or jazz rock. The listeners tend to be Heavy Metal graduates—youths ranging in age into the early 20s, who know and care about musicianship. Sedated by grass, Seconals and Quaaludes, they tend to applaud rather than scream their approval.

Squeaky Cleans. A description used by Singer Bette Midler to characterize fans of the soft, often poetic songs of such bards as Cat Stevens, James Taylor, Joni Mitchell, Melanie. This is an orderly dating crowd in its late teens and early 20s who are interested in love songs. Girls generally outnumber the boys by 2 to 1. Melanie's ethereal fans tend to invade the stage, only to sit quietly at her feet, perhaps lighting candles. Mitchell's following emulates her. "Since Joni started wearing gowns," says Wolf, "the girls have started wearing dresses and makeup."

Glitter Trippers. Glitter stars do not seem so much to have created their fandom as to have been created by it. The fastest-growing audience in rock dotes on the finery of such brocade-, sequin-, mascara- and rouge-wearing performers as Todd Rundgren, Suzi Quatro, Alice Cooper and the New York Dolls. Occasionally a glitter singer like England's bisexual David Bowie is actually good. Mostly, though, admits the Dolls' David Johansen, "the whole glitter trip is just jive." A concert can also be simply an excuse for youngsters to come out for a reasonably harmless masquerade party. The kids go on parade to show off their white tuxedos and top hats, feather boas, and of course glitter, lavishly applied to face and body.

The Evening-Outers. These are the young marrieds, who, says one New York promoter, "are dressed to the nines and smoke where they're supposed to." As mellowed graduates of the 1960s rock revolution, they will naturally show up to hear the Stones or Dylan, but mostly they turn out for the Carpenters, or The Fifth Dimension. Promoters like the Evening-Outers because they spend money generously at the concession bars.

10   Begun by the Beatles a decade ago, the rock revolution succeeded beyond everyone's wildest dreams. Rock defined an emerging segment of America, financed a counterculture, and spawned a $2 billion industry. Its principal gift to those who were young in the 1960s was to provide a common means of expression—a common music, a common language, even a kind of cathartic theater in which a Janis Joplin assumed almost mythic dimensions as a tragic heroine and Dylan strolled the stage like an Orpheus. It is no secret that rock's classic era is gone forever, along with the social bonds that nurtured it. The current fragmentation of the rock audience certifies that. In fairness, it must be added that it also signifies a diversity of personal taste and musical style unknown previously in American pop music. If rock can be described as being in a somewhat self-expressive romantic era, can its neoclassic period—or a pop Stravinsky—be far behind?

Questions About Meaning

1. How did the name "Heavy Metal" come to be used to describe those who enjoy "simplistic blues"?
2. In which group do the girls outnumber the boys two to one?
3. Which group spends the most money at the concession stand?
4. Which of the rock groups mentioned in the article are still popular? Which have retired? Which have changed their styles? (This article was originally published in 1974.)
5. What was rock's "principal gift to those who were young in the 1960s"?

Matters of Technique

1. What generalization does the author introduce in paragraph 1? How does he introduce it?
2. Where does the author announce the characteristics he is going to use to distinguish among the five groups? Why does he wait this long?
3. What is the function of the second paragraph?
4. Copy the sentence structures used to introduce the quotations in paragraphs 1 and 9—but make up your own sentences and quotes.
5. What is similar about the technique of the essay's opening and closing? Do you find the technique effective? Why?

Vocabulary

1. somnolently (2)
2. ecstatically (2)
3. hallowed (3)
4. wallowed (4)
5. lingua franca (4)

6. *de rigueur* (5)
7. ethereal (7)
8. emulates (7)
9. cathartic (10)

Suggestions for Writing

1. Describe the characteristics of students in three kinds of college classes (such as biology, art, composition, computer science, history, philosophy, or business). In discussing each category, describe the same characteristics, such as dress habits, reaction to test grades, behavior while listening to lectures, and note-taking. Look over "Faces in the Crowd" again if you need to.
2. Write an essay in which you classify your friends or acquaintances on the basis of their attitudes toward life, or toward their college careers. Be sure to use at least three categories.
3. Classify the employers you or your friends have had on the basis of their attitudes toward their employees. Use at least three categories.

Three Ways of Responding to Oppression

Martin Luther King, Jr.

Martin Luther King, Jr. was awarded the Nobel Peace Prize in 1964 for his work in the civil rights movement and his advocacy of passive resistance. He was assassinated in Memphis, Tennessee in 1968. "Three Ways of Responding to Oppression" (our title) comes from Stride Toward Freedom: The Montgomery Story *(1958).*

There is an additional King essay in Chapter 11.

1   Oppressed people deal with their oppression in three characteristic ways. One way is acquiescence: the oppressed resign themselves to their doom. They tacitly adjust themselves to oppression, and thereby become conditioned to it. In every movement toward freedom some of the oppressed prefer to remain oppressed. Almost 2800 years ago Moses set out to lead the children of Israel from the slavery of Egypt to the freedom of the promised land. He soon discovered that slaves do not always welcome their deliverers. They become accustomed to being slaves. They would rather bear those ills they have, as Shakespeare pointed out, than flee to others that they know not of. They prefer the "fleshpots of Egypt" to the ordeals of emancipation.

2   There is such a thing as the freedom of exhaustion. Some people are so worn down by the yoke of oppression that they give up. A few years ago in the slum areas of Atlanta, a Negro guitarist used to sing almost daily: "Ben down so long that down don't bother me." This is the type of negative freedom and resignation that often engulfs the life of the oppressed.

3   But this is not the way out. To accept passively an unjust system is to coöperate with that system; thereby the oppressed become as evil

as the oppressor. Noncoöperation with evil is as much a moral obligation as is coöperation with good. The oppressed must never allow the conscience of the oppressor to slumber. Religion reminds every man that he is his brother's keeper. To accept injustice or segregation passively is to say to the oppressor that his actions are morally right. It is a way of allowing his conscience to fall asleep. At this moment the oppressed fails to be his brother's keeper. So acquiescence—while often the easier way—is not the moral way. It is the way of the coward. The Negro cannot win the respect of his oppressor by acquiescing; he merely increases the oppressor's arrogance and contempt. Acquiescence is interpreted as proof of the Negro's inferiority. The Negro cannot win the respect of the white people of the South or the peoples of the world if he is willing to sell the future of his children for his personal and immediate comfort and safety.

A second way that oppressed people sometimes deal with oppres-   4
sion is to resort to physical violence and corroding hatred. Violence often brings about momentary results. Nations have frequently won their independence in battle. But in spite of temporary victories, violence never brings permanent peace. It solves no social problem; it merely creates new and more complicated ones.

Violence as a way of achieving racial justice is both impractical and   5
immoral. It is impractical because it is a descending spiral ending in destruction for all. The old law of an eye for an eye leaves everybody blind. It is immoral because it seeks to humiliate the opponent rather than win his understanding; it seeks to annihilate rather than to convert. Violence is immoral because it thrives on hatred rather than love. It destroys community and makes brotherhood impossible. It leaves society in monologue rather than dialogue. Violence ends by defeating itself. It creates bitterness in the survivors and brutality in the destroyers. A voice echoes through time saying to every potential Peter, "Put up your sword." History is cluttered with the wreckage of nations that failed to follow this command.

If the American Negro and other victims of oppression succumb to   6
the temptation of using violence in the struggle for freedom, future generations will be the recipients of a desolate night of bitterness, and our chief legacy to them will be an endless reign of meaningless chaos. Violence is not the way.

The third way open to oppressed people in their quest for freedom   7
is the way of nonviolent resistance. Like the synthesis in Hegelian philosophy, the principle of nonviolent resistance seeks to reconcile the truths of two opposites—acquiescence and violence—while avoiding the extremes and immoralities of both. The nonviolent resister agrees with the person who acquiesces that one should not be physically aggressive toward his opponent; but he balances the equation by

agreeing with the person of violence that evil must be resisted. He avoids the nonresistance of the former and the violent resistance of the latter. With nonviolent resistance, no individual or group need submit to any wrong, nor need anyone resort to violence in order to right a wrong.

8   It seems to me that this is the method that must guide the actions of the Negro in the present crisis in race relations. Through nonviolent resistance the Negro will be able to rise to the noble height of opposing the unjust system while loving the perpetrators of the system. The Negro must work passionately and unrelentingly for full stature as a citizen, but he must not use inferior methods to gain it. He must never come to terms with falsehood, malice, hate, or destruction.

9   Nonviolent resistance makes it possible for the Negro to remain in the South and struggle for his rights. The Negro's problem will not be solved by running away. He cannot listen to the glib suggestion of those who would urge him to migrate en masse to other sections of the country. By grasping his great opportunity in the South he can make a lasting contribution to the moral strength of the nation and set a sublime example of courage for generations yet unborn.

10   By nonviolent resistance, the Negro can also enlist all men of good will in his struggle for equality. The problem is not a purely racial one, with Negroes set against whites. In the end, it is not a struggle between people at all, but a tension between justice and injustice. Nonviolent resistance is not aimed against oppressors but against oppression. Under its banner consciences, not racial groups, are enlisted.

11   If the Negro is to achieve the goal of integration, he must organize himself into a militant and nonviolent mass movement. All three elements are indispensable. The movement for equality and justice can only be a success if it has both a mass and militant character; the barriers to be overcome require both. Nonviolence is an imperative in order to bring about ultimate community.

12   A mass movement of a militant quality that is not at the same time committed to nonviolence tends to generate conflict, which in turn breeds anarchy. The support of the participants and the sympathy of the uncommitted are both inhibited by the threat that bloodshed will engulf the community. This reaction in turn encourages the opposition to threaten and resort to force. When, however, the mass movement repudiates violence while moving resolutely toward its goal, its opponents are revealed as the instigators and practitioners of violence if it occurs. Then public support is magnetically attracted to the advocates of nonviolence, while those who employ violence are literally disarmed by overwhelming sentiment against their stand.

Questions About Meaning

1. According to King, how do some slaves regard slavery?
2. What does King call "negative freedom and resignation"?
3. What part does the concept of moral obligation play in King's philosophy?
4. Why does King think that nonviolent resistance can change the behavior and attitudes of oppressors? See paragraph 3.
5. What does King mean by saying, "The old law of an eye for an eye leaves everybody blind"?
6. What does the author mean by the statement, "Violence ends by defeating itself"?
7. What is King's ultimate goal? See paragraphs 5, 11, and 12.
8. To what is King's appeal ultimately directed? See paragraphs 3, 10, and 12.

Matters of Technique

1. Which of the ways of responding to oppression does King save for last? Why does he arrange his "ways" in that manner?
2. Since King does not agree with the first two ways of responding to oppression, why does he bring them up?
3. How do the topic sentences in various paragraphs clarify the initial thesis statement? (See paragraphs 1, 4, and 7.)
4. What use does King make of varying sentence lengths in paragraph 3? In paragraph 6?

Vocabulary

1. acquiescence (1)
2. tacitly (1)
3. emancipation (1)
4. glib (9)
5. en masse (9)

Suggestions for Writing

1. Write an appeal for a change in public attitude toward some controversial subject. Approximate King's method by developing at least three aspects of the subject (explaining, say, three *ways* in which the prevailing public attitude should change, or three *reasons* it should change), and try to be as cool and moderate in tone as King.

2. Develop a classification of the various attitudes held by people on some subject, then develop each category. Make sure that you have at least three categories. You might wish to classify your friends and acquaintances according to the categories you establish.

Cross-Reference

Compare, on the basis of its style and tone, King's essay to Lincoln's "Second Inaugural Address."

Communication Among the Naked Apes

Desmond Morris

Desmond Morris's The Naked Ape *(1967), subtitled* A Zoologist's Study of the Human Animal, *is a book of interesting—though sometimes far-fetched—speculation on the origins of human behavior. "Communication Among the Naked Apes" (our title) comes from that book.*

The behaviour pattern of talking evolved originally out of the increased need for the co-operative exchange of information. It grew out of the common and widespread animal phenomenon of non-verbal mood vocalization. From the typical, inborn mammalian repertoire of grunts and squeals there developed a more complex series of learnt sound signals. These vocal units and their combinations and re-combinations became the basis of what we can call *information talking.* Unlike the more primitive non-verbal mood signals, this new method of communication enabled our ancestors to refer to objects in the environment and also to the past and the future as well as to the present. To this day, information talking has remained the most important form of vocal communication for our species. But, having evolved, it did not stop there. It acquired additional functions. One of these took the form of *mood talking.* Strictly speaking, this was unnecessary, because the non-verbal mood signals were not lost. We still can and do convey our emotional states by giving vent to ancient primate screams and grunts, but we augment these messages with verbal confirmation of our feelings. A yelp of pain is closely followed by a verbal signal that 'I am hurt'. A roar of anger is accompanied by the message 'I am furious'. Sometimes the non-verbal signal is not performed in its pure state but instead finds expression as a tone of voice. The words 'I am hurt' are whined or screamed. The words 'I am furious' are roared or bellowed. The tone of voice in such cases is so unmodified by learning and so close to the ancient non-verbal mammalian signalling system that even a dog can understand the message, let alone a foreigner from another race of our own species. The actual words used in such instances are almost superfluous. (Try snarling 'good dog', or cooing 'bad dog' at your pet, and you will see what I mean.) At its crudest and most intense level, mood talking is little more than a 'spilling over' of verbalized sound signalling into an area of communication that is already taken care of. Its value lies in the increased possibilities it provides for more subtle and sensitive mood signalling.

2   A third form of verbalization is *exploratory talking*. This is talking for talking's sake, aesthetic talking, or, if you like, play talking. Just as that other form of information-transmission, picture-making, became used as a medium for aesthetic exploration, so did talking. The poet paralleled the painter. But it is the fourth type of verbalization that we are concerned with in this chapter, the kind that has aptly been described recently as *grooming talking*. This is the meaningless, polite chatter of social occasions, the 'nice weather we are having' or 'have you read any good books lately' form of talking. It is not concerned with the exchange of important ideas or information, nor does it reveal the true mood of the speaker, nor is it aesthetically pleasing. Its function is to reinforce the greeting smile and to maintain the social togetherness. It is our substitute for social grooming. By providing us with a non-aggressive social preoccupation, it enables us to expose ourselves communally to one another over comparatively long periods, in this way enabling valuable group bonds and friendships to grow and become strengthened.

3   Viewed in this way, it is an amusing game to plot the course of grooming talk during a social encounter. It plays its most dominant role immediately after the initial greeting ritual. It then slowly loses ground, but has another peak of expression as the group breaks up. If the group has come together for purely social reasons, grooming talk may, of course, persist throughout to the complete exclusion of any kind of information, mood or exploratory talk. The cocktail party is a good example of this, and on such occasions 'serious' talking may even be actively suppressed by the host or hostess, who repeatedly inter-vene to break up long conversations and rotate the mutual-groomers to ensure maximum social contact. In this way, each member of the party is repeatedly thrown back into a state of 'initial contact', where the stimulus for grooming talk will be strongest. If these non-stop social grooming sessions are to be successful, a sufficiently large num-ber of guests must be invited in order to prevent new contacts from running out before the party is over. This explains the mysterious minimum size that is always automatically recognized as essential for gatherings of this kind. Small, informal dinner parties provide a slightly different situation. Here the grooming talk can be observed to

wane as the evening progresses and the verbal exchange of serious information and ideas can be seen to gain in dominance as time passes. Just before the party breaks up, however, there is a brief resurgence of grooming talk prior to the final parting ritual. Smiling also reappears at this point, and the social bonding is in this way given a final farewell boost to help carry it over to the next encounter.

Questions About Meaning

1. Why, according to Morris, did "the behaviour pattern of talking" develop?
2. What type of talking does Morris call "the most important form of vocal communication for our species"? What are the advantages of this type of communication?
3. Morris makes a number of unqualified generalizations that are actually debatable. What are they?

Matters of Technique

1. Morris uses a number of strong concrete verbs in the latter half of paragraph 1. Point these out.
2. Which of Morris's "forms of verbalization" do you find the least clear? Help Morris clarify the concept by adding an example.
3. What technique does Morris use to introduce his discussion of each type of communication? Can you improve on this sequence of introductions?

Vocabulary

1. vocalization (1)
2. repertoire (1)
3. superfluous (1)

Suggestions for Writing

1. Using the actual words spoken to you and by you during the course of one day, write an essay on the advantages of "grooming talk."
2. Classify the various levels of your own language on the basis of the purposes for which you use them. Use plenty of examples and at least three categories.

Cross-Reference

Discuss the parallels and differences between Morris's classification of the purposes of language and Roberts' classification of the functions of various types of vocabulary.

The Candy Man

Alexander Theroux

The charm of Theroux's whimsical classification essay lies in his nostalgic lists of candy brand names. His essay originally appeared in a 1979 issue of Harper's.

I believe there are few things that show as much variety—that there is so much of—as American candy. The national profusion of mints and munch, pops and drops, creamfills, cracknels, and chocolate crunch recapitulates the good and plenty of the Higher Who.

Candy has its connoisseurs and critics both. To some, for instance, it's a subject of endless fascination—those for whom a root-beer lozenge can taste like a glass of Shakespeare's "brown October" and for whom little pilgrims made of maple sugar can look like Thracian gold—and to others, of course, it's merely a wilderness of abominations. You can sample one piece with a glossoepiglottic gurgle of joy or chew down another empty as shade, thin as fraud.

In a matter where tastes touch to such extremes one is compelled to seek through survey what in the inquiry might yield, if not conclusions sociologically diagnostic, then at least a simple truth or two. Which are the best candies? Which are the worst? And why? A sense of fun can feed on queer candy, and there will be no end of argument, needless to say. But, essentially, it's all in the *taste*.

The trash candies—a little lobby, all by itself, of the American Dental Association—we can dismiss right away: candy cigarettes, peanut brittle, peppermint lentils, Life Savers (white only), Necco Wafers (black especially), Christmas candy in general, gumballs, and above all that glaucous excuse for tuck called ribbon candy, which little kids, for some reason, pounce on like a duck on a June bug. I would put in this category all rock candy, general Woolworthiana, and all those little nerks, cupcake sparkles, and decorative sugars like silver buckshot that, though inedible, are actually eaten by the young and indiscriminate, whose teeth turn eerie almost on contact.

In the category of the most abominable tasting, the winner—on both an aesthetic and a gustatory level—must surely be the inscribed Valentine candy heart ("Be Mine," "Hot Stuff," "Love Ya," et cetera). In high competition, no doubt, are bubble-gum cigars, candy corn, marshmallow chicks (bunnies, pumpkins, et cetera), Wacky Wafers (eight absurd-tasting coins in as many flavors), Blow Pops—an owl's pellet of gum inside a choco-pop!—Canada Mints, which taste like petrified Egyptian lime, and, last but not least, those unmasticable beige near-candy peanuts that, insipid as rubber erasers, not only have no bite—the things just give up—but elicit an indescribable antitaste that is best put somewhere between stale marshmallow and dry wall. Every one of these candies, sweating right now in a glass case at your corner store, is to my mind proof positive of original sin. They can be available, I suggest, only for having become favorites of certain indiscriminate fatties at the Food and Drug Administration who must buy them by the bag. But a bat could see they couldn't be a chum of ours if they chuckled. . . .

6   There are certain candies, however—counter, original, spare, strange—that are gems in both the bite and the taste, not the usual grim marriage of magnesium stearate to lactic acid, but rare confections at democratic prices. Like lesser breeds raising pluperfect cain with the teeth, these are somehow always forgiven; any such list must include: Mary Janes, Tootsie Rolls, Sky Bars, Squirrels, Mint Juleps, the wondrous B-B Bats (a hobbit-sized banana taffy pop still to be had for 3¢), and other unforgettable knops and knurls like turtles, chocolate bark, peanut clusters, burnt peanuts, and those genius-inspired pink pillows with the peanut-butter surprise inside for which we're all so grateful. There's an *intelligence* here that's difficult to explain, a sincerity at the essence of each, where solid line plays against stipple and a truth function is solved always to one's understanding and always— *O altitudo!*—to one's taste.

7   Candy is sold over the counter, won in raffles, awarded on quiz shows, flogged door to door, shipped wholesale in boxes, thrown out at ethnic festivals, and incessantly hawked on television commercials by magic merrymen—clownish pied-pipers in cap-and-bells—who inspirit thousands of kids to come hopping and hurling after them, singing all the way to Cavityville. Why do w eat it? Who gets us started eating it? What sexual or social or semantic preferences are indicated by which pieces? The human palate—tempted perhaps by Nature *herself* in things like slippery elm, spruce gum, sassafras, and various berries—craves sweetness almost everywhere, so much so, in fact, that the flavor of candy commonly denominates American breath-fresheners, throat discs, mouthwash, lipstick, fluoride treatments, toothpaste, cough syrup, breakfast cereals, and even dental floss, fruit salts, and glazes. It's with candy—whether boxed, bottled, or bowed—that we say hello, goodbye, and I'm sorry. There are

regional issues, candies that seem at home only in one place and weirdly forbidden in others (you don't eat it at the ballpark, for instance, but on the way there), and of course seasonal candies: Christmas tiffin, Valentine's Day assortments, Thanksgiving mixes, and the diverse quiddities of Easter: spongy chicks, milk-chocolate rabbits, and those monstrositous roc-like eggs twilled with piping on the outside and filled with a huge blob of neosaccharine galvaslab! Tastes change, develop, grow fixed. Your aunt likes mints. Old ladies prefer jars of crystallized ginger. Rednecks wolf Bolsters, trollops suck lollipops, college girls opt for berries-in-tins. Truck drivers love to click Gobstoppers around the teeth, pubescents crave sticky sweets, the viler the better, and of course great fat teenage boys, their complexions aflame with pimples and acne, aren't fussy and can gorge down a couple of dollars' worth of Milky Ways, $100,000 Bars, and forty-eleven liquid cherries at one go!

The novelty factor can't be discounted. The wrapper often memorizes a candy for you; so capitalism, with its Hollywood brain, has devised for us candies in a hundred shapes and shocks—no, I'm not thinking of the comparatively simple Bit-O-Honey, golden lugs on waxed paper, or Little Nips, wax tonic bottles filled with disgustingly sweet liquid, or even the Pez, those little units that, upon being thumbed, dispense one of the most evil-tasting cacochymicals on earth. Buttons-on-paper—a trash candy—is arguably redeemed by inventiveness of vehicle. But here I'm talking about packaging *curiosa*—the real hype! Flying Saucers, for example, a little plasticene capsule with candy twinkles inside! Big Fake Candy Pens, a goofy fountain pen cartridged with tiny pills that taste like canvatex! Razzles ("First It's a Candy, Then It's a Gum")! Bottle Caps ("The Soda Pop Candy")! Candy Rings, a rosary of cement-tasting beads strung to make up a fake watch, the dial of which can be eaten as a final emetic. Rock Candy on a String, blurbed on the box as effective for throat irritation: "Shakespeare in *Henry IV* mentions its therapeutic value." You believe it, right?

And then there's the pop group: Astro Pops, an umbrella-shaped sugar candy on a stick; Whistle Pops ("The Lollipop with the Built-in Whistle"); and Ring Pops, cherry- or watermelon-flavored gems on a plastic stick—you suck the jewel. So popular are the fizzing Zotz, the trifling Pixie Stix with its powdered sugar to be lapped out of a straw, the Lik-M-Aid Fun Dip, another do-it-yourself stick-licker, and the explosion candies like Space Dust, Volcano Rocks, and Pop Rocks that candy-store merchants have to keep behind the counter to prevent them from getting nobbled. Still, these pale next to the experience of eating just plain old jimmies (or sprinkles or chocolate shot, depending on where you live), which although generally reserved for, and ancillary to, ice cream, can be deliciously munched by the fistful for a

real reward. With jimmies, we enter a new category all its own.
M&M's, for example: you don't eat them, you mump them.

10   Other mumping candies might be sugar babies, hostia almonds,
bridge mixes, burnt peanuts, and pectin jelly beans (Jelloids in general
lend themselves well to the mump.) I don't think Goobers and Raisi-
nets—dull separately—are worth anything unless both are poured
into the pocket, commingled, and mumped by the handful at the movies. (The clicking sound they make is surely one of the few pleasures
left in life.) This is a family that can also include Pom Poms, Junior
Mints, Milk Duds, Boston Baked Beans, Sixlets ("Candy-coated choc-
olate-flavored candies"—a nice flourish, that), and the disappoint-
ingly banal Jujubes—which reminds me. There are certain candies,
Jujubes for instance, that one is just too embarrassed to name out loud
(forcing one to point through the candy case and simply grunt), and
numbered among these must certainly be Nonpareils, Jujyfruits, Hore-
hound Drops, and Goldenberg's Peanut Chews. You know what I
mean. "Give me a *mrmrglpxph* bar." And you point. Interesting, right?

11   Interesting. The very word is like a bell that tolls me back to more
trenchant observations. Take the Sugar Daddy—it curls up like an elf-
shoe after a manly bite and upon being sucked could actually be used
for flypaper. (The same might be said for the gummier but more exquisite Bonomo's Turkish Taffy.) The Heath bar—interesting again—a
knobby little placket that can be drawn down half-clenched teeth with
a slucking sound for an instant chocolate rush, whereupon you're left
with a lovely ingot of toffee as a sweet surprise. The flaccid Charleston
Chew, warm, paradoxically becomes a proud phallus when cold (Isn't
there a metaphysics in the making here?) Who, until now, has ever
given these candies the kind of credit they deserve? . . .

12   You may reasonably charge me, in conclusion, with an insensibility
for mistreating a particular kind of candy that you, for one reason or
another, cherish, or bear me ill will for passing over another without
paying it due acknowledgment. But here it's clearly a question of taste,
with reasoning generally subjective. Who, after all, can really explain
how tastes develop? Where preferences begin? That they exist is sufficient, and fact, I suppose, becomes its own significance. Which leads
me to believe that what Dr. Johnson said of Roman Catholics might
less stupidly be said of candies: "In every thing in which they differ
from us, they are wrong."

Questions About Meaning

1. Theroux's categories are arbitrary and whimsical. Make up a candy
   category of your own that Theroux doesn't mention.
2. What seems to be the basis, the principle, of Theroux's classification? Where does he make this clear?

Matters of Technique

1. Theroux is almost too clever for his own good. For instance, the words "counter, original, spare, strange" in the first sentence of paragraph 6 are taken from a 19th-century poem, "Pied Beauty," by Gerard Manley Hopkins, while the Latin phrase "O altitudo!" in the last sentence of the same paragraph is an exclamation used by Sir Francis Bacon and Sir Thomas Browne. What does Theroux gain or lose by using such arcane allusions?
2. Point out words and phrases that would support the view that Theroux's vocabulary is a touch precious and pretentious.
3. The author's paragraphs consist basically of lists of candies that belong to certain categories. How exactly does he make these "lists" interesting? Analyze the nonlist aspects of paragraph 10.

Vocabulary

1. connoisseurs (2)
2. glaucous (4)
3. gustatory (5)
4. insipid (5)
5. hype (8)
6. emetic (8)
7. banal (10)
8. trenchant (11)
9. flaccid (11)

Suggestions for Writing

1. Write a paper in which you classify various sweets (such as candies, fruit, and desserts) according to the kind of hunger pangs they satisfy.
2. Write a paper in which you classify types of food (such as soup, steak, pizza, ice cream, bacon and eggs, and pie) according to the appetites they satisfy.
3. Write a classification theme that uses "There are three kinds of _____" as your topic sentence.

CHAPTER EIGHT

Definition

Definitions are troublesome things, knotty and unsafe. Nobody knew this better than Samuel Johnson, England's great 18th-century lexicographer. After working for seven years constructing definitions for his dictionary, he still believed that

> all definitions are hazardous. I see a cow. I define her: Animal quadrupes ruminans cornutum (a four-footed, horned animal that chews the cud). But a goat ruminates and a cow may not have horns.

If "cow" is difficult to define, imagine how much more difficult an abstraction like "sweet" is. (Try defining "sweet" without the help of a dictionary.)

Despite the hazards, attempts to define words are usually helpful, sometimes indispensable, and occasionally a matter of life and death. (A hospital's definition of "life" tells them when to unplug someone's life-support system, and a person's freedom sometimes hangs on a definition of "insanity.")

The definitions you write won't be as crucial, but they very well may help you survive college. In history classes you may be asked to define the Turnerian thesis. Your sociology professor may ask you to discuss the meaning of "introvert." And you will probably be asked to write an essay based on an extended definition in your composition class.

Forms Definitions Take

Let's begin with how to write a formal definition, the most logical and direct way of defining something. A formal definition has three parts: term, genus, and differentiation. For example:

Term: the word that needs defining	Genus: the class that the term falls into	Differentiation: characteristics that separate the term from others in its class
dibromide	a binary chemical compound	containing two bromine atoms per molecule
fremitus	a vibration	in the chest, as in speaking
gnu	an African antelope	having a drooping beard, tufted tail, and curved horns
foundling	a deserted child	left by parents whose identity is unknown
ideal	a conception of something	in its absolute perfection

Writing formal definitions isn't as formidable as it looks. Try a few and see. Try "ballpoint pen." (You see, don't you, that it falls into the class of "writing instruments," and that the characteristic that separates it from others in that class is its tiny steel ball bearing that transfers ink from a storage chamber to the paper?) Now try "hammer," "photograph," and "happiness" on your own.

The problem with formal definitions is that though they work very well for concrete terms like "gnu" and "foundling" and scientific terms like "dibromide," they don't work very well for abstractions like "ideal" or "happiness." And they don't work at all for parts of speech other than nouns.

When used in essays, definitions sometimes consist simply of a synonymous word or phrase placed within a parenthesis immediately following a crucial word in your essay: "The animal showed signs of being in estrus (in heat)." Even more common is the use of the appositive without the parenthesis: "The lamprey, a primitive eel-shaped fish with a sucking mouth, clamped onto my belly."

Our primary concern in this chapter, however, is with definitions that are developed at greater length and in greater detail. Even dictionary definitions, as precise as they are, often need to be expanded if the writer is to communicate his meaning fully and effectively.

Let's trace one word, "dialect," to note, in particular, that the way a writer defines a word depends on his purpose for defining it.

We can begin with an anonymous *American Heritage* lexicographer, who says that a "dialect" is a "regional variety of language, distinguished from other varieties by pronunciation, grammar, or vocabulary, especially." This is just right for its purpose—to provide a writer or reader with a quick, ready-to-use meaning.

People who have a special interest in language and dialects, however, may need a definition longer than one that the dictionary affords. For them there is C. Hugh Holman's *A Handbook to Literature*, which spends three paragraphs defining "dialect." Naturally, Holman begins with a brief dictionary-type definition. But he quickly goes on to discuss problems with the common definition of "dialect" when he says that "no scientific method has been devised which will make it possible in all cases to distinguish between a language and a dialect." (The dictionary, quite naturally, didn't want to get into that sticky mess.) Holman also gives categories of actual dialects, something the dictionary example didn't do. And finally, Holman develops part of his definition of "dialect" through cause and effect: "The chief cause of the development of dialects is isolation. . . ."

The lesson to be learned from Holman is that the writer should use whatever method of development seems useful and appropriate.

Roger Shuy's "Dialects: What They Are" (reprinted in this chapter) is yet another step up. Shuy's definition is a full-blown essay, sixteen paragraphs in length, of the type that you might be asked to write.

Essay-length definitions usually have a purpose outside the definition itself. They may be intended, for instance, to correct a common misconception about a word, or perhaps to make concrete what is normally abstract by defining words like freedom, joy, grief, or love. (Look at Paul's letter to the Corinthians, reprinted in this chapter, for a magnificent definition of "love.") Or the writer may want to argue a case by presenting a definition. Extended definitions need this outside purpose. They would be awfully dreary without it.

Roger Shuy, for instance, seems at least as concerned that his readers' attitudes about dialects be improved as he is with formally defining the term, though he does get to a formal definition in his concluding paragraph. He is, in effect, trying to raise our consciousness; he is really talking about language chauvinism when he writes that the "northern Illinois informants felt that the southern pronunciation [of greasy] was crude and ugly." Through a definition of "dialect," then, Shuy believes he can raise our tolerance level by getting us to accept what the "real" meaning of dialect is.

Special Problems in Defining

1. Keep the part of speech of the definition consistent with that of the term being defined:

> *Don't:* a marathon *is when* a group of people run a cross-country footrace over 26 miles, 385 yards.
>
> *Do:* a marathon *is a* cross-country footrace over a distance of 26 miles, 385 yards.

2. Don't include in your definition the word that is being defined. This is called "circular" definition. Don't define "jungle fever" as "fever caught in the jungle" or a "frying pan" as a "flat, circular pan used for frying."

3. Put quotation marks around words when they are used for their own sake rather than for what they represent. Example: "Frying pan" should be defined accurately.

4. Try to use simpler and more familiar words in the definition than are used in the term itself. Samuel Johnson's infamous definition of "network" as "anything reticulated or decussated, at equal distances, with interstices between the intersections" is not a good way to define "network." *The American Heritage Dictionary's* definition of "network" is much better: "An openwork fabric or other structure in which rope, thread, wires, or other materials cross at regular intervals."

5. Avoid opening an essay with "Perhaps it would be appropriate to begin by defining our terms." It may be appropriate, but it is also likely to scare away half your readers. Benjamin Disraeli's comment, "I hate definitions," is probably a widespread sentiment. If your essay needs a short definition, work it in unobtrusively, perhaps in a parenthesis immediately following the word that needs defining.

6. You can occasionally define through negation, as Paul does in 1st Corinthians: "Charity . . . doth not. . . ."

7. Stay away from happiness-is-a-warm-puppy definitions. These have seen their better days, and even on their best days they weren't very good.

8. In extended definitions, stay within the limits of the commonly accepted meaning for a term. You can't say, for instance, that pride in one's accomplishments is actually arrogance.

MODEL DEFINITION PARAGRAPH

Here Come the Voutians

Voutians (pronounced *Vowshuns*) are a growing group of . . . college students who are uninhibited admirers of jazz musician Slim Gaillard, composer of "Cement Mixer Put-ti, Put-ti," "Flat Foot Floogie with a Floy Floy." They play his records, talk his outlandish rhyming language. A pretty girl is a rootie-voutie, or viddle vop. Onions are reetie-pooties. Reeny, roony and aureenie are used as complementary suffixes. (Hamburgeraureenie is a good hamburger.)

LIFE Magazine, © *Time Inc. Reprinted with permission.*

ANALYSIS

This paragraph from *Life* follows the classic structure of a definition paragraph or essay. The author begins with the term that requires defining ("Voutians"), goes on to the term's genus, or class (college students), and then differentiates the term from others in its class. He does this by telling us that *these* college students are followers of Slim Gaillard. The latter part of the paragraph is an elaboration on the formal definition. In this case, the author tells us who Slim Gaillard is and describes the special language that Voutians have picked up from him.

ASSIGNMENT

Write a definition paragraph of your own in which you define a slang term through an imitation of the structure of the *Life* paragraph.

Where Hell Begins

Norman Cousins

Long the editor of Saturday Review, *Norman Cousins recently turned his attention, in* The Anatomy of an Illness *(1979), to the self-healing mechanisms in the mind and body. "Where Hell Begins " (1950) is one of the hundreds of editorials that Cousins wrote during the almost four decades that he was editor of* Saturday Review.

Gian-Carlo Menotti came up with an intriguing personal definition of hell a few weeks ago at New York's Town Hall. Mr. Menotti said that "hell begins on the day when God grants us a clear vision of all that we might have achieved, of all the gifts which we have wasted, of all that we might have done which we did not do. . . . For me, the conception of hell lies in two words: 'too late.'" 1

Another definition of hell is furnished by T. S. Eliot in that highly polished and meticulously written but frosty and detached play, *The Cocktail Party.* "What," asks the leading character, "is hell?" Then he proceeds to supply his own answer: "Hell is oneself. Hell is alone, the other figures in it merely projections. There is nothing to escape from and nothing to escape to. One is always alone." Later another character in Mr. Eliot's play supplements this conception of hell by picturing it as "the final desolation of solitude in the phantasmal world of imagination, shuffling memories, and desires." 2

It is a fascinating game, these personal definitions of hell. The other day I found myself playing this game in a somewhat inappropriate place—a strato-cruiser plane high up above the earth, high above a flooring of light-colored clouds. Here in a gleaming fairyland of skyscape and heaven I dwelled on hell. 3

I began by agreeing with Mr. Menotti. But even on his own terms I felt there was a hell more fiendish than the one he described. The torture that comes with a sudden vision or realization of squandered talent and unfulfilled creativeness is bad enough, but not nearly so bad as the torture of knowing what needs to be done, and not being able to dislodge the deep internal block that prevents it from being done. There is a locked door somewhere shutting the talent off from 4 the will. It is not true that genius will always out: genius can decay and destroy itself in the rust of its own corrosive juices. The retrospective hell over the unachieved is a small oven compared to the living hell of coping with a mysterious inner vault which volition alone cannot unlock.

5   Mr. Eliot's hell has this much in common with Mr. Menotti's: both are intensely personal. At the core center of Mr. Eliot's Gehenna man is aware that he will never be able to shatter his loneliness. He discovers the "final desolation of solitude." Here, too, it seemed to me that there must be hotter and sharper thorns at hell's center than those that stab at the naked loneliness of man. My intensified hell begins where man actually worships his solitude—because he fears his fellow man. He shrinks from the sight of men because he detects cunning in their eyes, designs in their minds, violence in their hands. He contemplates his brothers and knows only primitive uncertainty. To be alone is his only refuge from the transience of their affections, the terror of their suspicions, the explosiveness of their antagonisms.

6   Even this section of hell has an inner circle where the anguish is further compounded. Here man attains the ultimate in fear: he fears himself. He believes he is imprisoned in his own body. He feels he is chained to qualities and impulses he can neither comprehend nor control. He is first baffled, then terrified, by his responses to situations which, in anticipation, he can measure against high principle but which, in reality, leave him bereft of any moral standard. He finds himself shackled to a tyranny more absolute than any he has known outside himself—an inner tyranny which enfeebles the conscience and dictates over it. In such a fear and in such a hell, self-hate is inevitable and indeed becomes a crusade.

7   There is yet another hell beyond the hell in which "one is always alone," in Mr. Eliot's phrase. It is a hell in which man succeeds in piercing his loneliness, succeeds in establishing his bond with the generality of men—only to discover a collective loneliness in the universe. The iron walls of the self may be torn down in a magnificent triumph of common purpose and common conscience as men discover they are but single cells in a larger and common body. But it is not enough. For hell begins where larger identification stops. No loneliness is as great as that which severs the society of man from identification with the totality of all life and all things.

8   We now come to hell's own hell. The torment experienced by those at this innermost station may not be easily described but at least the sufferers may be recognized. This is the hell of those who possess a natural idealism yet turn their backs on it; who know the meaning of nobility yet resist it; who can comprehend dignity yet shun it. Finally, it is the hell of those who have an awareness of what is meant by the gift of life, yet fail to justify it.

Questions About Meaning

1. What does Cousins regard as worse than wasted talent?
2. How does Cousins qualify Eliot's definition of hell? (See paragraph 5.)
3. How does the author narrow his definition of hell still further in paragraph 6? In paragraph 7?
4. What is Cousins' ultimate hell, "hell's own hell"?

Matters of Technique

1. Notice that Cousins begins the essay by quoting two carefully stated definitions of hell. Do you find this technique an effective introduction to the subject? Why?
2. What function does paragraph 3 serve?
3. Improve Cousins' definition of "hell's own hell" (paragraph 8) by inserting an example or two into the paragraph.

Vocabulary

1. meticulously (2)
2. frosty (2)
3. detached (2)
4. desolation (2)
5. phantasmal (2)
6. retrospective (4)
7. volition (4)
8. Gehenna (5)
9. transience (5)
10. bereft (6)

Suggestions for Writing

1. Develop a personal definition of a commonly accepted abstraction by going beyond the usual definitions.
2. Begin your essay by quoting someone else's definition of an abstraction, a definition you generally agree with, then qualify and deepen the definition so that it more correctly expresses your own viewpoint.
3. Develop a definition, with examples, of one of the following abstract concepts: love, courage, faith, hatred, generosity, cowardice, envy, selfishness, or selflessness.

Dialects: What They Are

Roger Shuy

Roger Shuy, a linguist who specializes in dialects, is the author of Discovering American Dialects *(1967) and the co-author, with Joan Baratz, of* Teaching Black Children to Read *(1969). In the following essay, Shuy weaves through his definition of "dialect" the argument that dialects are what we all speak, not just what someone else speaks.*

1   Many Americans are unaware that they and their friends speak a variety of English which can be called a dialect. Many even deny it and say something like this: "No, we don't speak a dialect around here. They speak more harshly and strangely out East and down South, but we just don't have anything like that in *our* speech."

2   Most Southerners know that people from other parts of the country are either pleased or annoyed by their Southern pronunciations and expressions. Many Easterners are aware of the reactions of people from west of the Alleghenies to typical Eastern speech patterns. On the other hand, many Midwesterners, for some reason, seem oblivious to the fact that Americans from other areas find something strange about the vocabulary, pronunciation, and grammar characteristic of the Midwest.

3   People tend to describe the differences between their speech and that of others in certain conventional terms. *Harshness* and *nasalized drawl* are often used to describe the speech of any area other than that of the speaker. Another popular term, *guttural,* is also used with little precision. Strangely enough, many people will insist that they hear a *guttural* quality in the speech of another person *even though they cannot define the term.*

4   Linguists who specialize in the study of dialects describe American speech systematically and with precision. They avoid terms like *harsh* and *dull,* for such words are closer to condemnation than description, and terms like *soft* and *musical,* for they are too general to be useful.

Like many common English terms, these words have been used so widely that it is difficult to say exactly what they *do* mean.

How, then, can linguists go about describing dialect differences systematically and precisely? Perhaps we should begin with what we already know. In an age in which people often move from one area of the country to another, it is rather common for us to have neighbors or classmates whose dialect may be somewhat "different." Furthermore, the summer (or winter) vacation has enabled many of us to enter different dialect areas. Television and radio have brought speakers from many social and geographical dialect areas into our homes. We may begin, then, by recognizing that there *are* dialect differences.

Besides the facts, however, we also begin with attitudes. Since language is a form of social behavior, we react to a person's speech patterns as we would react to any of his actions. If his dialect differs from our own, we may consider him quaint, naive, stupid, suave, cultivated, conceited, alien, or any number of other things. Most frequently, however, our attitude toward the outsider tends to be negative, since, after all, he is not one of *our* group. Recently a graduate school professor at a large Midwestern university asked his students to describe various unidentified persons whose voices were recorded on tape. The class described one voice as rustic and uncultivated. The voice was that of their professor!

It is clear, then, that most people recognize dialect differences of some sort and have certain feelings or attitudes toward them. A classic example of this recognition and reaction occurred during a survey of Illinois speech conducted in 1962. Many people from the middle of the state and most from the southern part pronounced *greasy* something like *greezy*. On the other hand, people in the northern counties of the state pronounced the word *greecey*. The northern Illinois informants felt that the southern pronunciation was crude and ugly; it made them think of a very messy, dirty, sticky, smelly frying pan. To the southern and midland speakers, however, the northern pronunciation connoted a messy, dirty, sticky, smelly skillet.

Which of the two pronunciations and reactions are right? The answer is easy: The southern Illinois pronunciation and reaction are appropriate in southern Illinois, and the northern Illinois pronunciation and reaction are proper in northern Illinois. Educated *and* uneducated speakers say *greezy* in southern Illinois. Educated *and* uneducated speakers say *greecey* in northern Illinois. Although we must not be surprised that people tend to believe their own way is the "right way," it should be clear that there are two acceptable pronunciations of this word in Illinois, reflecting different dialects.

The word "dialect" is associated with speech communities, groups of people who are in constant internal communication. Such a group speaks its own dialect; that is, the members of the group have certain language habits in common. For example, a family is a speech community; the members of the family talk together constantly, and certain words have certain special meanings within the family group. The people who belong to your class in school form a speech community, sharing certain special ways of talking together—the latest slang, for instance. The people who work together in a single office are a speech community. Larger speech communities may be the members of a single occupation or profession. Carpenters share certain typical carpentry terms; lawyers use special legal terms.

10   An even larger speech community is made up of people who live in a particular geographic region. Such regional speech communities are the special concern of this book. The study of these communities is called "dialect geography" or "linguistic geography" or, simply "dialectology." The scholar who studies varieties of a language is called a "dialect geographer," or a "linguistic geographer," or a "dialectologist."

11   Dialectology is concerned with the regional and social aspects of language. The intermingling of these regional and social aspects is clearly illustrated in American English. We are all aware of the fact that relatively uneducated people tend to use certain pronunciations, grammar, and vocabulary which easily identify them as uneducated. We know, furthermore, that people from certain areas speak in such a way that we can make a good general guess as to where they are from. The speech of any such person, then, is a mixture of social and geographical features. The educated person will undoubtedly share some of the geographical features found in the speech of his uneducated townsman, but he will probably *not* share the speech features which label the other man uneducated (at least not in his more formal utterances). Here we discover two different aspects of dialectology— *regional* dialects and *social dialects*.

12   We might say that there are at least three degrees of understanding of what dialects are. First, some people think that a dialect is something spoken by a white-bearded old man in an out-of-the-way area.

13   Once we become aware of the fact that we *all* speak a dialect of some sort, we recognize dialects in a geographical sense, the second degree of understanding.

14   The third degree of understanding comes when we realize that social layers exist *within* regional dialect areas. That is, well-educated, partly-educated, and uneducated people may all live within the boundaries of a well-defined dialect area. In one sense, they all speak dialect X. It is also true, however, that they speak different varieties of this dialect. Certain aspects of the dialect are shared by all social levels; others are used by only one or two of the groups.

A case in point is the past tense of the verb *climb*. Well-educated 15 people in all dialect areas favor *climbed* as the past tense form. Some uneducated speakers in certain Northern dialect areas may say *clim*. In some parts of the Midland and Southern dialect areas, many uneducated speakers say *clum*; in Virginia, many uneducated speakers say *clome*. With this verb, then, we find dialect variants only among uneducated speakers. The variants, *clim*, *clum*, and *clome*, have geographical *and* social patterns. Both must be taken into account.

A dialect, then, is a variety of a language. It differs from other varieties in certain features of pronunciation, vocabulary, and grammar ("grammar" will be used to mean both word construction *and* syntax). It may reveal something about the social or regional background of its speakers, and it will be generally understood by speakers of other dialects of the same language.

Questions About Meaning

1. What does the author say are generally recognized dialects of American English?
2. What area's speakers often seem unaware that speakers from other regions of the United States find their speech habits strange?
3. What factors does Shuy say have caused Americans to become increasingly exposed to and aware of dialect variations in American English?
4. How does Shuy define what he means by the term "dialect"? See paragraphs 9, 10, and 16.
5. What is the difference between a social and a regional dialect?
6. Using Shuy's reasoning, why are the pronunciations of *greezy* and *greecey* both correct?
7. Shuy's purpose in writing this essay was more than definition. What was that additional purpose?

Matters of Technique

1. What is Shuy's purpose in his first four paragraphs?
2. In the three opening sentences in Shuy's first three paragraphs, he refers to Americans, Southerners, and people. How are these three groups qualified? Do you see that without those qualifications, Shuy would come across as dogmatic?
3. Shuy's extended definition of "dialect" ends with a formal definition. Why do you suppose Shuy didn't begin with his last paragraph?

Vocabulary

1. nasalized (3)
2. guttural (3)
3. linguists (4)
4. quaint (6)
5. suave (6)
6. syntax (16)

Suggestions for Writing

1. Write an essay on an incident that made you aware of your own social or regional dialect.
2. Select a dialect which you find most distasteful (or most pleasing) to you, and account for your reaction to it.

Tongues of Men and Angels

Paul

"Tongues of Men and Angels," Chapter 13 of Paul's First Letter to the Corinthians, is taken from the King James Version of the Bible, published first in 1611. An alternate translation of "charity" is love, which is favored by recent translators.

Though I speak with the tongues of men and of angels, and have not charity, I am become as sounding brass, or a tinkling cymbal. **1**

And though I have the gift of prophecy, and understand all mysteries, and all knowledge; and though I have all faith, so that I could remove mountains, and have not charity, I am nothing. **2**

And though I bestow all my goods to feed the poor, and though I give my body to be burned, and have not charity, it profiteth me nothing. **3**

Charity suffereth long, and is kind; charity envieth not; charity vaunteth not itself, is not puffed up, **4**

Doth not behave itself unseemly, seeketh not her own, is not easily provoked, thinketh no evil; **5**

Rejoiceth not in iniquity, but rejoiceth in the truth; **6**

Beareth all things, believeth all things, hopeth all things, endureth all things. **7**

Charity never faileth: but whether there be prophecies, they shall fail; whether there be tongues, they shall cease; whether there be knowledge, it shall vanish away. **8**

For we know in part, and we prophesy in part. **9**

But when that which is perfect is come, then that which is in part shall be done away. **10**

When I was a child, I spake as a child, I understood as a child, I thought as a child: but when I became a man, I put away childish things. **11**

For now we see through a glass, darkly; but then face to face: now I know in part; but then shall I know even as also I am known. **12**

And now abideth faith, hope, charity, these three; but the greatest of these is charity. **13**

Questions About Meaning

1. What point does Paul make about human motives by saying that, though one may give all his goods to the poor and "give [his] body to be burned," he may still possess no charity?
2. What do you suppose Paul means by saying that charity "seeketh not her own"?
3. What are the other things "charity" does not do? What are the things it does do?

Matters of Technique

1. What *method* does Paul use to define charity?
2. The rhetorical effectiveness of Chapter 13 of Paul's letter depends partly on rhythm. Point out a couple of particularly strong examples of rhythm.
3. Point out sections that are highly repetitious. What is the effect of these sections?
4. Note carefully Paul's opening metaphor (the gong and cymbal). Now finish the sentence after the word "charity" with a metaphor of your own that conveys a similar meaning.
5. The first three verses contain a number of "though" clauses; each withholds the most important part of the sentence until the final few words. Write a sentence of your own, based on the same sentence structure, using at least as many words as the second verse.

Vocabulary

1. vaunteth (verse 4)   3. iniquity (verse 6)
2. unseemly (verse 5)

Suggestions for Writing

1. Write a paper in which you define what "charity" (or "love") means to you. Use the relationships of family member, neighbor, and friend to develop your definition. You may find it useful to clarify your definition by showing what charity is *not*.
2. Write a paper in which you define what "faith," "hope," or some other abstract concept means to you. Again, you may wish to use the principle of negative contrast to help you develop your definition.
3. Define through description an object that is in your classroom or an object your teacher brings into the classroom.

The Nobel Prize Address

William Faulkner

Faulkner was awarded the Nobel Prize for Literature in 1950. His address on that occasion, reprinted here, gave him the opportunity to communicate to a worldwide audience what, in one form or another, he had been saying for years—that man will prevail "because he has a soul, a spirit capable of compassion and sacrifice and endurance" and that "the writer's duty is to write about these things." His best-known works of literature include The Sound and the Fury *(1929),* The Hamlet *(1940), and* Go Down, Moses *(1942).*

1   I feel that this award was not made to me as a man, but to my work— a life's work in the agony and sweat of the human spirit, not for glory and least of all for profit, but to create out of the materials of the human spirit something which did not exist before. So this award is only mine in trust. It will not be difficult to find a dedication for the money part of it commensurate with the purpose and significance of its origin. But I would like to do the same with the acclaim too, by using this moment as a pinnacle from which I might be listened to by the young men and women already dedicated to the same anguish and travail, among whom is already that one who will some day stand here where I am standing.

2   Our tragedy today is a general and universal physical fear so long sustained by now that we can even bear it. There are no longer problems of the spirit. There is only the question: When will I be blown up? Because of this, the young man or woman writing today has forgotten the problems of the human heart in conflict with itself which alone can make good writing because only that is worth writing about, worth the agony and the sweat.

3   He must learn them again. He must teach himself that the basest of all things is to be afraid; and, teaching himself that, forget it forever, leaving no room in his workshop for anything but the old verities and truths of the heart, the old universal truths lacking which any story is

"Address upon Receiving the Nobel Prize for Literature" by William Faulkner, from *Essays, Speeches & Public Letters,* edited by James B. Meriwether (Random House, Inc., 1965).

ephemeral and doomed—love and honor and pity and pride and compassion and sacrifice. Until he does so, he labors under a curse. He writes not of love but of lust, of defeats in which nobody loses anything of value, of victories without hope and, worst of all, without pity or compassion. His griefs grieve on no universal bones, leaving no scars. He writes not of the heart but of the glands.

4   Until he relearns these things, he will write as though he stood among and watched the end of man. I decline to accept the end of man. It is easy enough to say that man is immortal simply because he will endure: that when the last ding-dong of doom has clanged and faded from the last worthless rock hanging tideless in the last red and dying evening, that even then there will still be one more sound: that of his puny inexhaustible voice, still talking. I refuse to accept this. I believe that man will not merely endure: he will prevail. He is immortal, not because he alone among creatures has an inexhaustible voice, but because he has a soul, a spirit capable of compassion and sacrifice and endurance. The poet's, the writer's, duty is to write about these things. It is his privilege to help man endure by lifting his heart, by reminding him of the courage and honor and hope and pride and compassion and pity and sacrifice which have been the glory of his past. The poet's voice need not merely be the record of man, it can be one of the props, the pillars to help him endure and prevail.

Questions About Meaning

1. In paragraph 1, how does Faulkner *define* his work?
2. In paragraph 1, what audience does Faulkner say he is addressing? Be specific.
3. Faulkner's address was delivered in 1950, a year or so after Russia had exploded its first atomic bomb. Why is this fact important in understanding the essay?
4. What type of problems does Faulkner say the writer tends to forget in the shadow of nuclear annihilation? (See paragraph 2.)
5. In paragraph 3, what does Faulkner say must be in a piece of writing if it is to have universal significance?
6. According to Faulkner, what must a writer infuse into his work if he is to distinguish between such qualities or emotions as love and lust?
7. In the last paragraph, what does Faulkner say distinguishes man from other "creatures"—his ability to talk—or something else?
8. State Faulkner's thesis in your own words. That is, what is the writer's job?

Matters of Technique

1. This essay is located in the section titled "Definition." What is Faulkner defining?
2. Rewrite sentence 3 in the first paragraph to make it clearer. Have you lost or gained anything?
3. Faulkner occasionally descends to the colloquial. Point out where this occurs in the second paragraph.
4. Point out Faulkner's use of a variety of sentence lengths in paragraphs 2 and 3.
5. What image in paragraph 4 sums up the idea that Faulkner attacks (that man will not prevail, he will merely endure)?

Vocabulary

1. commensurate (1)
2. acclaim (1)
3. anguish (1)
4. travail (1)
5. verities (3)
6. ephemeral (3)

Suggestions for Writing

1. Write a paper that is an extended definition of one of the abstractions that Faulkner uses in paragraph 3: love, honor, pity, pride, compassion, sacrifice.
2. Assume that you have been chosen to deliver the Nobel Prize address. Write a speech in which you discuss your vision of the future of mankind. Do this in four paragraphs.
3. Write a paper in which you point out the similarities between Lincoln's vision of humanity in the "Second Inaugural Address" and Faulkner's in the "Nobel Prize Address."
4. Write an extended definition of what "happiness" (or "sorrow") means to you.

Cross-References

1. What is the similarity between Faulkner's "universal truths" and C. S. Lewis's "law of human nature"?
2. What similarity do you find between Faulkner's "old verities and truths of the heart" and those qualities Lincoln calls on the nation to exercise in the concluding paragraph of his "Second Inaugural Address"?

CHAPTER NINE

Cause and Effect

Nothing happens without a cause. Your water hose bursts during a cold night. What caused it? Your skirt is torn. What caused it? A large scorched circle appears one morning in your front yard. What caused it? A man is suffering from boils on his skin, low blood pressure, and convulsions. What caused his symptoms? The pebbles in the stream are round. What caused their roundness?

Even when we don't know the cause of something, we always assume there is one. We assume, for instance, that the giant footprints that people find in the snow in the Cascades in Oregon were caused by something. Perhaps, we think, they were bear prints that have been enlarged by being melted in the sun. Or we think that they were made by pranksters. Or even that they were made by a huge human-like animal that, for lack of a better word, we call "Bigfoot." Whatever the reason for the prints, we assume there was a reason.

For our purposes, not every cause of something or effect of something is worth writing about. Only those causes and effects that are open-ended in some way are worth it. A woman attends a religious revival in California and her crippled legs are healed during the service. Now there's a cause you can sink your teeth into. Because of conflicting opinions about religious healings, you can actually discuss the cause-and-effect relationship instead of giving a pat, simple answer.

Quite obviously, you wouldn't want to write about what causes water hoses to burst on cold nights, or what caused the Black Death in Europe in the Middle Ages, or what caused all the darkened houses on Tuesday nights in 1952. (Uncle Miltie was on TV.) Effects with only one simple cause that everyone agrees on make effective medical research papers and interesting detective stories. But they make rather dreary cause-and-effect essays.

However, the one simple cause that few people agree on often makes a good cause-and-effect essay. There may indeed be a simple cause for the image on the Shroud of Turin, a simple cause for the bent spoons of Uri Geller, a simple reason for the Hindenburg disaster—but the causes for these events are controversial, which is to say that no single cause is accepted as definitive.

Effects that have a multiplicity of causes (or vice versa) also make good essays. What is the effect of banning prayer in the schools? Why did SAT scores decline for sixteen years? What caused the Watts riots? Why did France elect a socialist president in 1981? In each of these cases, the causes (or effects) are numerous and complex—and therefore interesting. (Naturally, for most writing assignments, the subjects you choose will not be as complex as these examples. Keep it simple.)

Beginning a Cause-and-Effect Essay

The simplest way to begin a cause-and-effect essay is to state, as clearly as possible, either the cause or the effect you are going to discuss. Make certain, however, that you qualify or limit your thesis. Don't, for instance, begin with "Total honesty in a society would have a number of disastrous effects." That obligates you to discuss all the effects of total honesty, an impossible job in a book, much less in a brief essay. However, if you begin with "Total honesty in a society would have a number of disastrous effects. I would like to discuss one of them," you will have no trouble satisfying your reader's expectations. If you want to be braver, you could begin with "Total honesty in a society would have a number of disastrous effects, but I would like to discuss the most significant one."

Another way of beginning a cause-and-effect essay is to run through the complex causes or effects of your subject to let readers know you're aware of all these factors, but then tell them you want to focus your attention on only two or three, or even one cause or effect (because of its significance, its interesting nature, its neglect, or what have you). Consider the following thesis statement: "Although most people agree that the invention of the telephone has saved lives, speeded business communication, brought people closer together, and helped to spread knowledge, most people have never considered a small but significant effect of Bell's invention: our loss of privacy."

Common Fallacies in Cause-and-Effect Thinking

Before you begin a cause-and-effect essay, you should be aware of a few of the more common mistakes in examining cause-and-effect relationships.

The fellow who says that it rained because he washed his car has committed what is known in logical circles as the *post hoc* fallacy. That is, he seems to believe that because A (washing his car) occurred before B (rain), then A must have caused B. Naturally, not many of us believe that washing cars causes rain. (It would be raining every day all over the world if that were the case.) But the same kind of *post hoc* reasoning does occur with some frequency in everyday thinking. The man who gets chilled in a draft and then comes down with a cold the next day sometimes blames his cold on the draft, even though he knows, in the back of his mind, that colds are not caused by drafts but by microbes.

The writer who blames the lack of discipline in schools on the banning of prayer in schools is committing the *reductive* fallacy. That is, he is looking for a single, simple cause when multiple causes are obviously at work. If the writer had said instead that the ban on school prayer is one of the possible causes of the discipline problem, he would have been on much firmer ground. He would also be more likely to persuade more people.

Likewise, the person who blames the decline in SAT scores on TV watching is oversimplifying the cause. He might have said, "the major cause" or "one of the causes" or "a significant cause." Or in a book-length work, he could have discussed all the possible causes, such as lowered expectations, poor teaching methods, too many electives in high schools, and the look-say method of reading. Naturally, you should keep the maxim of Occam's Razor in mind: Cut away to the significant; don't multiply matters unnecessarily to explain the reason for something.

Suggestions: The Cause-and-Effect Essay

1. *Don't exaggerate the effects of something.* The invention of the hair-dryer no doubt had some small effects. It didn't change the world. A U.S. Senator recently attributed drug abuse, teenage pregnancies, assaults on teachers, and falling test scores to the banning of prayer in the schools. That is an exaggeration.

2. *Choose a manageable thesis.* Avoid one that is too broad ("What caused the violence in the 1960s?") or too narrow and straightforward ("What caused the San Andreas Fault?"). If possible, choose an open-ended thesis, one that has no definitive cause or effect.

3. *Don't merely state that something is a cause or an effect.* Unsupported assertions are not convincing, so offer some support to make them

plausible. It is through the offering of evidence that you convert your generalizations or assertions into *demonstrations*—so reason with your reader, present specific details, use examples, make comparisons: follow through.

MODEL CAUSE-AND-EFFECT PARAGRAPH

Such a Climate!

They [the Pilgrims] fell upon an ungenial climate, where there were nine months of winter and three months of cold weather, and that called out the best energies of the men, and of the women too, to get a mere subsistence out of the soil, with such a climate. In their efforts to do that they cultivated industry and frugality at the same time—which is the real foundation of [their] greatness. . . .

Ulysses S. Grant, 1880

ANALYSIS

Grant presents a remarkably clear cause-and-effect relationship in just two sentences, combining specifics with abstractions—and even a little humor. Naturally, in a short paragraph a writer can do little more than be casually suggestive about causes and effects; he needs far more room to argue convincingly that a certain cause has had a certain effect, particularly when he is claiming the kind of complicated and tenuous relationship that Grant is claiming.

Just to get things straight in your mind before you try a cause-and-effect paragraph, write down in your own words the cause and the effect in Grant's paragraph.

ASSIGNMENT

Write a paragraph of your own, about twice the length of Grant's, in which you *suggest* the effect of frugality or industry on someone you know. This effect might be a positive one, a negative one, or a mixture of the two.

My Wood

E. M. Forster

*Originally published in 1926, "My Wood" shows Forster's skill at turning dry
and abstract political issues—in this case the controversy about whether private property is corrupting—into small personal matters that he can lay his
hands on.*

1   A few years ago I wrote a book which dealt in part with the difficulties
of the English in India. Feeling that they would have had no difficulties in India themselves, the Americans read the book freely. The more
they read it the better it made them feel, and a cheque to the author
was the result. I bought a wood with the cheque. It is not a large
wood—it contains scarcely any trees, and it is intersected, blast it, by
a public footpath. Still, it is the first property that I have owned, so it
is right that other people should participate in my shame, and should
ask themselves, in accents that will vary in horror, this very important
question: What is the effect of property upon the character? Don't let's
touch economics; the effect of private ownership upon the community
as a whole is another question—a more important question, perhaps,
but another one. Let's keep to psychology. If you own things, what's
their effect on you? What's the effect on me of my wood?

2   In the first place, it makes me feel heavy. Property does have this
effect. Property produces men of weight, and it was a man of weight
who failed to get into the Kingdom of Heaven. He was not wicked,
that unfortunate millionaire in the parable, he was only stout; he stuck
out in front, not to mention behind, and as he wedged himself this
way and that in the crystalline entrance and bruised his well-fed
flanks, he saw beneath him a comparatively slim camel passing
through the eye of a needle and being woven into the robe of God.
The Gospels all through couple stoutness and slowness. They point
out what is perfectly obvious, yet seldom realized: that if you have a
lot of things you cannot move about a lot, that furniture requires dust-
ing, dusters require servants, servants require insurance stamps, and

the whole tangle of them makes you think twice before you accept an invitation to dinner or go for a bathe in the Jordan. Sometimes the Gospels proceed further and say with Tolstoy that property is sinful; they approach the difficult ground of asceticism here, where I cannot follow them. But as to the immediate effects of property on people, they just show straightforward logic. It produces men of weight. Men of weight cannot, by definition, move like the lightning from the East unto the West, and the ascent of a fourteen-stone bishop into a pulpit is thus the exact antithesis of the coming of the Son of Man. My wood makes me feel heavy.

In the second place, it makes me feel it ought to be larger.   3

The other day I heard a twig snap in it. I was annoyed at first, for I   4
thought that someone was blackberrying, and depreciating the value of the undergrowth. On coming nearer, I saw it was not a man who had trodden on the twig and snapped it, but a bird, and I felt pleased. My bird. The bird was not equally pleased. Ignoring the relation between us, it took fright as soon as it saw the shape of my face, and flew straight over the boundary hedge into a field, the property of Mrs. Henessy, where it sat down with a loud squawk. It had become Mrs. Henessy's bird. Something seemed grossly amiss here, something that would not have occurred had the wood been larger. I could not afford to buy Mrs. Henessy out, I dared not murder her, and limitations of this sort beset me on every side. Ahab did not want that vineyard—he only needed it to round off his property, preparatory to plotting a new curve—and all the land around my wood has become necessary to me in order to round off the wood. A boundary protects. But—poor little thing—the boundary ought in its turn to be protected. Noises on the edge of it. Children throw stones. A little more, and then a little more, until we reach the sea. Happy Canute! Happier Alexander! And after all, why should even the world be the limit of possession? A rocket containing a Union Jack, will, it is hoped, be shortly fired at the moon. Mars. Sirius. Beyond which . . . But these immensities ended by saddening me. I could not suppose that my wood was the destined nucleus of universal dominion—it is so very small and contains no mineral wealth beyond the blackberries. Nor was I comforted when Mrs. Henessy's bird took alarm for the second time and flew clean away from us all, under the belief that it belonged to itself.

In the third place, property makes its owner feel that he ought to   5
do something to it. Yet he isn't sure what. A restlessness comes over him, a vague sense that he has a personality to express—the same sense which, without any vagueness, leads the artist to an act of creation. Sometimes I think I will cut down such trees as remain in the wood, at other times I want to fill up the gaps between them with new

trees. Both impulses are pretentious and empty. They are not honest movements towards money-making or beauty. They spring from a foolish desire to express myself and from an inability to enjoy what I have got. Creation, property, enjoyment form a sinister trinity in the human mind. Creation and enjoyment are both very very good, yet they are often unattainable without a material basis, and at such moments property pushes itself in as a substitute,: saying, "Accept me instead—I'm good enough for all three." It is not enough. It is, as Shakespeare said of lust, "The expense of spirit in a waste of shame": it is "Before, a joy proposed; behind, a dream." Yet we don't know how to shun it. It is forced on us by our economic system as the alternative to starvation. It is also forced on us by an internal defect in the soul, by the feeling that in property may lie the germs of self-development and of exquisite or heroic deeds. Our life on earth is, and ought to be, material and carnal. But we have not yet learned to manage our materialism and carnality properly; they are still entangled with the desire for ownership, where (in the words of Dante) "Possession is one with loss."

6   And this brings us to our fourth and final point: the blackberries.

7   Blackberries are not plentiful in this meagre grove, but they are easily seen from the public footpath which traverses it, and all too easily gathered. Foxgloves, too—people will pull up the foxgloves, and ladies of an educational tendency even grub for toadstools to show them on the Monday in class. Other ladies, less educated, roll down the bracken in the arms of their gentlemen friends. There is paper, there are tins. Pray, does my wood belong to me or doesn't it? And, if it does, should I not own it best by allowing no one else to walk there? There is a wood near Lyme Regis, also cursed by a public footpath, where the owner has not hesitated on this point. He has built high stone walls each side of the path, and has spanned it by bridges, so that the public circulate like termites while he gorges on the blackberries unseen. He really does own his wood, this able chap. Dives in Hell did pretty well, but the gulf dividing him from Lazarus could be traversed by vision, and nothing traverses it here. And perhaps I shall come to this in time. I shall wall in and fence out until I really taste the sweets of property. Enormously stout, endlessly avaricious, pseudo-creative, intensely selfish, I shall weave upon my forehead the quadruple crown of possession until those nasty Bolshies come and take it off again and thrust me aside into the outer darkness.

Questions About Meaning

1. What is the question raised about one's property in the first paragraph?

2. What contrast in values does Forster set up in paragraph 2 by his reference to "the Kingdom of Heaven"?
3. What does Forster mean by saying the woodlot he owns makes him "feel heavy"?
4. In the fourth paragraph, how does Forster manage to make fun of the idea that one can "own" the natural world?
5. *How* can "possession [be] one with loss," that is, the *same* as "loss"?

Matters of Technique

1. The second and fourth topic sentences are set off from their paragraphs (3 and 6), while the first and third are attached to theirs (paragraphs 2 and 5). Why?
2. Point out the repetitive structures used in these topic sentences.
3. At a certain point in the last paragraph, Forster's fourth point ends and the conclusion begins. Where is that point? Would it have been more effective to put the conclusion in a separate paragraph?
4. Each paragraph in the body of the essay is developed through examples and allusions to literary and historical figures. Explain the following references: (1) the man of weight who failed to get into Heaven; (2) the slim camel who got through the eye of the needle; (3) "a bathe in the Jordan"; (4) Tolstoy; (5) "a fourteen-stone bishop" and "the coming of the Son of Man"; (6) "lightning from the East unto the West"; (7) Dives and Lazarus.

Vocabulary

1. parable (2)
2. asceticism (2)
3. ascent (2)
4. stone ("*fourteen-stone bishop*"; 2)
5. antithesis (2)
6. pretentious (5)
7. carnality (5)
8. traverses (7)
9. Bolshies (*see* "*Bolshevik*"; 7)

Suggestions for Writing

1. Write an essay on how a possession changed you either for the worse or for the better. Base the organization of your essay on Forster's.
2. Forster writes that "creation and enjoyment . . . are often unattainable without a material basis. . . ." Discuss the good effects of property ownership on individuals and on society as a whole.

3. Explain in detail what Forster means by suggesting that property "is forced on us by our economic system as the alternative to starvation."

Cross-Reference

What does the irony in Forster's essay have in common with that in Twain's "The War Prayer"?

The War Prayer

Mark Twain

Mark Twain has two reputations: To most people he is the untroubled comic writer of novels like Huckleberry Finn *and* Tom Sawyer; *to others he is one of America's darkest satirists in works like* What Is Man? *(1906) and* The Mysterious Stranger *(1916). Our selection is from that dark side of Twain.*

It was a time of great and exalting excitement. The country was up in arms, the war was on, in every breast burned the holy fire of patriotism; the drums were beating, the bands playing, the toy pistols popping, the bunched firecrackers hissing and spluttering; on every hand and far down the receding and fading spread of roofs and balconies a fluttering wilderness of flags flashed in the sun; daily the young volunteers marched down the wide avenue gay and fine in their new uniforms, the proud fathers and mothers and sisters and sweethearts cheering them with voices choked with happy emotion as they swung by; nightly the packed mass meetings listened, panting, to patriot oratory which stirred the deepest deeps of their hearts, and which they interrupted at briefest intervals with cyclones of applause, the tears running down their cheeks the while; in the churches the pastors preached devotion to flag and country, and invoked the God of Battles, beseeching His aid in our good cause in outpouring of fervid eloquence which moved every listener. It was indeed a glad and gracious time, and the half dozen rash spirits that ventured to disapprove of the war and cast a doubt upon its righteousness straightway got such a stern and angry warning that for their personal safety's sake they quickly shrank out of sight and offended no more in that way. 1

Sunday morning came—next day the battalions would leave for the front; the church was filled; the volunteers were there, their young faces alight with martial dreams—visions of the stern advance, the gathering momentum, the rushing charge, the flashing sabers, the flight of the foe, the tumult, the enveloping smoke, the fierce pursuit, the surrender!—then home from the war, bronzed heroes, welcomed, 2 adored, submerged in golden seas of glory! With the volunteers sat their dear ones, proud, happy, and envied by the neighbors and friends who had no sons and brothers to send forth to the field of honor, there to win for the flag, or, failing, die the noblest of noble deaths. The service proceeded; a war chapter from the Old Testament was read; the first prayer was said; it was followed by an organ burst that shook the building, and with one impulse the house rose, with glowing eyes and beating hearts, and poured out that tremendous invocation—

"God the all-terrible! Thou who ordainest, Thunder thy clarion and lightning thy sword!"

Then came the "long" prayer. None could remember the like of it for passionate pleading and moving and beautiful language. The burden of its supplication was, that an ever-merciful and benignant Father of us all would watch over our noble young soldiers, and aid, comfort, and encourage them in their patriotic work; bless them, shield them in the day of battle and the hour of peril, bear them in His mighty hand, make them strong and confident, invincible in the bloody onset; help them to crush the foe, grant to them and to their flag and country imperishable honor and glory—

3   An aged stranger entered and moved with slow and noiseless step up the main aisle, his eyes fixed upon the minister, his long body clothed in a robe that reached to his feet, his head bare, his white hair descending in a frothy cataract to his shoulders, his seamy face unnaturally pale, pale even to ghastliness. With all eyes following him and wondering, he made his silent way; without pausing, he ascended to the preacher's side and stood there, waiting. With shut lids the preacher, unconscious of his presence, continued his moving prayer, and at last finished it with the words, uttered in fervent appeal, "Bless our arms, grant us the victory, O Lord our God, Father and Protector of our land and flag!"

4   The stranger touched his arm, motioned him to step aside—which the startled minister did—and took his place. During some moments he surveyed the spellbound audience with solemn eyes, in which burned an uncanny light; then in a deep voice he said:

5   "I come from the Throne—bearing a message from Almighty God!" The words smote the house with a shock; if the stranger perceived it he gave no attention. "He has heard the prayer of His servant your shepherd, and will grant it if such shall be your desire after I, His messenger, shall have explained to you its import—that is to say, its full import. For it is like unto many of the prayers of men, in that it asks for more than he who utters it is aware of—except he pause and think.

"God's servant and yours has prayed his prayer. Has he paused and   6
taken thought? Is it one prayer? No, it is two—one uttered, the other
not. Both have reached the ear of Him Who heareth all supplications,
the spoken and the unspoken. Ponder this—keep it in mind. If you
would beseech a blessing upon yourself, beware! lest without intent
you invoke a curse upon a neighbor at the same time. If you pray for
the blessing of rain upon your crop which needs it, by that act you are
possibly praying for a curse upon some neighbor's crop which may
not need rain and can be injured by it.

"You have heard your servant's prayer—the uttered part of it. I am   7
commissioned of God to put into words the other part of it—that part
which the pastor—and also you in your hearts—fervently prayed
silently. And ignorantly and unthinkingly? God grant that it was so!
You heard these words: 'Grant us the victory, O Lord our God!' That
is sufficient. The *whole* of the uttered prayer is compact into those
pregnant words Elaborations were not necessary. When you have
prayed for victory you have prayed for many unmentioned results
which follow victory—*must* follow it, cannot help but follow it. Upon
the listening spirit of God the Father fell also the unspoken part of the
prayer. He commandeth me to put it into words. Listen!

"O Lord our Father, our young patriots, idols of our hearts, go forth   8
to battle—be Thou near them! With them—in spirit—we also go forth
from the sweet peace of our beloved firesides to smite the foe. O Lord
our God, help us to tear their soldiers to bloody shreds with our shells;
help us to cover their smiling fields with the pale forms of their patriot
dead; help us to drown the thunder of the guns with the shrieks of
their wounded, writhing in pain; help us to lay waste their humble
homes with a hurricane of fire; help us to wring the hearts of their
unoffending widows with unavailing grief; help us to turn them out
roofless with their little children to wander unfriended the wastes of
their desolated land in rags and hunger and thirst, sports of the sun
flames of summer and the icy winds of winter, broken in spirit, worn
with travail, imploring Thee for the refuge of the grave and denied
it—for our sakes who adore Thee, Lord, blast their hopes, blight their
lives, protract their bitter pilgrimage, make heavy their steps, water
their way with their tears, stain the white snow with the blood of their
wounded feet! We ask it, in the spirit of love, of Him Who is the
Source of Love, and Who is the ever-faithful refuge and friend of all
that are sore beset and seek His aid with humble and contrite hearts.
Amen."

(*After a pause.*) "Ye have prayed it; if ye still desire it, speak! The   9
messenger of the Most High waits."

It was believed afterward that the man was a lunatic, because there   10
was no sense in what he said.

Questions About Meaning

1. In the first paragraph, Twain describes the enthusiasm with which a country's citizens may welcome a war. How does he suggest that this enthusiasm may be misplaced and naive?
2. What is the thesis of Twain's satire?
3. What do the young soldiers Twain describes imagine war will be like?
4. What is the irony involved in praying to "the ever-merciful ... Father of us all" for help in achieving victory in war?
5. Is there any hint anywhere in the essay that there might be such a thing as a righteous war?
6. What is Twain's point in the last sentence?

Matters of Technique

1. Where is Twain's thesis stated? How is it presented?
2. What difference do you notice about the paragraphing of Twain's piece—written in the 19th century—and a modern essay?
3. How effective do you find the first paragraph? What is its function?
4. How effective do you find Twain's device for presenting his view of war? Can you think of another method of presenting the same view?

Vocabulary

1. oratory (1)
2. fervid (1)
3. martial (2)
4. invocation (2)
5. clarion (2)
6. benignant (2)
7. import (*noun*; 5)
8. supplications (6)
9. ponder (6)
10. beseech (6)

Suggestions for Writing

1. Write an essay on this idea: One person's joy is often another person's pain.
2. Write a short satiric piece that depends for its effectiveness on a messenger from Heaven coming down to announce God's point of view.
3. Discuss what you believe would be a just cause for war.

Cross-Reference

Irony is saying one thing and meaning another. Twain makes heavy use of it. What other authors in this book use it?

The Perfect Crime

Tom Wolfe

Tom Wolfe's books include a satiric look at some of the more bizarre facets of popular culture in The Kandy-Kolored Tangerine-Flake Streamline Baby *(1965), a satiric dissection of modern art in* The Painted Word *(1975), and an analysis of U.S. astronauts in* The Right Stuff *(1979). Wolfe's analysis of the hostage taker's motives in the following essay sounds reasonable enough. Unfortunately, just because a problem can be explained doesn't mean it can be solved. As a matter of fact, hostage taking seems to be one of those insoluble problems that the 20th century keeps coming up with.*

1   Remember the old idea of the Perfect Crime? The wife kills her husband by hitting him over the head with a frozen leg of lamb. Then she puts the leg of lamb in the stove and sets the temperature at 450 degrees. When the detective comes by to investigate the murder, she takes the murder weapon out of the oven and garnishes it with parsley and mint sauce and puts it on a Spode platter and serves it to the detective. The detective himself devours and digests the evidence! And eliminates it! The wife—the widow—has only to tote up in her mind the fortune that will be coming her way as soon as her husband's will is probated. How cool! How clever! She scores big! leaves not a trace! is never caught!—the Perfect Crime.

2   The criminal mind has come a long way since then. Not up, not down; just a long way. Consider the Perfect Crime of the 1970's:

3   On July 17, 1972, a twenty-two-year-old hair stylist shampooed his own hair and hot-combed it down over his forehead and ears into a John Denver bob, put on a groovy shirt striped with an intricate leaf-repeat pattern and a pair of bell-bottoms with fine chalk-and-pin stripes picking up the tones of the shirt, and walked into a suburban bank near Richmond, Virginia, with a 12-gauge shotgun. He fired two blasts into a wooden door to show he meant business. He took nine women and one man as hostages and herded them into a back room. He spent about five minutes terrifying them and about four hours trying to charm them with jokes and the story of his life. He offered them steak dinners.

4   "The bank's paying for it!" he said, casting himself in the role of Tyrone Power as Jesse James.

5   He was disappointed when they asked for pizzas and beer instead, but he got these Low Rent items for them anyway by shouting orders to the bank officials and policemen waiting outside. He also ordered $500,000 in cash and a 1972 white Lincoln Continental to drive away in. He ordered full television and radio coverage of all events, especially the loading of the money into the trunk of the Lincoln. Said conditions having been met, he put down the shotgun, said goodbye to the hostages, and emerged from the bank smiling and waving to the TV cameras and talking a mile a minute into the microphones, right up until the moment when federal officers grabbed him. He put up no struggle at all. They ushered him into the back seat of the white Lincoln Continental, the very one with the half million in the trunk, and drove him off to jail. He was still smiling and waving as the car pulled off.

6   What on earth, one may ask, could be "perfect" about any such zany, feckless, giddy, goofy attempt at extortion? Nevertheless, it was a casebook example of the Perfect Crime of the 1970's, which is: taking hostages.

7   Taking hostages is the common core of many different crimes peculiar to the late 1960's and the 1970's: the more than two hundred airplane hijackings since November 1967; most of the prison riots of the same period, such as the Attica uprising; much of the political terrorism, such as the kidnappings at the 1972 Olympics and in Uruguay; and many attempted bank robberies, such as the incident in Stockholm in which two convicts named Olsson and Olofsson kept four hostages in a bank vault for six days.

8   Most of the Hostage Takers have been people at the ends of their ropes in struggles against what they regard as the enormity of "the system." Moreover, they seem to think that if they can beat the system, they can also deal with more traditional frustrations, i.e., those involving class, love, and money. One of the most sensational of the airplane hijackings was pulled off by an Italian-born U.S. Marine named Raffaele Minichiello. He took his hostages from Los Angeles to Rome in a wild trip that involved many stops and several changes of crew. Minichiello had grown up in the United States but had never learned English properly and felt like a hopelessly awkward Italian country boy (class); felt too gauche to ask American girls out on dates (love); was decorated for bravery while fighting in Vietnam, only to discover that (by his count) he had been euchred out of $200 in the G.I. savings plan (money); drank six beers and broke into a PX, stole an even $200 worth of merchandise; passed out nearby; was cleared by a local civil judge who simply threw the case out; felt elated; rushed to his com-

manding officer to bring him the good news; was astounded to hear the C.O. start dictating to his secretary orders for a court-martial, felony level, which would ruin his service career (((((((((((((the unbeatable freaking system!)))))))))))))))).

So what does the modern Master Criminal do? He *takes hostages*. Ostensibly he takes hostages in order to achieve some goal at the end of the line, but in many cases even the internal logic is bananas. Minichiello said his plan was to hijack a plane to Italy, then hide in the countryside and live off the land like a guerrilla. Palestinian and Uruguayan terrorists take hostages ostensibly to call attention to their causes and gain sympathy. The effect, quite predictably, is the opposite, so far as sympathy is concerned, even among true believers. But so what? The master criminal does not really take hostages in order to accomplish such goals. He dreams up such goals in order to Take Hostages. The formula is turned around: the means justify the end.

With one stroke the Hostage Taker creates his own society, his own system: in the bank vault, in the Olympic quarters, in the airplane, in the prison courtyard. On his own small scale the Hostage Taker accomplishes the classic coup d'état as described by Machiavelli: the sudden, short-term use of terror, cold steel, and bloodletting, if necessary, in order to gain respect—then the long charm course . . . to turn respect into love, thereby making it easy to govern. On the face of it, it is astonishing how often hostages come away from their ordeal describing the Hostage Taker as "nice," "considerate," even "likeable," as in the case of both Minichiello and the groovy hair stylist. A female hostage named Kristin Enmark left the Stockholm bank vault on a stretcher waving to one of the Hostage Takers, Clark Olofsson, telling him, "We'll see each other again!" and informing one and all that he had been kind, hadn't harmed her in the slightest, hadn't been as big a threat as the police, in fact. A psychiatrist immediately explained that she was suffering from shell shock, like a line soldier who has been at the front too long, and was repressing her actual feelings as a "defense mechanism." Is the same to be said of the twenty-nine American passengers and airline crewmen who were held hostage by Palestinian terrorists in Jordan for almost a month and who, *after being freed*, sent a telegram to Israel's Prime Minister Golda Meir saying: "We wish to affirm that our guards treated us humanely and always did their utmost to protect us against harm and to meet our basic needs"—and urging her to give fresh consideration to the Arab cause in Palestine? Thirteen of the twenty-nine signers were Jews.

Far from being a "defense mechanism," such examples are a grand-scale display of a phenomenon well known to police detectives. One of the techniques of the "third degree" involves the Goon & the Nice Guy. The suspect is put into an interrogation room with two detectives, one of whom plays the role of the violent goon while the other plays the nice guy who seeks to protect him. In a remarkably short time, a few hours, in fact, the victim may form an emotional attachment to the Nice Guy, his "protector," and pour out his soul. In precisely the same manner, the Hostage Taker may soon have the hearts and minds of his subjects as well as their hides. The hostage responds like a dog. He has an urge not only to obey but to be obliging and ingratiating in the bargain. What a delightful and emboldening new world!—especially if one has been for so long as helpless as a Palestinian radical up against the complexities of Cold War politics or a Uruguayan radical up against the endless exfoliations of American power in South America. No possible "ransom" or "prisoner release" could compare with the ecstasy of this moment—when for a change I have these people whimpering like dogs at my feet!

12   All at once I am not the lowliest subject but the head of state. I demand to negotiate with chiefs of police, mayors, governors, and I get my wish. I even have support on the outside. Nelson Rockefeller was heavily criticized for not coming to Attica and negotiating directly with the Hostage Taker inmates. Many hijackers have demanded to talk to the President of the United States. One hijacked a plane to Dulles International Airport and demanded "a million dollars from Lyndon Johnson." At the very least I finally cut through the red tape. I put an end to the eternal runaround. I make the System spin to my number. At last the top people are listening to *me* . . . and answering . . . quite politely, too, and with quite a little choke in their miserable voices . . .

13   Above all: as long as I have my hostages, as long as the drama has not been played out, I have the ultimate certification that my new status is real and true—that in the most modern sense my class position is secure: *I am a celebrity!* My existence fills the very atmosphere of the city, the state, the nation. As long as Olsson and Olofsson had their hostages in the Stockholm bank vault, Sweden's national election campaign (one of the more crucial since World War II) came to a halt. Who had time for politics, what with O. & O.'s World on TV around the clock? Nor does my celebrity status end with the event itself. Not necessarily! Minichiello became a hero in Italy and served only a year and a half in jail. He appeared continually on television and in magazines. He was signed up for a book and the leading role in an Italian Western. More impressive, he rated the best tables at all the smart restaurants near the Via del Babuino. His troubles with the chicks were over. Marriage proposals were passed in under his door. Movie actresses thrilled to his courage and good looks in the daily pictorials. *Children want my autograph! Everybody loves me!*

14   At Attica we Hostage Takers custom-ordered our news coverage.

For example, we asked for, and got, Tom Wicker of *The New York Times* and he was obliging. He wrote about us as if we were all Prometheuses in noble deathlock with the forces of repression in a battle for the soul of man. As journalism it was pretty embarrassing stuff—but not half bad as a back rub for the boys in Cellblock D!

The groovy at the suburban bank also custom-ordered his news coverage, asking for certain local broadcasters by name. He was in a jolly mood from the moment he first heard live coverage of his escapade over a transistor radio. When the television crews arrived, he made the hostages stick their heads out the window to be filmed, then acted as if he had done them another service, of the magnitude of the beer & pizzas. When the police brought up the white Lincoln Continental, as he demanded, he broke into a grin and announced to his subjects: "You see what you can get with a gun!" The more intense the radio and television coverage became, the better the Hostage Taker's mood became. The police chief characterized it as the turning point— the pressure that finally flushed him out smiling and unarmed, beaming, waving to pals & gals everywhere, to fans, subjects, devotees from border to border and coast to coast . . . and now, the star of our show . . . a sunny day, a perfect crime.

Questions About Meaning

1. What motivation does Wolfe see for hostage taking? (See paragraph 8.)
2. Explain how Wolfe's essay is based on a cause-and-effect relationship.
3. What, according to Wolfe, is the hostage taker's ultimate satisfaction? (See paragraph 13.)

Matters of Technique

1. Why is another kind of "perfect crime" (the leg-of-lamb murder) introduced in the first paragraph?
2. How does Wolfe achieve emphasis in paragraph 6?
3. What in the world is the purpose of those strings of parentheses in paragraph 9?
4. How effective do you find Wolfe's alternation of the third person and the first person point of view? Point out a paragraph in which both viewpoints are used.

Vocabulary

1. Spode (1)
2. tote (1)
3. probated (1)
4. feckless (6)
5. extortion (6)
6. gauche (8)
7. euchred (8)
8. ostensibly (9)
9. coup d'état (10)
10. ingratiating (11)
11. exfoliations (11)
12. certification (13)

Suggestions for Writing

1. Write your own analysis of the causes of some form of antisocial behavior. Imitate Wolfe's style.
2. Violent crime by juveniles is increasing. Discuss your view of the causes of this trend. Or discuss your view of the probable effects.

Back to Reticence!

Lance Morrow

Morrow's argument for a return to old-fashioned virtues like good manners and decorum appeared originally as a "Time Essay" in 1980.

Cultivated to a high degree by art and science, we are civilized to the point where we are overburdened with all sorts of social propriety and decency.

—*Immanuel Kant, 1784*

Jimmy Connors does not labor under Kant's burden. Sometimes when the tennis gets intense, Connors grabs his crotch and shakes it for the crowd. He pelts the linesmen and judges with rotten language. He shoots his finger. The umpire usually responds with the flustered and ineffectual dismay of a curate who has discovered the servants copulating in his study. 1

This sort of court behavior, also indulged in by John McEnroe and Ilie Nastase, is what kindergarten teachers call "age inappropriate." It is punk tennis, the transformation of a formerly pristine game into the moral equivalent of roller derby. The spectacle is symptomatic of something that has befallen the American's idea of how one ought to behave. What would once have been intolerable and impermissible public conduct has now become commonplace. If it is not exactly accepted, then at least it is abjectly and wearily endured. 2

Social habit in the U.S. has taken decisive turns toward the awful. Since the end of World War II, Americans have been steadily relinquishing their inhibitions about the social consequences of their actions. They have lost a crucial sense of community, even while highways, jets, satellite TV signals and leisure travel have brought them physically closer together. The social environment has grown polluted along with the natural; a headlong greed and self-absorption have sponsored both contaminations. Somehow, Americans have also misplaced the moral confidence with which to condemn sleaziness and stupidity. It is as if something in the American judgment snapped, and has remained so long unrepaired that no one notices any more. 3

4   The daily grind of the offensive is both tiring and obscurely humiliating. It is impossible to watch the nightly news on network television without being treated to a stream of 30-second treatises on hemorrhoids, tampons, feminine deodorant sprays and constipation. "I want to talk to you about diarrhea," says the earnest pitchman. T shirts, sweatshirts and bumper stickers proclaim their aggressive little editorials. Some are mildly funny (a woman's T shirt, for example, that says SO MANY MEN, SO LITTLE TIME). But often they are crude with a faintly alarming determination to affront, even sometimes to menace. They are filled with belligerent scatology. Something or other always SUCKS.

5   Constitutionally protected grossness—edible underwear, the vibrators in the drugstore window, massage parlors, sex merchandised in its pervasive richness—has spread the pornographic spirit widely. The Twelfth Night Masque, the oldest private subscription ball in Chicago and hitherto a bastion of Midwestern decorum, has suffered a recent rash of crudity. Last year some guests showed up at the ball dressed as hemorrhoids when President Carter was so afflicted; two years before, when the masque theme was "The Father of Our Country," a number of Lake Shore socialites appeared as penises or sperm. No one proposes calling out a SWAT team to deal with this sort of whoopee-cushion wit. It is not sullenly antisocial, like the blaring radios the size of steamer trunks that adolescents haul onto public buses to cook up a small pot of community rage, or the occasional pistols that got waved in gas lines.

6   Much of today's offensiveness began in the guise of a refreshing virtue: honesty. The doctrine of "letting it all hang out" got propagated in the headlong idealism of the late '60s. The result is a legacy of insufferable and interminable candor. The idealism has vanished into the mainstream of the culture or into thin air. We are left with the residue of bad habits, ugly noises and moral slackness.

7   As in some burlesque science fiction, the nation seems to have been injected with a truth serum designed to make people bore one another to death; it has given them a compulsion to confide embarrassing intimacies, has led them on to endless emotional ostentations, as if, as Saul Bellow once wrote, "to keep the wolf of insignificance from the door." A man sits down at a New Jersey dinner party, beside a woman he met half an hour before, and hears in elaborately explicit detail from soup through coffee, how the woman and her husband managed to conquer their sexual incompatibility with the help of a sex therapist. A magazine writer not long ago met the new young husband of Novelist Erica Jong at a party and realized with a disagreeable little jolt that she knew from Jong's novel *How to Save Your Own Life* just how large the husband's penis was.

8   The book racks are filled with volumes of confession and revenge.

People rush to destroy their own privacy, possibly judging that loneliness is worse. In the past ten or twelve years, everything has tumbled out of the closet in a heap. Some homosexuals parade themselves like walking billboards, the placement of the keys and handkerchiefs in their back pockets acting as a semaphore to signal the specific secrets of their sexual tastes.

The depressing quality of much American public behavior—from Connors to T shirts—is its edgy meanness. Bad enough that it is calculatedly cheap. Worse is the stolid nastiness of it, the rock in the snowball, the compulsion to affront. Even relentless candor—wounding friends or family by telling them their defects in the name of honesty—is a symptom not only of stupidity but also of unkindness and buried anger. 9

There are doubtless profound cultural reasons for such anger: the aggressive self-regard of the era now perhaps passing, the centrifugal individualism, the loss of authority, the sense of alienation from "the System," a precipitous disenchantment that tended to discredit all rules, including those of social behavior. It is possible that the price of a certain amount of personal liberty is excess and mess, all the frictions and bad smells generated by social change and people exercising their constitutional rights. Jefferson had an idea that democracy should be genteel, but it did not work out that way. And today, there is no point in growing as mistily sentimental as a Soviet realist hack about the pleasures of right thinking and conformity. 10

Still, it is possible that the '80s are going to demand some virtues unknown in the '60s and '70s—self-control, self-discipline, stoicism, decorum, even inhibition and a little puritanism. It may be time for a touch of reticence. Coercion cannot produce such attitudes, but the mood of the time may. Americans may find themselves agreeing in some paraphrase of Elihu Root when he walked through a squalid Siberian village as Woodrow Wilson's emissary in the first Soviet revolutionary dawn. "I'm a firm believer in democracy," he said, as he skeptically eyed his surroundings. "But I do not like filth." 11

Questions About Meaning

1. What does Morrow think has led to what he calls "today's offensiveness"?
2. What examples does Morrow use to show what he means by what he calls "the depressing quality of much American public behavior"?
3. Morrow's reference to the "aggressive little editorials" displayed

on T-shirts, sweatshirts, and bumper stickers suggests that this practice may be a form of aggression. Can you think of other examples of such "editorials" that illustrate his point?

Matters of Technique

1. Prefacing an essay with a quote is often an effective way to begin. But it also has drawbacks. Can you think of any? Did you read the quotation before you read the essay?
2. In what two paragraphs does Morrow deal with the causes of the boorish behavior he describes?
3. Study the author's copious examples of offensive behavior. Can you think of others which would be equally effective in illustrating his point?
4. Morrow isn't very reticent himself. Why not?

Vocabulary

1. pristine (2)
2. abjectly (2)
3. inhibitions (3)
4. scatology (4)
5. bastion (5)
6. decorum (5)
7. propagated (6)
8. candor (6)
9. ostentations (7)
10. stolid (9)
11. reticence (11)

Suggestions for Writing

1. If you find refreshing what Morrow finds offensive, write an essay illustrating this point of view. Use many of the same examples he does.
2. Write a paper that illustrates the quotation with which Morrow prefaces his essay.
3. Discuss your view of the probable effects of total honesty in social and personal relations. Adopt a personal viewpoint if it helps you organize your paper more effectively.
4. Discuss the probable causes of the development of the social conventions and courtesies known as "good manners."

CHAPTER TEN

Argumentation: Appeals to Reason

In *Huckleberry Finn* the "King" and the "Duke" are attempting to bilk some orphans out of money when the town doctor begins to get suspicious.When the Duke tells the King of the doctor's suspicions, the King replies, "Cuss the doctor! What do we k'yer for *him*? Hain't we got all the fools in town on our side? And ain't that a big enough majority in any town?"

It may be that the fools in any town are a majority, but even fools like to think of themselves as reasonable chaps, eager to distinguish the sensible from the senseless. (We wouldn't hold our opinions unless they were true, would we?)

The fact that fools and nonfools alike pride themselves on their reason is something that a writer can count on, perhaps even capitalize on. To seek truth through reason in an argumentative essay is therefore not only a virtuous act, but it is also a sound rhetorical strategy. We can go about this in two basic ways: through inductive logic and through deductive logic. Let's begin with the former.

Inductive Reasoning

Induction is the process of arriving at a conclusion by observing a number of particulars. As you know, political pollsters use inductive reasoning as the basis for their predictions. Although a pollster may sample only a part of the population, from that sample he infers that the votes or opinions of the remainder of the population will match the sample. On a simpler level, the woman who finds that five apples from a barrel are pithy will probably conclude, through inductive logic, that the rest of the apples are.

Naturally, if the sample is too small or not representative, the conclusion might be wrong. If the woman who picked the five apples had picked only one, she might have made an incorrect conclusion and walked away from a barrel of crisp Washington apples. She also could have made an inductive error by testing apples taken from only the top row; these top-row apples might not have been representative of the apples from the middle and the bottom.

But enough of apples. Faulty inductive thinking can have more serious consequences. In 1936 pollsters who worked for *The Literary Digest* predicted that Alf Landon would defeat Franklin D. Roosevelt. Unfortunately, the people they polled were chosen from telephone books and car registrations and thus tended to be of a higher social and economic class than the general population. In effect, the pollsters picked only apples from the top row. When Roosevelt was elected in a landslide, the magazine's reputation was severely damaged and it soon folded.

Take the lesson of *The Literary Digest* to heart. In your essays, don't jump too quickly to conclusions based on small or unrepresentative samples. If you have had two friends attacked while they were walking home from night classes, don't immediately conclude that the campus is becoming increasingly dangerous after dark. Ask around, visit the campus police and ask them questions, compare this year's statistics with last year's. It may be that your two friends were the only people attacked all year, and that the campus is actually safer than it was last year. Watch what apples you pick.

Deductive Reasoning

Deductive reasoning is the other side of the coin. It moves not from particular instances but from a general truth (usually based on inductive principles, of course) to a conclusion. In its formal form, it is called a syllogism and consists of two premises and a conclusion based on those premises:

premise: All mammals breathe oxygen.
premise: The porpoise is a mammal.
conclusion: The porpoise breathes oxygen.

A syllogism, then, is just a way of stripping an argument down to its essentials, and then arranging those essentials in a sequence to see if they make sense. Because the syllogism makes explicit what otherwise might be dark and convoluted, it reveals hidden assumptions and chains of reasoning. Naturally, it can be used to analyze the essential argument in an essay—yours or someone else's.

The appeal of deductive reasoning is that if you follow the rules of the syllogism, your conclusion will be valid. Unfortunately, a conclusion may be valid and still not be true. Early astronomers were fond of this deductive sequence:

The planets move in perfect circles.
The earth is a planet.
Therefore, the earth moves in a perfect circle.

The problem here is with the first premise, an assumption that doesn't happen to be true. (Planets move in ellipses.)

Let's go back now and analyze Twain's King's logic by putting his argument in the form of a syllogism:

In every town, most people are fools.
We have all the fools in this town on our side.
Therefore, we have a majority in this town on our side.

The King's deductive sequence is perfect, and his conclusion is therefore valid. However, what the syllogism reveals is that a critical term in his first premise is imprecise: What exactly is a "fool"? Furthermore, even if the term could be defined precisely, the King's statement that most people are fools is revealed for what it is: an assumption, which may or may not be true. As a matter of fact, the Duke and the King are finally run out of town. They should have been more careful with their logic.

Naturally, we never see a syllogism in our everyday reading. However, all arguments can be broken down into some form of a syllogism. To illustrate, let's take apart the reasoning in Bertrand Russell's essay, "Do We Survive Death?" (reprinted in this chapter) and put it in syllogistic form:

premise: The "self," which is the heredity and the acquired parts of the personality, is bound up with bodily structures.
premise: Bodily structures disintegrate after death.
conclusion: Therefore, the "self" doesn't survive death.

The truth of Russell's syllogism, of course, rests on the truth of his first premise—that there is no self without heredity and acquired characteristics, a premise that most major religions reject.

Ways of Developing an Appeal to the Reader's Reason

1. *Develop a tolerant tone.* Truth, after all, comes in many forms, is often influenced by the vantage point of the observer, and usually reflects probability instead of certainty. If you're cocksure and intolerant, you'll get the expected kneejerk agreement from those who are already on your side, but you'll also antagonize those who might have been persuaded if you had adopted a more tolerant tone. In fact, go ahead and admit—if you can stand it—that the other side of the argument is not *pure* nonsense. That admission won't kill you. Indeed, it might even leave your reader with the impression that you're a person who actually listens to all sides of an argument before making up your mind.

2. *Develop a reasoned tone.* Leave your reader with the impression that you're a searcher after truth instead of someone who is merely loading his argument. Let's assume that you need to use the statistics on deaths caused by the Hiroshima atomic bomb blast for an argument you're making, and let's further assume that the higher this death total is, the better your argument will sound. But then you find that one book gives the figure of 79,000 deaths, another says 80,000 to 200,000, and yet another says 240,000. Since the authorities disagree, and your argument is best served by the largest figure, it would be tempting to use the largest figure. But what if you said instead, "There is no way of telling exactly how many died at Hiroshima, but estimates range from 79,000 to 240,000." That kind of fair-minded comment is not only honest, but it leaves your reader with the impression that what you're after is the truth, not just a strong argument. It is critically important that your reader believe that you're fair and honest.

3. *Don't overstate your case.* This means that you shouldn't claim too much from your evidence. Be especially careful of words like "proves," "obviously," and "certainly." Few things in this world are proven, obvious, or certain. Instead, begin your sentences with modest qualifying phrases:

> These examples *suggest* that . . .
> The *most likely* result will be . . .
> This *probably* means that . . .

Or identify your statements, especially critical ones, as your opinions:

> There is little doubt *in my mind* that . . .
> I have therefore *come to believe* that . . .

4. *Get things right.* Nothing will destroy a reader's confidence in your argument sooner than an error in fact. Once the reader sees that you've been careless with a statistic or a quotation, he begins to lose trust in you, and that loss of trust undermines his faith in your argument.

MODEL PARAGRAPH BASED ON AN APPEAL TO REASON

Which Is the Greater Miracle?

... no testimony [by witnesses] is sufficient to establish a miracle unless the testimony be of such a kind that its falsehood would be more miraculous than the fact which it endeavors to establish.... When anyone tells me that he saw a dead man restored to life, I immediately consider with myself whether it be more probable that this person should either deceive or be deceived, or that the fact which he relates should really have happened. I weigh the one miracle against the other, and according to the superiority which I discover, I pronounce my decision, and always reject the greater miracle. If the falsehood of his testimony would be more miraculous than the event which he relates, then, and not till then, can he pretend to command my belief or opinion.

David Hume, 1748

ANALYSIS

For the moment, don't worry too much about trying to decipher the argument in Hume's paragraph. Just listen to its reasoned tone. That's what we're looking for here, the *sound* of an appeal being made to the reader's reason.

No one in the eighteenth century, the Age of Reason, tried harder to achieve a reasoned tone than Hume. As you can see, his prose is almost bare of colored words and rhetorical flourishes. He tries to lead the reader, reasoned step by reasoned step, to an inevitable conclusion.

Now let's take a look at meaning. Hume's philosophical writings are not easy to follow, but stripping the paragraph down to the form of a syllogism will help clarify the argument:

premise: A miracle can only be proved through witnesses if it is more likely that the miracle happened than it is that the person who related the miracle is inaccurate.

premise: It is always more likely that the person who related the miracle is inaccurate than it is that the miracle happened.

conclusion: Therefore, testimony is insufficient to prove the truth of a miracle.

As you can see, cutting away to the bones of an argument reveals the argument's strengths and weaknesses, which makes syllogisms particularly useful.

ASSIGNMENT

In a single paragraph, construct a coolly reasoned argument in which you make a case the opposite of Hume's. That is, argue that in certain cases witnesses can serve as reasonable proof of the occurrence of a miracle. After you have written your paragraph, put your argument in the form of a syllogism to make clear its essential points.

Do We Survive Death?

Bertrand Russell

Although Russell will surely be remembered for his work in math and philosophy, he will also likely be remembered as one of the 20th century's great heretics. Throughout his life he was an opponent of Christianity, expressing his views in articles like "Why I Am Not a Christian" (1927), "A Free Man's Worship" (1903), and the piece we have reprinted here, "Do We Survive Death?" (1936).

Before we can profitably discuss whether we shall continue to exist 1
after death, it is well to be clear as to the sense in which a man is the same person as he was yesterday. Philosophers used to think that there were definite substances, the soul and the body, that each lasted on from day to day, that a soul, once created, continued to exist throughout all future time, whereas a body ceased temporarily from death till the resurrection of the body.

The part of this doctrine which concerns the present life is pretty 2
certainly false. The matter of the body is continually changing by processes of nutriment and wastage. Even if it were not, atoms in physics are no longer supposed to have continuous existence; there is no sense in saying: this is the same atom as the one that existed a few minutes ago. The continuity of a human body is a matter of appearance and behavior, not of substance.

The same thing applies to the mind. We think and feel and act, but 3
there is not, in addition to thoughts and feelings and actions, a bare entity, the mind or the soul, which does or suffers these occurrences. The mental continuity of a person is a continuity of habit and memory: there was yesterday one person whose feelings I can remember, and that person I regard as myself of yesterday; but, in fact, myself of yesterday was only certain mental occurrences which are now remembered and are regarded as part of the person who now recollects them.

All that constitutes a person is a series of experiences connected by memory and by certain similarities of the sort we call habit.

4   If, therefore, we are to believe that a person survives death, we must believe that the memories and habits which constitute the person will continue to be exhibited in a new set of occurrences.

5   No one can prove that this will not happen. But it is easy to see that it is very unlikely. Our memories and habits are bound up with the structure of the brain, in much the same way in which a river is connected with the riverbed. The water in the river is always changing, but it keeps to the same course because previous rains have worn a channel. In like manner, previous events have worn a channel in the brain, and our thoughts flow along this channel. This is the cause of memory and mental habits. But the brain, as a structure, is dissolved at death, and memory therefore may be expected to be also dissolved. There is no more reason to think otherwise than to expect a river to persist in its old course after an earthquake has raised a mountain where a valley used to be.

6   All memory, and therefore (one may say) all minds, depend upon a property which is very noticeable in certain kinds of material structures but exists little if at all in other kinds. This is the property of forming habits as a result of frequent similar occurrences. For example: a bright light makes the pupils of the eyes contract; and if you repeatedly flash a light in a man's eyes and beat a gong at the same time, the gong alone will, in the end, cause his pupils to contract. This is a fact about the brain and nervous system—that is to say, about a certain material structure. It will be found that exactly similar facts explain our response to language and our use of it, our memories and the emotions they arouse, our moral or immoral habits of behavior, and indeed everything that constitutes our mental personality, except the part determined by heredity. The part determined by heredity is handed on to our posterity but cannot, in the individual, survive the disintegration of the body. Thus both the hereditary and the acquired parts of a personality are, so far as our experience goes, bound up with the characteristics of certain bodily structures. We all know that memory may be obliterated by an injury to the brain, that a virtuous person may be rendered vicious by encephalitis lethargica, and that a clever child can be turned into an idiot by lack of iodine. In view of such familiar facts, it seems scarcely probable that the mind survives the total destruction of brain structure which occurs at death.

7   It is not rational arguments but emotions that cause belief in a future life.

8   The most important of these emotions is fear of death, which is instinctive and biologically useful. If we genuinely and wholeheartedly believed in the future life, we should cease completely to fear

death. The effects would be curious, and probably such as most of us would deplore. But our human and subhuman ancestors have fought and exterminated their enemies throughout many geological ages and have profited by courage; it is therefore an advantage to the victors in the struggle for life to be able, on occasion, to overcome the natural fear of death. Among animals and savages, instinctive pugnacity suffices for this purpose; but at a certain stage of development, as the Mohammedans first proved, belief in Paradise has considerable military value as reinforcing natural pugnacity. We should therefore admit that militarists are wise in encouraging the belief in immortality, always supposing that this belief does not become so profound as to produce indifference to the affairs of the world.

Another emotion which encourages the belief in survival is admi- 9
ration of the excellence of man. As the Bishop of Birmingham says, "His mind is a far finer instrument than anything that had appeared earlier—he knows right and wrong. He can build Westminster Abbey. He can make an airplane. He can calculate the distance of the sun. . . . Shall, then, man at death perish utterly? Does that incomparable instrument, his mind, vanish when life ceases?"

The Bishop proceeds to argue that "the universe has been shaped 10
and is governed by an intelligent purpose," and that it would have been unintelligent, having made man, to let him perish.

To this argument there are many answers. In the first place, it has 11
been found, in the scientific investigation of nature, that the intrusion of moral or aesthetic values has always been an obstacle to discovery. It used to be thought that the heavenly bodies must move in circles because the circle is the most perfect curve, that species must be immutable because God would only create what was perfect and what therefore stood in no need of improvement, that it was useless to combat epidemics except by repentance because they were sent as a punishment for sin, and so on. It has been found, however, that, so far as we can discover, nature is indifferent to our values and can only be understood by ignoring our notions of good and bad. The Universe may have a purpose, but nothing that we know suggests that, if so, this purpose has any similarity to ours.

Nor is there in this anything surprising. Dr. Barnes tells us that man 12
"knows right and wrong." But, in fact, as anthropology shows, men's views of right and wrong have varied to such an extent that no single item has been permanent. We cannot say, therefore, that man knows right and wrong, but only that some men do. Which men? Nietzsche argued in favor of an ethic profoundly different from Christ's, and some powerful governments have accepted his teaching. If knowledge of right and wrong is to be an argument for immortality, we must first settle whether to believe Christ or Nietzsche, and then argue that

Christians are immortal, but Hitler and Mussolini are not, or vice versa. The decision will obviously be made on the battlefield, not in the study. Those who have the best poison gas will have the ethic of the future and will therefore be the immortal ones.

13   Our feelings and beliefs on the subject of good and evil are, like everything else about us, natural facts, developed in the struggle for existence and not having any divine or supernatural origin. In one of Aesop's fables, a lion is shown pictures of huntsmen catching lions and remarks that, if he had painted them, they would have shown lions catching huntsmen. Man, says Dr. Barnes, is a fine fellow because he can make airplanes. A little while ago there was a popular song about the cleverness of flies in walking upside down on the ceiling, with the chorus: "Could Lloyd George do it? Could Mr. Baldwin do it? Could Ramsay Mac do it? Why, NO." On this basis a very telling argument could be constructed by a theologically-minded fly, which no doubt the other flies would find most convincing.

14   Moreover, it is only when we think abstractly that we have such a high opinion of man. Of men in the concrete, most of us think the vast majority very bad. Civilized states spend more than half their revenue on killing each other's citizens. Consider the long history of the activities inspired by moral fervor: human sacrifices, persecutions of heretics, witch-hunts, pogroms leading up to wholesale extermination by poison gases, which one at least of Dr. Barnes's episcopal colleagues must be supposed to favor, since he holds pacifism to be un-Christian. Are these abominations, and the ethical doctrines by which they are prompted, really evidence of an intelligent Creator? And can we really wish that the men who practiced them should live forever? The world in which we live can be understood as a result of muddle and accident; but if it is the outcome of deliberate purpose, the purpose must have been that of a fiend. For my part, I find accident a less painful and more plausible hypothesis.

Questions About Meaning

1. What, according to Russell, accounts for "belief in a future life"?
2. In paragraph 6, Russell mentions the effects of injury, disease, and lack of iodine on the brain. How are these effects relevant to his argument?
3. What objection does Russell raise to the idea that the universe shows evidence of an intelligent design and purpose?
4. What does Russell mean when he says that the "ethic of the future" belongs to those who will have the best poison gas?
5. What does Russell think is the origin of "our feelings and beliefs on the subject of good and evil"?

6. Why does Russell conclude that, "if [the Universe] is the outcome of deliberate purpose, the purpose must have been that of a fiend"?
7. In paragraph 11, Russell notes that it used to be believed that heavenly bodies traveled in perfect circles. Why, according to Russell, did men believe this?
8. What relationship does Russell see between spirit and matter—in his terms, between memory and the brain's material structure? (See paragraphs 5 and 6.)

Matters of Technique

1. Russell's thesis is preceded by a lengthy introduction. Given the complexity of the thesis, does this technique seem an effective way to begin his essay? Why?
2. Analyze the analogy in paragraph 5. What is being compared to what? What purpose does the analogy serve?
3. Paragraph 7 is a transition paragraph. Show how it ends one part of Russell's argument and begins another.
4. Has Russell drifted off the topic in his concluding paragraph? If he has not, explain the connection between the major idea in the final paragraph and the thesis of the entire essay.

Vocabulary

1. pugnacity (8)
2. immutable (11)
3. ethic (12)
4. heretics (14)

5. pogroms (14)
6. pacifism (14)
7. plausible (14)

Suggestions for Writing

1. Using the same kind of cool and reasoned tone that Russell uses, argue against one of these beliefs: (1) That stepping on a crack breaks a mother's back; (2) that planets influence human behavior; (3) that a black cat crossing your path means bad luck.
2. Without recourse to your religion, show why life after death is a reasonable expectation. Give your reasons for your opinion a good deal of thought before you begin.
3. In saying that "it is not rational arguments but emotions that cause belief in a future life," Russell is saying that there is only one kind of truth—that arrived at by the logical mind. Other thinkers have argued that our emotional nature (or "spirit" or "unconscious

mind"—other labels for the nonrational) is also a means of apprehending truth—an intuitive truth. Write an essay in which you agree or disagree with Russell's statement. If you disagree, you will be arguing for the validity of the concept of intuitive truth.

4. Russell argues that the *human* capacity for evil cancels out the possibility of belief in God. Write an essay in which you argue for or against his point of view.

5. Discuss your view of the probable effects on human conduct produced by belief—or disbelief—in a life after death.

Cruel Lib

D. Keith Mano

D. Keith Mano writes for magazines as diverse as the libertarian Oui *(as a film critic) and the conservative* National Review *(as a columnist on American manners). "Cruel Lib" appeared in the* Newsweek *"My Turn" section in 1975.*

Let's call him Fred. I met Fred during his junior year in college. All **1**
Fred wanted was love and a rewarding sexual relationship—is that not
an inalienable right by now? Fred was purposelessly big, overweight.
His arm flesh hung down, white as a brandy Alexander, full of stretch
marks. His face, in contrast, was bluish: acne scars that might have
been haphazard tattooing. A nice guy, intelligent enough, but the
coeds were put off. Fred wooed them at mixers with his face half-
averted, as if it were an illicit act.

Fred was without sexual prejudice: as they say, he could go both **2**
ways. There was a militant gay-lib branch on campus. For months,
struck out at mixers, he had considered joining. It was a painful decision: if he came out of the closet, Fred knew, his mother and father
would probably go in—hidden there for shame. Yet mimeo sheets
from gay lib offered a tacit, thrilling promise: new life, freedom. I
remember the day Fred told me he had come out: he was relieved,
optimistic. But being gay and free didn't cosmetize his face. When
Fred let it all hang out, it just dangled there. After a while he noticed
the good-looking gays dated the good-looking gays, as a first-string
quarterback goes out with a homecoming queen. Fred had caused his
family anguish for small compensation: he was now a wallflower in
both sexes. Liberation. The tacit promise had been empty, and it had
cracked his fragile spirit. Three months later Fred committed suicide.

Let's call her Gwen. The usual: $40,000 bilevel house, three kids, **3**
married to a good provider. Her unwed sister-in-law, however, ran the
local women's-lib cell. Gwen's sister-in-law made fun of the drudgery:
dishes; that unending double-play combo, hamper to washer to dryer;
the vacuum she used and the one she lived in. It seemed so *uncreative.*
Creativity, you know, is another inalienable American right. Gwen

was 34 and, good grief, only a housewife. There were wonderful, though unspecified, resources inside her. After some time marriage, in Gwen's mind, became a kind of moth closet.

4   Ms. Gwen is divorced now. Mr. Gwen still loves her; he has taken the children. Gwen enrolled in a community college, but she didn't do well. Term papers were drudgery. For some time she made lop-sided ashtrays at a Wednesday-night ceramics class. She was free and bored to death with herself. Now Gwen drinks a lot; she has some talent in that direction. Her children, well . . . all three understand, of course, that they were exploiting Gwen for twelve and nine and seven years respectively.

5   It's an unattractive human truth, but every now and then someone should put it on record: most people—Christians used to acknowledge this fact without embarrassment—most people are not particularly talented or beautiful or charismatic. Set free to discover "the true self," very often they find nothing there at all. Men and women who determine "to do their own thing" commonly learn that they have little of note to do. Yet these people are harassed, shamed by the Zeitgeist and its glib armies into disparaging their conventional roles. The bubble-gum tune goes like this: American civilization, through some spiteful, stupid conspiracy, means to thwart self-expression. We are all frustrated painters, explorers, starlets, senators. But there are times when it's more healthful to be frustrated than to have one's mediocrity confirmed in the light of common day.

6   Roles don't limit people; roles protect them. And, yes, most people need protection: deserve it. Not so long ago our society honored the husband and the wife, the mother and the father. These were titles that carried merit enough to justify a full human life. Remember the phrase? "It's like attacking motherhood." Times have changed. On the lecture circuit today, you can pull down a nice income plus expenses attacking motherhood.

7   Yet probably the cruelest of libs is education lib. Ed lib hasn't been formally incorporated, but it's very well sustained by an immense bureaucracy of teachers, professors, administrators, foundations, Federal agencies. Strike a match and you learn inside the pad how John earned respect from his bowling team as a correspondence-school computer executive. And on the crosstown bus they tell you DON'T PREPARE FOR TOMORROW WITH YESTERDAY'S SKILLS (picture of a wheelbarrow). Or, A MIND IS A TERRIBLE THING TO WASTE. Sure. But what about a pair of hands, damn it? Even at fifteen bucks per hour, we humiliate our labor force in a programmatic way. The elitism of it all is pernicious and disgusting.

8   Some few centuries ago another kind of lib prevailed. Christianity, they called it. Christian lib isn't a "now" item; it comes due in another life. Prerequisites are faith, works, humility: children are raised,

things are made, to God's glory. Christians know personal gratification for what it is: a brummagem trinket. And this has been the shrewd beauty of Communism. Lenin cribbed his tactics from the New Testament. Liberation is promised through an arduous class struggle—but not in anyone's lifetime. This lib movement, moreover, functions within a powerfully structured, oppressive social system. Not only do totalitarian governments curtail personal liberty, but they are downright prissy when it comes to permissive sex. Yet people, in general, accept. Their roles are clear, and those roles are esteemed.

In this country, circa 1975, lib has become a growth industry. Many who are otherwise talentless have made it their profession. But what Ralph Nader will hold them accountable for the Freds and the Gwens, for those who have been dispirited by a society that no longer prizes sexual restraint or menial labor or the nuclear family? We have, I hold it self-evident, an inalienable right to be unliberated. This nation—another unattractive truth—doesn't need more personal freedom. The human spirit can be an unruly beast; a little restraint is wholesome. Let people be cherished for what they are, not for ambiguous thwarted gifts, or for the social responsibilities they default on. The men and women of Middle America have earned that small consideration. Really "creative" people will surface anyway. They usually do. And they will have their great rewards.

9

Questions About Meaning

1. What is Mano's thesis?
2. What does Mano say may be the uncomfortable result of trying to find one's true self, and to "liberate" it?
3. What does Mano mean by saying that people can be "harassed, shamed by the Zeitgeist and its glib armies into disparaging their conventional roles"?
4. What is Mano's view of the idea that their roles in life limit people?
5. What does Mano call "the cruelest" of the libs? Why? (A physician once told his son, who was marveling over how many fine professional men their state university had turned out, "Yes. But we've ruined a lot of good blacksmiths.")
6. What ethic does Mano propose as a healthy alternative to "self-expression"?

Matters of Technique

1. What advantages does Mano's technique of beginning with two examples have? What are the disadvantages?
2. At what point does Mano first state his thesis?

3. How does paragraph 8 fit Mano's thesis?
4. Where does Mano set up his contrast with the "Liberation" ethic? How effectively does he do so?

Vocabulary

1. inalienable (1)
2. illicit (1)
3. tacit (2)
4. charismatic (5)
5. Zeitgeist (5)
6. glib (5)
7. disparaging (5)
8. programmatic (7)
9. elitism (7)
10. pernicious (7)
11. brummagem (8)
12. cribbed (8)

Suggestions for Writing

1. Write an argumentative essay in which you attack or defend the ethic of self-expression as a guide to the conduct of life. Emphasize the effects, good or bad, which you believe will follow from practice of the ethic.
2. Write an argumentative essay which uses the same organizational structure that Mano's does. That is, begin with an example or two and then explain what that example or those examples mean.
3. Write an essay on this sentence from Mano's sixth paragraph: "Roles don't limit people; roles protect them."
4. Write an essay based on this sentence from paragraph 5: "But there are times when it's more healthful to be frustrated than to have one's mediocrity confirmed in the light of common day." Use your own experiences or relate the experiences of someone you know.

Cross-References

What are the similarities between Mano's views and those of Lance Morrow? What are the similarities to Faulkner's views? To C. S. Lewis's?

Is a Crime Against the Mind No Crime at All?

Judith Plotz

Judith Plotz, as you might be able to tell from her article, is a professor who specializes in Romantic literature. At the time she wrote the following 1976 article for The Chronicle of Higher Education, *she was an English teacher at George Washington University.*

Twenty research papers are submitted in one freshman composition **1** section; nine are plagiarized. A sharp-eyed history professor, disheartened by yearly bumper crops of plagiarists, gives up on the term paper: "I even have graduate students do annotated bibliographies now." Another professor in the social sciences retains papers, but with cynical fatalism: "Plagiarism? Sure, there's lots of it, but I'm busy and try not to look too closely." An allegedly original English paper is submitted bearing a fresh top-sheet over the unaltered text of a roommate's year-old paper, unaltered even to the roommate's name and the original instructor's comments and grade.

These are representative examples of university life in the '70's, **2** where plagiarism is epidemic. The academic community has proffered a number of explanations for the plague, each more dismal than the last. The general decline in moral standards is a recurrent theme: something is rotten—the students, the country, even the university. The students, one argument goes, are intellectually corrupt; growing up in unearned ease, they have never learned to respect the hard-earned achievements of intellect. Or, more vastly, the nation, as the Watergate affair illustrates, is corrupt and has taught its children to seek success at any price. Alternatively, or additionally, the university is corrupt in employing a judgmental grading system that encourages students to jockey for grades rather than to seek truth. Less moralistically, others trace the problems to a presumed drop in standards of admissions. Traditional university programs demand too much of poorly prepared students, who plagiarize out of panic.

3   These explanations may account for some cases, but not all. Actually, the very concept of plagiarism, a relatively new phenomenon, has grown up with modern ideas of individuality.

4   In the medieval and Renaissance periods, the concept of plagiarism—the *illegitimate* borrowing from another author—was virtually unknown. With the exception of direct comma-for-comma copying of another writer's work, most sorts of borrowing were legitimate, even laudable. An authoritarian social system nurtured literary authoritarianism. To model one's style, one's plots, one's ideas on a literary master was the time-honored way of learning to write well. One rather boasted of than tried to hide one's appropriations from the masters. Medieval poets, recognizing Virgil as a supreme craftsman, believing that one could not have too much of a good thing, translated and versified great swatches of the *Aeneid;* rather than condemning such poets for theft, their audiences praised them for pleasing versions of an honored favorite.

5   The classical masters were regarded, as nature itself was regarded, as a writer's resource. The writer foolish enough to aim at total individuality was not admirable, but an eccentric deliberately impoverishing himself.

6   Plagiarism first came into existence as a significant literary problem only toward the end of the 17th century. Like Renaissance writers, critics of this period were predominantly authoritarian and held that all the major subjects for literature had already been pre-empted, seized upon by writers of genius when the world was young, when "nature," as Samuel Johnson said of Shakespeare, "was still open" to them. But a favorite Latin tag of the age, *"Pereant qui ante nos nostra dixerunt"* (Damn those who had all our best ideas before we did), captures the increasing discontent with this situation. Eighteenth-century writers, despite their traditionalism, also felt an envious esteem for originality, the power to look at something in a new way, and for invention, the power to discover a new subject. Originality, now held to be a prime literary virtue, was despairingly deemed typical only of young civilizations and virtually unattainable in a modern age. Despite their desire for originality, modern writers could never be much more than copyists of the past, or so the prevailing theory went.

7   It was during this period of reluctant traditionalism and longing for originality that critics began fervidly to hunt down plagiarists. Whether out of a thirst for originality or out of an aggrieved desire to show originality impossible to anyone, critics began to make accusations of plagiarism against writers who did no more than echo a word or phrase from an earlier writer. The presence of plagiarism was held to be an inevitability in a period which was a reluctant heir to the treasures of the ages. Nevertheless, it was fiercely derided as an enemy

of originality. The failure to be original became culpable only when originality became desirable.

By the Romantic age plagiarism should have become unnecessary. **8** The early 19th-century Romantics took a high view of the potential creativity of every human soul. Originality, they argued, is the birthright of every individual. So liberating, so anti-authoritarian a theory of creativity should have set a writer free from the necessity of literary theft. Yet the greatest plagiarist in literary history—great in the number of his depredations, great in his genius—Samuel Taylor Coleridge, is a product of the age of originality. As Norman Fruman's recent book, *Coleridge, the Damaged Archangel,* makes plain, Coleridge compulsively appropriated the materials of other writers, notably German critics and philosophers, and equally compulsively protested his absolute originality.

Like Coleridge, contemporary undergraduates labor under a double **9** burden: the burden of originality imposed by the age and the burden of intellectual coherence imposed by the university. That the burdens often prove intolerable, the present state of academic morality attests.

American undergraduates of the '70's are heirs to the by-now sleazy **10** and dilapidated Romantic ideal of creativity. I call the ideal sleazy because it has degenerated from its original heroic summons to immense productive and synthetic efforts into a slack and sentimental invitation to self-complacent ease. It is one thing to hold that every child is innately imaginative and another to argue that all self-expression, no matter how feeble, is artistic creation. To believe that the inner spirit, the child-like soul in and of itself, untouched by any particular knowledge, is alone creative, has led in much contemporary secondary education to a loss of confidence in forms and in substantive knowledge. Since creativity comes from the naked self, it is no longer necessary to furnish that self with facilitating knowledges (grammar, German, Latin, calculus, physics) and forms (syntax, the sonnet, the book report). With "writing" in secondary schools largely confined to English class (though extracts copied from encyclopedias and other unimpeachable sources frequently surface as "research" papers in various other subject areas) and with English dedicated to evoking individual creativity, students are losing the habit of unselfconscious writing as a means of communication, as a mechanical knack in which the deepest self is not necessarily involved.

Habitually to write free verse, impressionistic responses to litera- **11** ture, and ruminative short stories without any compensatory training in the mere prose of communication is to hole up the self in a very narrow cell. Originality has been confounded with the spontaneous, unmediated productions of the sole self, and the real experience of the sole self has been identified with pre-verbal incommunicable states which are impossible to express discursively. To be true to one's self, therefore, to be appropriately original, is to draw back from the world of facts and forms, the world of science and high culture. Authenticity lies in expressing the self rather than in expressing the world.

12   Parallel with the development of this solipsistic idea of originality has been the knowledge explosion. The first-hand knowledge of any individual, even if he has the curiosity of a Leonardo and the stamina of a Casanova, is puny beside the vast stores of genuine scholarship that are piling up with unprecedented speed and to an unprecedented density in our libraries. The act of synthesizing preceding knowledge requires humility, ardor, and dedication to the life of the mind. Even a seasoned scholar feels intimidated by the mass of materials he must master and comprehend.

13   When a student is asked to write an essay synthesizing or assessing literary or historical or political data, he finds himself facing materials on which considerable authoritative commentary may already exist. To write a good essay, the student must digest the data and commentary, synthesize them, and then go beyond them. The process, once second nature to well-trained college students, has by now become remarkably difficult for them. My guess is that the act of writing is increasingly tied up with the idea of self-expression and has little connection with the comprehension of any external aspect of the world. Because the presumably true, the creative self, exists most fully in isolation from the multiple intellectual constructions and historical accumulations with which liberal education is concerned, many students find all questions involving comment on a body of knowledge artificial, mechanical, and alien. When a student regards a paper assignment as merely mechanical, he quite consistently feels something of a hypocrite in devoting his full strength to so empty a pursuit. To many students it seems no greater a self-violation to commit fraud and plagiarize their papers than to push themselves through an exercise personally meaningless.

14   If my hypothesis is correct, if plagiarism does derive from a perverted ideal of creativity, is there anything at all the university can do? Clearly, the plagiarist's contempt for earned intellectual distinction, his assumption that a crime against the mind is no crime, his theft from his sources and his fraud against his professors destroy any possible value from his education.

15   The quick way to abolish the problem, of course, is to abolish term papers; but this is decapitation for a headache. The problem goes so deep that individual actions may be only palliative, but some new approaches to writing might help. Three kinds of papers might be useful. In order to combat the association between the act of writing and self-expression, I suggest that numerous small exercises be

demanded—quizzes, summaries, paraphrases—all cast in consecutive prose. I also suggest the revival of the deliberate Imitation, an educational device so old, so aboriginal, as to be new. Students might be asked to write about English history in the manner of Macaulay, about the Vietnam war as Karl Marx. This would give the aid an established form always provides while still demanding the expression of individual judgment.

With exercises and imitations encouraging impersonal prose, major paper assignments might be made more personal. The rote assignment, the question unreal both to instructor and student, might be replaced by assignments that deliberately cross the subjective self with the objective world, assignments that demand a reaching out into the world from a frankly acknowledged personal center. One might even try tapping the tremendous energy of animus, of anger, and ask students to write on those aspects of subjects they find most objectionable. 16

One might, one might . . . In any case, one must. The epidemic of plagiarism is sad testimony to student estrangement from the goals of education. The increasing inability of students to leap the gap between their sole selves and the realm of knowledge means that it is vital to build more bridges, more crossings, to ease the passage. 17

Questions About Meaning

1. What are some of the suggested explanations the author mentions for widespread plagiarism in university classes?
2. What does the author say are the shortcomings of the concept of the unique, creative self in the environment of a modern university?
3. In paragraph 10, what criticism does the author make of the teaching of English as a means of evoking students' self-expression and "individual creativity"? What does the author mean by the phrase, "unselfconscious writing"?
4. What does Plotz mean by saying (paragraph 11) that "originality has been confounded with the spontaneous"?
5. What cause (paragraph 13) does Plotz suggest for the apparently increasing difficulty university students have in writing about, assimilating, and synthesizing a body of objective knowledge?
6. What does Plotz say in paragraph 14 is the effect of plagiarism on the value of one's education?
7. What sorts of exercises does the author suggest be used to give the student practice in "impersonal prose"? What does she mean by "impersonal prose"?

Matters of Technique

1. It's now considered rather old-fashioned to include a lengthy history of your subject at the beginning of an essay. Plotz's history of plagiarism is about one-third of her essay; how do you feel about this as a technique?
2. Notice, once again, that professional writers often begin with examples. Why?
3. Plotz writes a relatively formal, impersonal prose that echoes her thesis. What makes her prose formal and impersonal? Study in particular paragraph 10.

Vocabulary

1. cynical (1)
2. fatalism (1)
3. proffered (2)
4. recurrent (2)
5. laudable (4)
6. derided (7)
7. culpable (7)
8. coherence (9)
9. substantive (10)
10. discursively (11)
11. palliative (15)
12. animus (16)
13. estrangement (17)

Suggestions for Writing

1. How is plagiarism a "crime against the mind"? Develop your answer in an essay.
2. What does Plotz mean by her phrase, "sleazy and dilapidated Romantic ideal of creativity"? Develop your answer in an essay.
3. Do what Plotz recommends in paragraph 15: Write an essay in imitation of a famous stylist like Hemingway, Dickens, Shakespeare, or Salinger, or of a type of literature, such as a fairy tale, a hard-boiled mystery, or a romantic novel.
4. Discuss your view of the reasons for the student plagiarism you have observed. Comment also on your view of the effects of such practices on the plagiarist and on the meaning of his education.

The Law of Human Nature

C. S. Lewis

*C. S. Lewis, an amazingly versatile writer, was known in the scholarly world as a prolific literary critic (*The Allegory of Love, *1936), among science fiction fans as the author of speculative fiction (*Out of the Silent Planet, *1938), and in religious circles as a Christian apologist (*The Screwtape Letters, *1943). Our selection from* Mere Christianity *(1952) may have been generated from Lewis's Christian experiences, yet it has obvious universal application.*

Every one has heard people quarrelling. Sometimes it sounds funny and sometimes it sounds merely unpleasant but however it sounds, I believe we can learn something very important from listening to the kind of things they say. They say things like this: "How'd you like it if anyone did the same to you?"—"That's my seat, I was there first"—"Leave him alone, he isn't doing you any harm"—"Why should you shove in first"—"Give me a bit of your orange, I gave you a bit of mine"—"Come on, you promised." People say things like that every day, educated people as well as uneducated, and children as well as grown-ups. 1

Now what interests me about all these remarks is that the man who makes them is not merely saying that the other man's behaviour does not happen to please him. He is appealing to some kind of standard of behaviour which he expects the other man to know about. And the other man very seldom replies: "To hell with your standard." Nearly always he tries to make out that what he has been doing does not really go against the standard, or that if it does there is some special excuse. He pretends there is some special reason in this particular case why the person who took the seat first should not keep it, or that things were quite different when he was given the bit of orange, or that something has turned up which lets him off keeping his promise. It looks, in fact, very much as if both parties had in mind some kind of Law or Rule of fair play or decent behaviour or morality or what- 2 ever you like to call it, about which they really agreed. And they have. If they had not, they might, of course, fight like animals, but they could not *quarrel* in the human sense of the word. Quarrelling means trying to show that the other man is in the wrong. And there would be no sense in trying to do that unless you and he had some sort of agreement as to what Right and Wrong are; just as there would be no sense in saying that a footballer had committed a foul unless there was some agreement about the rules of football.

3   Now this Law or Rule about Right and Wrong used to be called the Law of Nature. Nowadays, when we talk of the "laws of nature" we usually mean things like gravitation, or heredity, or the laws of chemistry. But when the older thinkers called the Law of Right and Wrong "the Law of Nature," they really meant the Law of *Human* Nature. The idea was that, just as all bodies are governed by the law of gravitation and organisms by biological laws, so the creature called man also had *his* law—with this great difference, that a body could not choose whether it obeyed the law of gravitation or not, but a man could choose either to obey the Law of Human Nature or to disobey it.

4   We may put this in another way. Each man is at every moment subjected to several different sets of law but there is only one of these which he is free to disobey. As a body, he is subjected to gravitation and cannot disobey it; if you leave him unsupported in mid-air, he has no more choice about falling than a stone has. As an organism, he is subjected to various biological laws which he cannot disobey any more than an animal can. That is, he cannot disobey those laws which he shares with other things; but the law which is peculiar to his human nature, the law he does not share with animals or vegetables or inorganic things, is the one he can disobey if he chooses.

5   This law was called the Law of Nature because people thought that every one knew it by nature and did not need to be taught it. They did not mean, of course, that you might not find an odd individual here and there who did not know it, just as you find a few people who are colour-blind or have no ear for a tune. But taking the race as a whole, they thought that the human idea of decent behaviour was obvious to every one. And I believe they were right. If they were not, then all the things we said about the war were nonsense. What was the sense in saying the enemy were in the wrong unless Right is a real thing which the Nazis at bottom knew as well as we did and ought to have practised? If they had had no notion of what we mean by right, then, though we might still have had to fight them, we could no more have blamed them for that than for the colour of their hair.

6   I know that some people say the idea of a Law of Nature or decent behaviour known to all men is unsound, because different civilisations and different ages have had quite different moralities.

But this is not true. There have been differences between their moralities, but these have never amounted to anything like a total difference. If anyone will take the trouble to compare the moral teaching of, say, the ancient Egyptians, Babylonians, Hindus, Chinese, Greeks and Romans, what will really strike him will be how very like they are to each other and to our own. Some of the evidence for this I have put together in the appendix of another book called *The Abolition of Man;* but for our present purpose I need only ask the reader to think what a totally different morality would mean. Think of a country where people were admired for running away in battle, or where a man felt proud of double-crossing all the people who had been kindest to him. You might just as well try to imagine a country where two and two made five. Men have differed as regards what people you ought to be unselfish to—whether it was only your own family, or your fellow countrymen, or everyone. But they have always agreed that you ought not to put yourself first. Selfishness has never been admired. Men have differed as to whether you should have one wife or four. But they have always agreed that you must not simply have any woman you liked.

But the most remarkable thing is this. Whenever you find a man who says he does not believe in a real Right and Wrong, you will find the same man going back on this a moment later. He may break his promise to you, but if you try breaking one to him he will be complaining "It's not fair" before you can say Jack Robinson. A nation may say treaties do not matter; but then, next minute, they spoil their case by saying that the particular treaty they want to break was an unfair one. But if treaties do not matter, and if there is no such thing as Right and Wrong—in other words, if there is no Law of Nature—what is the difference between a fair treaty and an unfair one? Have they not let the cat out of the bag and shown that, whatever they say, they really know the Law of Nature just like anyone else?

It seems, then, we are forced to believe in a real Right and Wrong. People may be sometimes mistaken about them, just as people sometimes get their sums wrong; but they are not a matter of mere taste and opinion any more than the multiplication table. Now if we are agreed about that, I go on to my next point, which is this. None of us are really keeping the Law of Nature. If there are any exceptions among you, I apologise to them. They had much better read some other work, for nothing I am going to say concerns them. And now, turning to the ordinary human beings who are left:

I hope you will not misunderstand what I am going to say. I am not preaching, and Heaven knows I do not pretend to be better than anyone else. I am only trying to call attention to a fact; the fact that this year, or this month, or, more likely, this very day, we have failed to

7

8

9

10

practise ourselves the kind of behaviour we expect from other people. There may be all sorts of excuses for us. That time you were so unfair to the children was when you were very tired. That slightly shady business about the money—the one you have almost forgotten—came when you were very hard up. And what you promised to do for old So-and-so and have never done—well, you never would have promised if you had known how frightfully busy you were going to be. And as for your behaviour to your wife (or husband) or sister (or brother) if I knew how irritating they could be, I would not wonder at it—and who the dickens am I, anyway? I am just the same. That is to say, I do not succeed in keeping the Law of Nature very well, and the moment anyone tells me I am not keeping it, there starts up in my mind a string of excuses as long as your arm. The question at the moment is not whether they are good excuses. The point is that they are one more proof of how deeply, whether we like it or not, we believe in the Law of Nature. If we do not believe in decent behaviour, why should we be so anxious to make excuses for not having behaved decently? The truth is, we believe in decency so much—we feel the Rule or Law pressing on us so—that we cannot bear to face the fact that we are breaking it, and consequently we try to shift the responsibility. For you notice that it is only for our bad behaviour that we find all these explanations. It is only our bad temper that we put down to being tired or worried or hungry; we put our good temper down to ourselves.

11   These, then, are the two points I wanted to make. First, that human beings, all over the earth, have this curious idea that they ought to behave in a certain way, and cannot really get rid of it. Secondly, that they do not in fact behave in that way. They know the Law of Nature; they break it. These two facts are the foundation of all clear thinking about ourselves and the universe we live in.

Questions About Meaning

1. What leads Lewis to think that people believe in a standard or rule of correct behavior?
2. What does Lewis think is the importance of the excuses we are constantly making to one another?
3. What, according to Lewis, is the crucial difference between the laws of nature and the "Law of Human Nature"?
4. What is Lewis's answer to the idea that different civilizations and societies "have had quite different moralities"?
5. How does the behavior of the person who disbelieves in a real "right" and "wrong" support Lewis's argument?

Matters of Technique

1. What technique does Lewis use in the first paragraph to get into his subject?
2. Note the use of parallel structures in the third and fourth sentences of paragraph 4. Write two sentences of your own modeled on the structure of these sentences.
3. Lewis uses the kind of conclusion that neatly summarizes his main points. What are the advantages of this kind of conclusion? The disadvantages?

Vocabulary

decent (5)

Suggestions for Writing

1. What do you think is necessary for people to get along with one another peacefully? Discuss your views in detail.
2. What do you think are the root causes of human hatred and envy? Discuss your assessment in detail.

Cross-Reference

Compare Lewis's view of the effects of belief in an objective universal moral standard with the views on this subject expressed by one of the following: Faulkner, Lincoln, or King.

CHAPTER ELEVEN

Argumentation : Appeals to Emotion

If we were all mind, like one of those science fiction beings of the future, with their gigantic balloon heads and tiny vestigial bodies, then writers would base all their arguments on pure, sweet reason. But the heart, as the saying goes, has reasons that reason itself doesn't know. And even our minds, thank goodness, don't operate with the cold logic of a computer chip. And that is why a good writer has to know how to appeal to the heart's reasons as well as to the mind's.

Patrick Henry knew it well when he stood in front of the Virginia Convention in 1775 to try to persuade its delegates to prepare for war with England. Listen to his plea in the justly famous "Liberty or Death" speech:

We have petitioned—we have remonstrated—we have supplicated—we have prostrated ourselves before the throne, and have implored its interposition to arrest the tyrannical hands of the ministry and parliament. . . . we must fight!—I repeat it, sir, we must fight! An appeal to arms and to the God of Hosts is all that is left us!

But so did Benito Mussolini when he announced in 1922 that it was time for the Fascists to march on Rome and take the government by force:

> Fascism bares its sword in order to cut the too-numerous Gordian knots that enmesh and sadden Italian life. We call upon the Supreme Lord and spirit of our five hundred thousand Dead to witness that only one impulse drives us, only one will brings us together, only one passion inflames us: to contribute to the safety and greatness of our Homeland.

Obviously, an essay or a speech that hinges on an emotional appeal is neither bad nor good in itself. The rhetorical devices that are used in the manipulation of the emotions of an audience are neutral and are available, like all tools, to both good and evil causes. They were available to St. Francis of Assisi, Joan of Arc, and Stalin; they are available today to Mother Theresa, African dictators, and advertising copywriters. The purpose of emotional rhetoric may be as pernicious as that of Hitler's speech at Nuremberg. Or it may be as benign as in Martin Luther King's "I Have a Dream" speech or in Abraham Lincoln's "Second Inaugural Address" (both reprinted in this chapter).

Naturally, there are some writing situations—eulogies, sermons, commencement addresses, political campaign speeches, dedications—which seem to demand an emotional appeal. But there are many other situations that at least invite one. When, for instance, an audience already shares the writer's assumptions and is ready to applaud foregone conclusions, it is not the time for a heavily reasoned argument. The original readers of Tom Paine's essay, "The American Crisis!" (with its stirring "summer soldier" figure of speech) were eager to have their flagging determination strengthened and their common values reaffirmed. They were not eager to read a fact-strewn, strictly reasoned essay on why America should continue to oppose British political domination of the Colonies.

The writer also doesn't need to construct a reason-based essay when the facts are so well known that their rehearsal seems obtrusive. Copywriters for antismoking campaigns, for instance, know that we have been given, time and again, the reasons and facts, so they try to scare us with descriptions of rotting lungs. Debates over environmental concerns are also often based almost entirely on emotional appeals because the facts and reasons are all so familiar.

Naturally, when a writer is discussing ethics, or how people ought to behave, his writing usually rests on an emotional appeal. Facts seem rather inappropriate when a writer is trying to persuade someone to help grandmothers across the street, or to be thrifty, brave, clean, and reverent.

A caution: emotional appeals can backfire if the writer is blatantly unfair, even when his audience shares most of his assumptions. In a famous debate over evolution with Thomas Huxley, Bishop Samuel Wilberforce chose to base his argument on an emotional appeal to his audience's shared assumptions about religion; but Wilberforce went too far. He thought that his audience also shared his scorn for Darwin's bulldog, Huxley, and would look past any shabby treatment of him. Wilberforce therefore concluded his argument by wondering if Huxley traced his descent from monkeys through his grandfather or his grandmother. When Huxley heard this, he whispered to the man seated next to him, "The Lord hath delivered him into mine hands," and then rose to present his side of the debate. He began by saying that he would not be ashamed to discover that he had a monkey for an ancestor, but he would be greatly ashamed to obscure the truth with "aimless rhetoric" and "appeals to religious prejudice." By most accounts, Huxley won the debate.

But a more important consideration than the possible loss of an argument through unfairness is the simple obligation a writer has to treat his subject and an opponent fairly. Even when a writer's audience shares his assumptions, he is obliged by the standards of fair play and honesty to search after truth, not to play heavily on people's base instincts or distort the truth for the sake of argument.

The Characteristics of Emotional Appeals

1. *the use of words with strong emotional associations.* (For a more thorough discussion of these "colored" words, turn to the latter part of Paul Roberts' essay in the Introduction): When Benito Mussolini called on the Fascists to contribute to the "greatness" of the "Homeland," he was using words with strongly positive associations. And when Patrick Henry described the Tory status quo as "chains and slavery," his opponents as having "tyrannical hands," and his cause as a "struggle for liberty," he too was using words with emotional associations.

2. *appeals to an audience's assumptions:* When Patrick Henry stood in front of the Virginia Convention and appealed to the "God of Hosts," he was, in effect, not only identifying his cause with God's, but he was also identifying his audience's assumptions with his cause. Likewise, when Mussolini called upon the "Supreme Lord" and "five hundred thousand Dead" as his witnesses, he was appealing to both religious and political assumptions that his Italian audience shared.

3. *the use of rhythm and repetition:* Though rhythm and repetition are usually thought the province of the poet, prose writers often use these

devices to good effect. Listen to the rhythm that Patrick Henry used in his "Liberty or Death" speech. (We have emphasized the rhythm by putting the clauses into poetic form.)

We have petitioned—
We have remonstrated—
We have supplicated—
We have prostrated . . .

And listen to Mussolini:

. . . only one impulse drives us,
only one will brings us together,
only one passion inflames us. . . .

Most emotional appeals, of course, are not so dramatic and blatant. As a matter of fact, appeals to emotion and appeals to reason are usually inextricably bound together, often in the same sentence. An emotional device like the use of "colored" words quite often lies atop, like frosting on a cake, a logical sequence of ideas.

In this chapter we have included two speeches, one by Abraham Lincoln and one by Martin Luther King, that are thoroughly emotional in their appeals. But we have also included two essays with more reasoned tones, by David Berg and Edward Abbey, to show that most arguments, however rational their surface, appeal to emotional convictions as well as to rationally held ones. The Berg and Abbey essays on gun control have rational frameworks and fairly reasoned tones. But they also contain a strong strain of subjectivity because the writers take the risk—and it is a risk—of identifying themselves closely with their positions. Naturally, when writers do this, they give away the objective tone that accompanies a heavily reasoned, emotionally distanced argument. But there are gains as well—as you will see when you read their essays—in forcefulness and sincerity.

The most important human issues—and gun control is one of these—involve morality and basic human freedoms, both of which usually lie beyond the reach of the most logical arguments. These issues live in a dark place where reason is an infrequent and often unwelcome visitor.

For these issues, reason is almost an afterthought, an instrument used to express what the heart feels. Working backwards, we add layers of reason to beliefs that grew up with us, that were a part of us before we knew the difference between a rational argument and a child's toy.

As you read Berg's and Abbey's arguments (and they should be read as a pair), look beyond the rational structure of their essays to those sentences that rest on emotional appeals. There are more of them than a cursory reading would suggest.

MODEL PARAGRAPH BASED ON AN EMOTIONAL APPEAL

Their Finest Hour

Upon this battle [the air war over Britain] depends the survival of Christian civilization. Upon it depends our own British life, and the long continuity of our institutions and our Empire. The whole fury and might of the enemy must very soon be turned on us. Hitler knows that he will have to break us in this island or lose the war. If we can stand up to him, all Europe may be free and the life of the world may move forward into broad, sunlit uplands. But if we fail, then the whole world, including the United States, ... will sink into the abyss of a new Dark Age made more sinister ... by the lights of perverted science. Let us therefore brace ourselves to our duties, and so bear ourselves that, if the British Empire and its Commonwealth last for a thousand years, men will still say, "This was their finest hour."

Winston Churchill, 1940

ANALYSIS

Churchill's use of colored words ("perverted science"), his appeal to shared national and religious sentiments ("Christian civilization"), and his heavy use of strong images and metaphors ("He will have to break us," "sunlit uplands," "sink into the abyss") show that his appeal is basically to the emotions of his listeners. Naturally, a heavily emotional appeal like Churchill's should be reserved for heavily emotional occasions. (Churchill's speech was delivered to England's House of Commons in 1940 when the country was being attacked by Germany's air force.) But milder versions of these techniques can be used by writers in less emotionally charged situations.

ASSIGNMENT

Using the three kinds of emotional appeals that Churchill uses (colored words, shared assumptions, striking images and figures of speech), write an emotionally loaded paragraph in which you try to persuade your readers that your town needs a new humane-society shelter. Naturally, unless you're going to write a humorous paragraph, you'll have to bring the emotional pitch down a few notches from Churchill's. If you do try a humorous paragraph, go all out; you might even want to use repetition and rhythm.

I Have a Dream

Martin Luther King, Jr.

"I Have a Dream" will likely outlive us all. Not only is it a stirring piece of rhetoric, but it is also one of the most significant historical documents that arose out of the civil rights movement of the 1960s. The speech was originally delivered in front of the Lincoln Memorial in Washington, D.C. on August 28, 1963.

Five score years ago, a great American, in whose symbolic shadow we stand today, signed the Emancipation Proclamation. This momentous decree came as a great beacon light of hope to millions of Negro slaves who had been seared in the flames of withering injustice. It came as a joyous daybreak to end the long night of their captivity. 1

But one hundred years later, the Negro still is not free. One hundred years later, the life of the Negro is still sadly crippled by the manacles of segregation and the chains of discrimination. 2

One hundred years later, the Negro lives on a lonely island of poverty in the midst of a vast ocean of material prosperity. One hundred years later, the Negro is still languished in the corners of American society and finds himself an exile in his own land. So we have come here today to dramatize a shameful condition. 3

In a sense we have come to our nation's capital to cash a check. When the architects of our republic wrote the magnificent words of the Constitution and the Declaration of Independence, they were signing a promissory note to which every American was to fall heir. This note was a promise that all men, yes, black men as well as white men, would be granted the unalienable rights of life, liberty, and the pursuit of happiness. 4

It is obvious today that America has defaulted on this promissory note insofar as her citizens of color are concerned. Instead of honoring this sacred obligation, America has given the Negro people a bad check—which has come back marked "insufficient funds." 5

But we refuse to believe that the bank of justice is bankrupt. We refuse to believe that there are insufficient funds in the great vaults of opportunity of this nation. So we have come to cash this check—a 6 check that will give us upon demand the riches of freedom and the security of justice.

7   We have also come to this hallowed spot to remind America of the fierce urgency of *now*. This is no time to engage in the luxury of cooling off or to take the tranquilizing drug of gradualism. *Now* is the time to make real the promises of democracy. *Now* is the time to rise from the dark and desolate valley of segregation to the sunlit path of racial justice. *Now* is the time to lift our nation from the quicksands of racial injustice to the solid rock of brotherhood. *Now* is the time to make justice a reality for all of God's children.

8   It would be fatal for the nation to overlook the urgency of the moment and to underestimate the determination of the Negro. This sweltering summer of the Negro's legitimate discontent will not pass until there is an invigorating autumn of freedom and equality. 1963 is not an end but a beginning. Those who hope that the Negro needed to blow off steam and will now be content will have a rude awakening if the nation returns to business as usual.

9   There will be neither rest nor tranquility in America until the Negro is granted his citizenship rights. The whirlwinds of revolt will continue to shake the foundations of our nation until the bright day of justice emerges.

10   But there is something that I must say to my people who stand on the warm threshold which leads into the palace of justice. In the process of gaining our rightful place we must not be guilty of wrongful deeds.

11   Let us not seek to satisfy our thirst for freedom by drinking from the cup of bitterness and hatred. We must forever conduct our struggle on the high plane of dignity and discipline. We must not allow our creative protest to degenerate into physical violence. Again and again we must rise to the majestic heights of meeting physical force with soul force.

12   The marvelous new militancy which has engulfed the Negro community must not lead us to a distrust of all white people, for many of our white brothers, as evidenced by their presence here today, have come to realize that their destiny is tied up with our destiny and they have come to realize that their freedom is inextricably bound to our freedom. We cannot walk alone.

13   And as we walk, we must make the pledge that we shall always march ahead. We cannot turn back. There are those who are asking the devotees of civil rights, "When will you be satisfied?" We can never be satisfied as long as the Negro is the victim of the unspeakable horrors of police brutality.

14   We can never be satisfied as long as our bodies, heavy with the fatigue of travel, cannot gain lodging in the motels of the highways

and the hotels of the cities. We cannot be satisfied as long as the Negro's basic mobility is from a smaller ghetto to a larger one.

We can never be satisfied as long as our children are stripped of 15 their selfhood and robbed of their dignity by signs stating "for whites only." We cannot be satisfied as long as a Negro in Mississippi cannot vote and a Negro in New York believes he has nothing for which to vote. No, we are not satisfied, and we will not be satisfied until justice rolls down like waters and righteousness like a mighty stream.

I am not unmindful that some of you have come here out of exces- 16 sive trials and tribulation. Some of you have come fresh from narrow jail cells. Some of you have come from areas where your quest for freedom left you battered by the storms of persecution and staggered by the winds of police brutality. You have been the veterans of creative suffering. Continue to work with the faith that unearned suffering is redemptive.

Go back to Mississippi; go back to Alabama; go back to South Car- 17 olina; go back to Georgia; go back to Louisiana; go back to the slums and ghettos of the Northern cities, knowing that somehow this situation can, and will be changed. Let us not wallow in the valley of despair.

So I say to you, my friends, that even though we must face the dif- 18 ficulties of today and tomorrow, I still have a dream. It is a dream deeply rooted in the American dream—that one day this nation will rise up and live out the true meaning of its creed: "We hold these truths to be self-evident, that all men are created equal".

I have a dream that one day on the red hills of Georgia, sons of 19 former slaves and sons of former slave-owners will be able to sit down together at the table of brotherhood.

I have a dream that one day, even the state of Mississippi, a state 20 sweltering with the heat of injustice, sweltering with the heat of oppression, will be transformed into an oasis of freedom and justice.

I have a dream that my four little children will one day live in a 21 nation where they will not be judged by the color of their skin but by the content of their character. I have a dream today!

I have a dream that one day, down in Alabama, with its vicious 22 racists, with its governor having his lips dripping with the words of interposition and nullification, that one day, right there in Alabama, little black boys and black girls will be able to join hands with little white boys and white girls as sisters and brothers. I have a dream today!

I have a dream that one day every valley shall be exalted, every hill 23 and mountain shall be made low, the rough places shall be made plain, and the crooked places shall be made straight and the glory of the Lord will be revealed and all flesh shall see it together.

24   This is our hope. This is the faith that I go back to the South with.

25   With this faith we will be able to hew out of the mountain of despair a stone of hope. With this faith we will be able to transform the jangling discords of our nation into a beautiful symphony of brotherhood.

26   With this faith we will be able to work together, to pray together, to struggle together, to go to jail together, to stand up for freedom together, knowing that we will be free one day. This will be the day when all of God's children will be able to sing with new meaning— "My country 'tis of thee, sweet land of liberty, of thee I sing. Land where my fathers died, land of the Pilgrims' pride, from every mountainside, let freedom ring." And if America is to be a great nation, this must become true.

27   So let freedom ring from the prodigious hilltops of New Hampshire!

28   Let freedom ring from the mighty mountains of New York!

29   Let freedom ring from the heightening Alleghenies of Pennsylvania!

30   Let freedom ring from the snow-capped Rockies of Colorado!

31   Let freedom ring from the curvaceous slopes of California!

32   But not only that.

33   Let freedom ring from Stone Mountain of Georgia!

34   Let freedom ring from Lookout Mountain of Tennessee!

35   Let freedom ring from every hill and molehill of Mississippi! From *every* mountainside, let freedom ring!

36   And when we allow freedom to ring, when we let it ring from every village and hamlet, from every state and city, we will be able to speed up that day when all of God's children—black men and white men, Jews and Gentiles, Catholics and Protestants—will be able to join hands and to sing in the words of the old Negro spiritual, "Free at last! Free at last! Thank God Almighty, we are free at last!"

Questions About Meaning

1. King says in paragraph 2 that the Negro in America, one hundred years after Lincoln's Emancipation Proclamation, still was not free. What are the types of bondage he mentions?
2. To what rights does King appeal in paragraph 4?
3. What warning does King deliver to his own people in paragraph 11? What does he mean by "creative protest"?
4. What does King say (in paragraph 15) that it will take to satisfy the Negro?
5. In paragraph 16, King speaks of "creative suffering" and says that "unearned suffering is redemptive." What does he mean?

6. What does King say (paragraph 18) is the relationship of the Negro's dream to the American dream?
7. What *is* King's dream?

Matters of Technique

1. The first few words of King's speech echo another famous speech. Which one? Given the subject and the setting, why is this an effective technique?
2. Dr. King's appeal to the emotions comes partly through his use of figures of speech. Identify those in paragraphs 2, 4, 5, and 6.
3. What are the two major rhetorical devices that begin with paragraph 19?
4. What repetitive structures are used in paragraphs 24 to 26, and 27 to 36?

Vocabulary

1. momentous (1)
2. languished (3)
3. unalienable (4)
4. hallowed (7)
5. inextricably (12)
6. tribulation (16)
7. redemptive (16)
8. interposition (22)
9. nullification (22)

Suggestions for Writing

1. Write a highly emotional political speech about freedom of speech or freedom of religion. Study the various rhetorical devices in King's speech (repetition, rhythm, slanted diction, emotional figures of speech) and use them in your speech.
2. Analyze, in an essay, the rhetorical devices in King's speech.
3. Write an essay in which you do these things: State your own version of "the American Dream," make an attempt to persuade your audience of its validity, and describe the means of fulfilling this dream.

Cross-References

How does King's concept of humanity compare with Faulkner's? With Lincoln's? With C. S. Lewis's?

Second Inaugural Address

Abraham Lincoln

The London Times *called Lincoln's "Second Inaugural Address" the "most sublime state paper of the century." It was delivered by Lincoln on March 4, 1865. Two months later it was read again, this time over Lincoln's grave.*

---

1   FELLOW-COUNTRYMEN: At this second appearing to take the oath of the Presidential office there is less occasion for an extended address than there was at the first. Then a statement somewhat in detail of a course to be pursued seemed fitting and proper. Now, at the expiration of four years, during which public declarations have been constantly called forth on every point and phase of the great contest which still absorbs the attention and engrosses the energies of the nation, little that is new could be presented. The progress of our arms, upon which all else chiefly depends, is as well known to the public as to myself, and it is, I trust, reasonably satisfactory and encouraging to all. With high hope for the future, no prediction in regard to it is ventured.

2   On the occasion corresponding to this four years ago all thoughts were anxiously directed to an impending civil war. All dreaded it, all sought to avert it. While the inaugural address was being delivered from this place, devoted altogether to *saving* the Union without war, insurgent agents were in the city seeking to *destroy* it without war— seeking to dissolve the Union and divide effects by negotiation. Both parties deprecated war, but one of them would *make* war rather than let the nation survive, and the other would *accept* war rather than let it perish, and the war came.

3   One-eighth of the whole population were colored slaves, not distributed generally over the Union, but localized in the southern part of it. These slaves constituted a peculiar and powerful interest. All knew that this interest was somehow the cause of the war. To strengthen, perpetuate, and extend this interest was the object for which the insurgents would rend the Union even by war, while the Government claimed no right to do more than to restrict the territorial enlargement of it. Neither party expected for the war the magnitude

or the duration which it has already attained. Neither anticipated that the *cause* of the conflict might cease with or even before the conflict itself should cease. Each looked for an easier triumph, and a result less fundamental and astounding. Both read the same Bible and pray to the same God, and each invokes His aid against the other. It may seem strange that any men should dare to ask a just God's assistance in wringing their bread from the sweat of other men's faces, but let us judge not, that we be not judged. The prayers of both could not be answered. That of neither has been answered fully. The Almighty has His own purposes. "Woe unto the world because of offenses; for it must needs be that offenses come, but woe to that man by whom the offense cometh." If we shall suppose that American slavery is one of those offenses which, in the providence of God, must needs come, but which, having continued through His appointed time, He now wills to remove, and that He gives to both North and South this terrible war as the woe due to those by whom the offense came, shall we discern therein any departure from those divine attributes which the believers in a living God always ascribe to Him? Fondly do we hope, fervently do we pray, that this mighty scourge of war may speedily pass away. Yet, if God wills that it continue until all the wealth piled by the bondsman's two hundred and fifty years of unrequited toil shall be sunk, and until every drop of blood drawn with the lash shall be paid by another drawn with the sword, as was said three thousand years ago, so still it must be said "the judgments of the Lord are true and righteous altogether."

With malice toward none, with charity for all, with firmness in the 4 right as God gives us to see the right, let us strive on to finish the work we are in, to bind up the nation's wounds, to care for him who shall have borne the battle and for his widow and his orphan, to do all which may achieve and cherish a just and lasting peace among ourselves and with all nations.

Questions About Meaning

1. How does Lincoln suggest, in paragraph 3, that people cannot always avoid disaster even when they wish to? What responsibility does he leave to man?
2. What does Lincoln say (paragraph 3) was the basic cause of the Civil War? What were the issues?
3. What is the thesis of the address?
4. What duty, and what mood, does Lincoln outline in his final paragraph?

Matters of Technique

1. The biblical quotation which Lincoln uses midway in paragraph 3 seems particularly appropriate for the historical setting and the content of Lincoln's speech. Why?
2. Read carefully and then paraphrase the complicated sentence that concludes paragraph 3.
3. Write a sentence of your own modeled on the structure of the final sentence of the address. Why would this sentence's structure be effective for oral delivery?

Vocabulary

1. deprecated (2)
2. insurgents (3)
3. rend (3)
4. discern (3)

5. scourge (3)
6. unrequited (3)
7. malice (4)

Suggestions for Writing

1. Your college is returning to separate dorms for male and female students (or is going to coed dorms). Write an impassioned speech in which you try to persuade your listeners to keep the coed dorm system (or to keep the separate dorms). You may find it useful to use figures of speech, rhythm, a quotation, and other rhetorical elements in your speech.
2. Write a speech on a political topic of your choice. Use one of the rhetorical flourishes that Lincoln uses in his "Second Inaugural Address" (short sentences for emphasis, parallelism, rhythm, quotation).
3. Suppose you are Jefferson Davis or Robert E. Lee and you must try to present a speech to the people of the South in April 1865, to lift up their hearts from despair and give them courage to go on. Your audience has endured terrible suffering and has made terrible sacrifices only to lose the war. Write a speech no longer than Lincoln's in which you try to give them hope.
4. Do the same thing as outlined in question 3, but consider as your audience the people of Japan (or Germany) after their surrender to the Allies in 1945. Imagine yourself a surviving Japanese or German leader (political or religious).
5. Analyze the rhetorical techniques in an emotion-laden speech or essay.

The Right to Arms

Edward Abbey

Edward Abbey has spent his life writing about the West in novels such as Fire on the Mountain *(1962) and* Good News *(1980), and in collections of essays such as* Desert Solitaire *(1968) and* Abbey's Road *(1979). He seems to dislike developers as much as he dislikes gun control advocates. In his comic novel* The Monkey Wrench Gang *(1975), a gang of ecologists go around destroying bulldozers in preparation for blowing up Glen Canyon Dam.*

If guns are outlawed
Only outlaws will have guns.
(True? False? Maybe?)

Meaning weapons. The right to own, keep, and bear arms. A sword 1
and a lance, or a bow and a quiverful of arrows. A crossbow and darts.
Or in our time, a rifle and a handgun and a cache of ammunition.
Firearms.

In medieval England a peasant caught with a sword in his posses- 2
sion would be strung up on a gibbet and left there for the crows.
Swords were for gentlemen only. *(Gentlemen!)* Only members of the
ruling class were entitled to own and bear weapons. For obvious reasons. Even bows and arrows were outlawed—see Robin Hood. When
the peasants attempted to rebel, as they did in England and Germany
and other European countries from time to time, they had to fight with
sickles, bog hoes, clubs—no match for the sword-wielding armored
cavalry of the nobility.

In Nazi Germany the possession of firearms by a private citizen of 3
the Third Reich was considered a crime against the state; the statutory
penalty was death—by hanging. Or beheading. In the Soviet Union,
as in Czarist Russia, the manufacture, distribution, and ownership of
firearms have always been monopolies of the state, strictly controlled
and supervised. Any unauthorized citizen found with guns in his
home by the OGPU or the KGB is automatically suspected of subver-

sive intentions and subject to severe penalties. Except for the land-owning aristocracy, who alone among the population were allowed the privilege of owning firearms, for only they were privileged to hunt, the ownership of weapons never did become a widespread tradition in Russia. And Russia has always been an autocracy—or at best, as today, an oligarchy.

4   In Uganda, Brazil, Iran, Paraguay, South Africa—wherever a few rule many—the possession of weapons is restricted to the ruling class and to their supporting apparatus: the military, the police, the secret police. In Chile and Argentina at this very hour men and women are being tortured by the most up-to-date CIA methods in the effort to force them to reveal the location of their hidden weapons. Their guns, their rifles. Their arms. And we can be certain that the Communist masters of modern China will never pass out firearms to *their* 800 million subjects. Only in Cuba, among dictatorships, where Fidel's revolution apparently still enjoys popular support, does there seem to exist a true citizen's militia.

5   There must be a moral in all this. When I try to think of a nation that has maintained its independence over centuries, and where the citizens still retain their rights as free and independent people, not many come to mind. I think of Switzerland. Of Norway, Sweden, Denmark, Finland. The British Commonwealth. France, Italy. And of our United States.

6   When Tell shot the apple from his son's head, he reserved in hand a second arrow, it may be remembered, for the Austrian tyrant Gessler. And got him too, shortly afterward. Switzerland has been a free country since 1390. In Switzerland basic national decisions are made by initiative and referendum—direct democracy—and in some cantons by open-air meetings in which all voters participate. Every Swiss male serves a year in the Swiss Army and at the end of the year takes his government rifle home with him—where he keeps it for the rest of his life. One of my father's grandfathers came from Canton Bern.

7   There must be a meaning in this. I don't think I'm a gun fanatic. I own a couple of small-caliber weapons, but seldom take them off the wall. I gave up deer hunting fifteen years ago, when the hunters began to outnumber the deer. I am a member of the National Rifle Association, but certainly no John Bircher. I'm a liberal—and proud of it. Nevertheless, I am opposed, absolutely, to every move the state makes to restrict my right to buy, own, possess, and carry a firearm. Whether shotgun, rifle, or handgun.

8   Of course, we can agree to a few commonsense limitations. Guns should not be sold to children, to the certifiably insane, or to convicted criminals. Other than that, we must regard with extreme suspicion any effort by the government—local, state, or national—to control our

right to arms. The registration of firearms is the first step toward confiscation. The confiscation of weapons would be a major and probably fatal step into authoritarian rule—the domination of most of us by a new order of "gentlemen." By a new and harder oligarchy.

The tank, the B-52, the fighter-bomber, the state-controlled police and military are the weapons of dictatorship. The rifle is the weapon of democracy. Not for nothing was the revolver called an "equalizer." *Egalité* implies *liberté*. And always will. Let us hope our weapons are never needed—but do not forget what the common people of this nation knew when they demanded the Bill of Rights: An armed citizenry is the first defense, the best defense, and the final defense against tyranny. 9

If guns are outlawed, only the government will have guns. Only the police, the secret police, the military. The hired servants of our rulers. Only the government—and a few outlaws. I intend to be among the outlaws. 10

Questions About Meaning

1. What is the answer that Abbey expects us to give to the question that precedes his essay?
2. What is Abbey suggesting through his use of historical references in paragraphs 2 and 3? Write a topic sentence for paragraph 2.
3. In the first sentence of paragraph 5 Abbey says, "There must be a moral in all this." What is that moral?
4. What historical episode is being alluded to by the sentence, "*Egalité* implies *liberté*"?
5. What are the limitations that Abbey would place on owning a gun?

Matters of Technique

1. What rhetorical device does Abbey use in the first paragraph? Is this device an appeal to the reader's emotions? (If you're stuck, look back to "The Characteristics of Emotional Appeals" in the introduction to this chapter.) Now revise the paragraph to remove the emotional appeal. What have you lost? What have you gained?
2. Abbey opens paragraphs 5 and 7 with an admission that he doesn't know what the meaning of the previous paragraphs is. Does he know the meaning? Why does he say he doesn't?
3. In paragraph 6 the logical connection between the second and third sentences is missing. Supply it. Why do you suppose Abbey left it out?

4. Abbey has the knack of constructing sentences that sound like aphorisms, or conventional wisdom: "The registration of firearms is the first step toward confiscation," "If guns are outlawed, only the government will have guns," "The rifle is the weapon of democracy," "An armed citizenry is the first defense against tyranny." Are these appeals to reason or appeals to emotion? How effective are they?

5. Abbey is very much a part of his argument. Not only does he often use "I" (beginning with paragraph 5), but he tells us about his political persuasion (liberal), his membership in the National Rifle Association, how many guns he owns, and his determination to be an "outlaw" if guns are outlawed. What does he lose by introducing this personal, subjective tone into his argument? What does he gain?

6. With whom does Abbey associate his cause in paragraphs 2 and 3? With whom does he associate the advocates of gun control? Why does he use these associations?

7. What colored words does Abbey use in paragraph 9? (See the introduction to this chapter for a discussion of colored words.)

8. In paragraph 5 Abbey lists a number of nations that have maintained their independence over hundreds of years. This list includes the British Commonwealth, Sweden, and Denmark—all of which have stricter gun control laws than the United States. Since that is the case, why does Abbey lump the United States with these countries?

Vocabulary

1. cache (1)
2. gibbet (2)
3. subversive (3)
4. autocracy (3)

5. oligarchy (3)
6. referendum (6)
7. *egalité* (9)

Suggestions for Writing

1. Write a two-part paper. In the first part, use emotional appeals almost exclusively to persuade your fellow students to stay away from alcohol while they are in college. (Refer back to the introduction to this chapter for a discussion of such appeals.) In the second half, use an almost exclusively reasonable and controlled tone to persuade them of the same thing.

2. Write an analysis paper in which you discuss those passages in Abbey's essay that rest mainly on emotional appeals. The "Matters of Technique" section will get you started in the right direction.
3. Abbey sees an intimate connection between "the right to arms" and personal liberty. Do you think his view is a valid one? Discuss your views in detail.

The Right to Bear Arms

David Berg

David Berg, a criminal lawyer, wrote "The Right to Bear Arms" for the "My Turn" page of Newsweek. *The essay originally appeared in the December 29, 1980 issue.*

---

1   Last year there were almost five times as many murders committed in my hometown, Houston, Texas, as in Northern Ireland. There were more murders in Houston in 1979 than in England and Wales combined. Nationwide, 20,000 Americans were murdered, over half of them by handguns. These statistics do more than mirror a national disgrace. They demonstrate that we have become one of the most violent nations on the face of the earth.

2   We respond to death out of order with a brief expression of alarm, then settle back with chilling detachment. "Everything," as W. H. Auden wrote, "turns away quite leisurely from the disaster."

3   In London, reporters questioned passersby after John Lennon was shot. They consistently responded that the assassination could happen "only in America."

4   As a result of violence, our political loss is incalculable. It is too simple to say that liberalism ran out of ideas and died; it is more accurate to say its leaders were shot away from us. After the murders of John Kennedy, Robert Kennedy and Martin Luther King Jr., no voices emerged to articulate new political directions. Predictably, their deaths created a void that transcends realpolitik or, perhaps, dictates it. Those of us on the left whose political initiation came during the '60s are without our own George Will or Jack Kemp. There is not even one recognized, compelling voice central to our generation on the editorial pages of major newspapers or on the floor of the United States Congress.

5   John Lennon represented to many of us what is best about my generation now: a mature understanding about country and change and a return to the more stable values of home and, ironically in his case, love of peace.

6   His slaying was simple. His assassin's primary qualification for

owning a gun was that he was not a felon. Now Mr. Lennon's lyric genius is gone and we do nothing as a nation to prevent the next killing. We do mourn his loss. While there has been great national outrage over his killing, this by itself is unlikely to bring an end to the proliferation of handguns.

The murder and maiming of national figures is only one dimension 7 of the fearsome legacy of firearms. As an attorney, I have tried many murder cases, but the first autopsy report I ever read was my brother's. The words had a kind of haunting poesy: "Gunshot wound to the head, through and through." He had been kidnapped in Houston, driven to a neighboring county and, in a senseless act of violence, shot to death with a handgun. He was missing for six months—we did not know he was dead. Our family was distraught. Finally, he was found and the wound described by the medical examiner was demonstrated vividly in one of our local papers. A deputy sheriff held my brother's skull for a photograph that appeared in the center of the front page, above the fold.

The suffering of my family is not unique. Someone is murdered by 8 a gunshot every 48 minutes in America, about 10,000 people a year, a figure that has quadrupled since my brother's death in 1968. The agony cannot be confined to the dead: it spreads inexorably through the family to friends and acquaintances. Those of us touched personally by these grotesque statistics cannot even console ourselves, as might the families of John and Robert Kennedy and Martin Luther King, that our relatives or friends died for causes they believed in. We must live forever with an agonizing truth: that someone we loved was killed for nothing at all and with a gun that was sold like groceries.

The very man who was accused but acquitted of killing my brother 9 was convicted of another murder three years later. He is now described by local officials as the principal suspect in the handgun slaying of Federal Judge John H. Wood, Jr.

We can drastically reduce the number of murders and all other 10 crimes committed with pistols by enacting legislation that provides for a three week "cooling off" period before the purchase of any firearm. During that time, a thorough background search of the buyer should be conducted to verify not only his qualifications to purchase the gun but also his sworn purpose for owning it. The process should be cumbersome, time consuming and a deterrent to gun and rifle sales. Sen. Edward Kennedy and Congressman Peter Rodino have introduced legislation that contains some of these requirements as well as others that set a limit on the maximum number of handguns an individual can buy in any given year (three) and establish mandatory prison sentences for violations of the act. Americans increasingly favor some form of gun control, yet this bill will probably never pass.

11   The Constitution does not confer on our people an unassailable right to bear arms. The National Rifle Association does. For at least a generation that organization has bullied state and national legislators out of passing effective gun-control laws. During the years that the NRA has successfully blocked gun-control legislation and effectively fought gun-control groups, weapons have proliferated and so has death. The NRA has increased the already swollen profits of the fire-arms industry by fostering the myth that handguns are for protection, when precisely the opposite is true. Precious few lives are saved by guns; pistols these days are for murder.

12   Columnists who have eloquently eulogized men such as Allard Lowenstein, Michael Halberstam and John Lennon have uniformly despaired of stopping the killing. Even those writers who favor restrictions on the sale of guns seem resigned that such laws cannot pass. Unless gun-control legislation gains the support of conservative legislators, the writers are probably correct. Like Richard Nixon's China initiative, the drive toward sensible gun-control laws will probably have to emerge from the right. That support may be a long time coming. Nonetheless, we can begin. We can write congressmen held captive by the NRA. We can join and financially support gun-control lobbies. And we can strive as a nation for the day when owning a handgun will be seen as the act of cowardice and stupidity it actually is.

Questions About Meaning

1. What part of the political spectrum does Berg imply (in paragraph 4) that George Will and Jack Kemp belong to?
2. What recommendations does Berg favor to reduce the number of crimes committed with pistols?
3. Where, according to Berg, will the drive for gun control probably have to begin if it is to be successful?
4. What does Berg mean statistically when he says, "Americans increasingly favor gun control"?

Matters of Technique

1. What does Berg gain by opening with statistics? What does he lose?
2. How does he make his statistics interesting?
3. What is the main emotional appeal in paragraph 3?
4. What is the main emotional appeal in paragraph 5?
5. What colored words (see the introduction to this chapter) does Berg use in paragraph 5? What connotations do these words have?

6. Why does Berg mention the photograph of the skull of his brother in paragraph 7? Is this primarily a logical or an emotional ploy?
7. At what point does Berg end his argument and begin his recommendations?
8. Search out unsupported generalizations in paragraphs 3, 5, 10, 11, and 12.
9. Why do you suppose Berg is willing to identify himself as a liberal in paragraph 4? What does he gain and what does he lose by this?

Vocabulary

1. incalculable (4)
2. liberalism (4)
3. realpolitik (4)
4. proliferation (6)

5. inexorably (8)
6. deterrent (10)
7. eulogized (12)

Suggestions for Writing

1. Write an analysis of those passages in Berg's essay that rest mainly on emotional appeals.
2. Gun control is presented by its advocates as an effective means of crime control. Write an argumentative paper supporting or attacking the assumptions underlying this view. You will probably wish to do some research on the issue before writing your paper.

Cross-References

Compare and contrast Berg's and Abbey's views on the issues implicit in gun control. A hint: David Berg's highest good seems to be security; Abbey's seems to be liberty.

CHAPTER TWELVE

The American Way of Death: Pros and Cons

In 1961 *The Saturday Evening Post* published an article with the shocking title, "Can You Afford to Die?" In it Roul Tunley dissected the funeral industry, charging it with selling extravagant, costly, and "morbidly sentimental" funerals. Although there had been sporadic attacks on the funeral industry through the years, Tunley's attack was particularly annoying. Not only was it published in one of the largest-circulation magazines in the United States, but, even worse from an industry standpoint, it showed its readers how they could plan for a cheap funeral by joining a cooperative burial association.

The *Post* article drew wails of protest from cemetery owners, funeral directors, and even florists. *Casket and Sunnyside*, a funeral industry journal, tried to rally funeral directors to the defense:

> There is little doubt that funeral service today, beset by powerful adversaries, will buckle under the strain unless there is united action in a common cause by all groups of funeral directors. If not, funeral service faces the danger of retrogressing to a point which we do not care to contemplate.

If 1961 was a bad year for funeral directors, 1963 was a horror. Ruth Harmer's *The High Cost of Dying* and Jessica Mitford's *The American Way of Death*, two lively muckraking books highly critical of the funeral industry, were published that year. Mitford's sardonic wit made her book especially devastating. In addition, a highly acclaimed documentary, "The Great American Funeral," was aired on TV. To those within the funeral industry, it must have looked like a deluge.

Despite the advice of *Casket and Sunnyside*, which this time advised its readers to "Stay silent," the funeral industry struck back loudly and energetically. Virtually the entire program of the 1963 convention of the National Funeral Directors Association was given over to rebuttals of Mitford. And the trade journals filled their editorial pages with justifications of the traditional funeral, interspersed with attacks on Mitford. (One wag named his cheapest casket "The Mitford.")

In this chapter we have reprinted selections from *The American Way of Death, The High Cost of Dying*, Tunley's "Can You Afford to Die?" and an article from *Casket and Sunnyside*—as well as some later responses to the continuing debate about the traditional American funeral.

We hope we have been fair to both sides. The "cons" seem to be better writers. Their ranks are largely filled with popular journalists like Al Morgan and Jessica Mitford—writers who know how to make a subject, even when it has been long dead, come alive. Their prose is sometimes satiric and always filled with marvelous examples displayed like curiosities floating in a jar of formaldehyde.

However, if the "cons" have the writing edge, the "pros" have the edge in authority. Their ranks contain a psychiatrist, a historian, a clergyman, and a pair of anthropologists. If their prose is not as lively, it is at least always competent, and occasionally eloquent. We have also included, among the pros, a fascinating view from "inside," which showed up in a 1975 *Esquire* article titled "Five Undertakers" (which we changed to "Four Undertakers" because one of the gentlemen didn't want to attack or defend funerals; he only wanted to complain about his job. So we left him out.)

One more thing: Following the essays in this chapter is a special section consisting of a large number of writing topics combined with a short lesson on a few simple research writing skills.

The Cons

The Bier Barons

Al Morgan

Forest Lawn, the subject of Al Morgan's essay, is a particularly inviting target for satirists. As the ne plus ultra *of funeral extravagance, Forest Lawn is so successful and so unashamedly proud of its display of the symbols of death that it has served many satirists well, including Evelyn Waugh, who used Forest Lawn as the central target of his novel* The Loved One *(1948).*

"Show me the manner in which a people bury their dead and I shall measure with mathematical exactness the degree of civilization attained by these people." The gent who uttered these ringing lines was British Prime Minister Gladstone, and it is a crying shame that we will never have the benefit of his mathematical measurement of the level of civilization of a certain city in the Western portion of the United States, in the sixth decade of the Twentieth Century.

That city is Hollywood, California, justly famous as a world-wide symbol of glamor and make-believe, and now equally famous for another major industry, the packaging and peddling of that most unsalable of all commodities: death.

The mortuary business has become a whopping industry, ranking just behind the making of motion pictures and the sale of used cars. The merchants of death—the plot salesmen, the tombstone hustlers, the embalming parlor proprietors—have turned what once was a quiet, necessary service and a solemn religious rite into a streamlined, klieg-lighted multi-billion-dollar industry. The hustlers of death, who have run an embalming school diploma, six feet of dirt plus the ethics of a snake-oil salesman into a bonanza, can give your old corner undertaker cards and spades in the business of merchandising his product, a product described in unctuous tones in Hollywood radio commercials as "the one purchase we must all make."

The facts of death, to even the casual tourist, are as inescapable as the facts of life in Hollywood. Billboards on all the major highways proclaim the virtues of one or another of the mortuary establishments competing for the death buck.

"We treat every woman like our sister. Every man like our brother or son. Female attendants!"

"Funerals on credit. As little as $2.85 a week. Nothing down."

"Spend Holy Week at Forest Lawn."

"Utter-McKinley—the only funeral home in the entire world located on internationally famous Hollywood Boulevard, near Vine."

"Paste this number on your telephone. Service twenty-four hours a day. One phone call does everything."

"In time of sorrow, understanding and experience are important."

Full-page ads in newspapers announce the opening of the newest, flashiest, smartest burial ground. Searchlights poke at the sky and door prizes (imitation-leather wallets with the name, address and phone number of the mortuary stamped in gold) are distributed to the first five hundred visitors. Radio commercials, practicing the soft sell, punctuate the rock-'n'-roll recordings seventeen hours a day. Ads on the benches at bus stops along Hollywood Boulevard tell you in detail what to do "when sorrow comes." The classified phone books have pages of mortuary listings and a growing listing for "Pet Cemeteries." (This subsidiary branch of the industry has become a profitable sideline. A funeral for a run-of-the-mill pound mongrel starts at a hundred and fifty bucks but can go into the thousands if you want refinements such as copper-lined caskets, a headstone carved in the image of the loved one or a chic plot close to some canine celebrity in residence in the burial ground. One enterprising hustler, tapping the parakeet-owning population, has specialized in funeral services for this species of bird. His most popular item is a gold urn for the ashes in the shape of the dear departed feathered friend that retails for a neat $2500.) . . .

In tracing the development of this concept of soft-selling death, it is impossible to ignore the high priest of the industry, Dr. Hubert Eaton, a bespectacled man of seventy-eight who likes to be called "The Builder" but is frequently referred to, irreverently, as "The Digger," and his creation, Forest Lawn. In Dr. Eaton and Forest Lawn we have the dream, the plan and the fulfillment. He is the elder statesman of the eternity hustling dodge and his creation is the General Motors of the Memorial Parks.

Forest Lawn itself dates back to the early days of Hollywood. When Eaton, who had just gone broke operating a silver mine in Nevada, arrived on the scene, it was just another run-down cemetery. In the forty-three years he has been its guiding spirit, he has turned it into a model (or a horrible example, depending on your point of view) of its kind.

Let's take a close look at this Paradise of Burying Grounds, with its nine hundred employees, its staff of cosmeticians who are better at gilding the lily than anyone who ever turned out the cookie-cutter glamor queens at the major studios. In the process, you may get a greater insight into the revolution that has taken place in the old-fashioned, frock-coated, serious business of burying the dead. . . .

Physically, Forest Lawn is overpowering. More than eighty miles of pipes are used to water and drain its three hundred acres. There are more than 100,000 shrubs and an uncounted number of evergreens (no leaf shall fall at Forest Lawn to remind anyone of death, even in the plant world). Hidden behind the shrubbery are loudspeakers that play recorded birdcalls and music (*Indian Love Call* and *Ah, Sweet Mystery of Life* are the two top tunes on the Forest Lawn Hit Parade). There are eight miles of winding roads and twenty-eight separate buildings with 370 stained-glass windows. There are no headstones and no crosses visible. Graves are marked by flat plaques.

There are separate areas called Eventide, Babyland (shaped, in Forest Lawn's words, like a mother's heart), Lullabyland (every Christmas, small decorated trees and toys are placed on each grave), Graceland, Inspiration Slope, Slumber Point, Sweet Memories, Vesper Land and Dawn of Tomorrow. Obviously the namers of housing developments could take a couple of lessons from the Forest Lawn phrasemakers. Dr. Eaton has gone in for architectural reconstructions in a big way. The three churches within the geographic limits of his Memorial Park are not just churches, they are replicas of historical buildings. There is, for instance, a reconstruction of the church in Stoke Poges, England, where Thomas Gray wrote his famous *Elegy*. There is another that is a replica of the Wee Kirk in the Heather, and the third resembles the parish church in Rottingdean, England, where Rudyard Kipling worshiped. . . .

Forest Lawn has one section set aside for the VIP trade, the Garden of Memories, which the trade magazine *American Cemetery* describes as "a room with the lawn for a carpet and the sky for a ceiling." Owners of memorials in this area are given Golden Keys to open the bronze gates that keep the casual tourists and gawkers out. Jean Harlow is buried here in a $25,000 mortuary chamber purchased by William Powell, who was to have been her fourth husband. Miss Harlow's tomb has been closed to the public. Too many of the worshiping pilgrims came to say a prayer and wound up chipping hunks of marble off the tomb as souvenirs. The Garden of Memories also contains the mortal remains of such names as Florenz Ziegfeld, Tom Mix (his horse, Tony, is buried in an equally posh Hollywood cemetery specializing in four-footed celebrities), John Gilbert, Joe Penner, Irving Thalberg, Marie Dressler, Carole Lombard, King Gillette (the inventor of the safety razor), Theodore Dreiser, Atwater Kent, Aimee Semple McPherson and Carrie Jacobs Bond.

Lon Chaney is buried beneath an unmarked marble plaque, the ano-
nymity being explained this way: "Mr. Chaney was a rather retiring
person who valued privacy." Despite that, Forest Lawn salesmen drop
his name into a sales pitch that suggests that what's good enough for
the top stars of Hollywood is certainly good enough for your old dead
Uncle Charley. The celebrities buried in Forest Lawn also contribute
to the public acceptance of it as an institution with that elusive something Hollywood calls "class." Evelyn Waugh, who wrote a scathing
satirical novel on Forest Lawn called *The Loved One* (the press agent
who showed him around was fired on publication day) summed it up
this way: "At Forest Lawn, the body does not decay. It lives on, more
chic in death than ever before."

Available in the more classy category are such refinements as a ven-
tilating system and arrangements to have tape-recorded music played
to the Loved One for all eternity. For the shoot-the-works, you-only-
die-once crowd, the tab can crowd a million dollars, as was the case
with the Irving Thalberg Mausoleum. . . .

Dr. Hubert Eaton, the guiding spirit behind this Technicolored Val-
halla, looks at first glance like the last man in the world you would
cast for the role he has been playing so successfully. Physically, he
would not be out of place leading the pep songs at any Rotary Club
meeting in the country, or as a member of Dale Carnegie's faculty.
Beneath the benign, slightly cornball exterior is a shrewd mind, cold-
blooded determination and what one Hollywood critic described as
"the divine gall of the successful card shark." As befits a leader of
industry, he is a man of awesome influence. To wit: the Eaton home
used to be just across the geographic boundary line of Beverly Hills, a
much-sought-after address to the status seeker in Hollywood. Dr.
Eaton is now, however, legally a resident of that prestigious community without having moved a stick of furniture. A zoning change happened to take place that annexed the block he lived on and made it
part of Greater Beverly Hills. On one occasion his influence extended
as far as Europe. During a vacation trip, the Eatons turned up in Rome
to look over some local works of art with an eye toward taking a few
of them back to Forest Lawn. (The Eatons collect statuary and other
works of art the way most tourists collect match covers or picture post-
cards.) They lusted after Michelangelo's mammoth masterpieces *David*
and *Moses* displayed at St. Peter's in Chains, but they realized they
were beyond the reach of even a mortuary millionaire. They decided
to settle for replicas. Not copies. Replicas. In order to cast these, it was
necessary to move in a pack of experts to measure and survey in preparation for making the necessary molds. That meant that Rome's
famous Church of St. Peter's in Chains would have to be closed for a
day. Eaton's agents admit to spreading a little money around Rome on

cocktail parties and to making several contributions to worthy causes. Whether this was effective or not (it had always worked back home), the fact is that for the first time in history, the church was closed for a day so that the casts could be made. The *David* statue (with fig leaf added) is on display in a section of Forest Lawn called—no surprise—the Court of David. The *Moses* statue is displayed in an area called the Cathedral Corridor in the Memorial Terrace, and Dr. Eaton uses either replica as a backdrop when he poses for official press pictures. . . .

Dr. Eaton loaded Forest Lawn with more works of art than the Louvre (more, not better). His globe-trotting vacations and the art savvy of his Mills College wife fulfill the dual purpose of adding culture to his business enterprise and supplying him with still another source of revenue. Dr. and Mrs. Eaton return from Europe loaded down with works of art. They buy them in wholesale lots, by the ton. Each new acquisition is placed around the park (with a little sign that says, "This statue may be purchased as a private memorial and moved to another location in Forest Lawn"), the way merchandise is put on display in a department store. The memorial shopper has his choice of nudes, angels and pieces of sculpture glorifying motherhood, marriage, old age, togetherness, innocence, cleanliness and joy. In Madison Avenue parlance, when the Eatons put them on display they are "sustaining" memorials. When they're sold and moved to another location, they're "sponsored." . . .

If the old Hollywood, the movie capital of the world, is disappearing (and one survey trip through the idle sound stages confirms it), a new Hollywood is growing up in its place. The land that has spawned many a fantastic, cynical, cold-blooded enterprise in its gaudy history is well on its way to becoming identified to future generations as the natural habitat of commercialized, gimmicked death, what one leader of the corpse brigade aptly calls "the packaging of immortality."

Can You Afford to Die?

Roul Tunley

Before Jessica Mitford there was Roul Tunley, whose article, "Can You Afford to Die?" was published in 1961, two years before Mitford's The American Way of Death. *Tunley's article had a particularly strong impact not only because it was a well-written piece, but also because it was published in* The Saturday Evening Post, *one of the largest-circulation family magazines in the United States. No article until that time had so provoked the ire of the funeral industry.*

In the opinion of many opponents of modern funeral arrangements, the increasing emphasis on show is much more serious than the cost. Clergymen, in particular, view with alarm the proliferation of elaborate burial practices—with embalming, cosmetology or the restoration of the remains, open-casket viewing, slumber rooms, costly coffins with innerspring mattresses, concrete vaults and sealers and other expensive accouterments. The Rev. Dr. Josiah Bartlett, of Berkeley, California, a Unitarian clergyman who is dean of a school for the ministry, told me, "I find my people are in increasing rebellion against the pagan atmosphere of the modern funeral. It is not so much the cost as the morbid sentimentality of dwelling on the physical remains."

One way in which clergymen and laymen have been successful in combating soaring costs and lavish funerals has been to organize cooperative, or memorial, societies, which insist on the kind of funeral they want. Such an organization, calling itself the Bay Area Funeral Society, was started a few years ago by Doctor Bartlett and others in Berkeley, California. By bargaining collectively and signing a contract with three local morticians, the society has reduced costs as much as 70 per cent for its members. Prices for dignified funerals are fixed in advance. Surviving relatives do not have to dicker when they are too emotional to resist high-pressure salesmanship.

At present there are perhaps fifty such societies in the nation—in California, Pennsylvania, New Jersey, New York, Ohio, Illinois, Minnesota, Indiana, Washington, Wisconsin and Washington, D.C. This is a small number when compared to the country's 24,000 funeral homes, but the list is growing. In the San Francisco area, for example, the Bay Area group has tripled its membership in the last two years and now includes 5000 persons. Its success has kindled both interest and alarm among members of the funeral profession, especially since local morticians under contract to the society can offer simple but complete funerals, including redwood casket, use of a chapel and transportation to the cemetery for $150. In shopping around in the area on my own, I was unable to obtain any estimate for similar services lower than $500. . . .

Last year Charles V. Gates, an engineer in San Luis Obispo, California, found that the mere threat of using a funeral society's services toppled prices for him by 50 per cent. His experience started when he began shopping around, at the insistence of his ninety-year-old parents, for a mortician who would take care of their cremation after death. Gates found that the local crematory would not accept his parents' remains unless they were embalmed and placed in caskets. The lowest estimate was $510 for each person. This price struck the elderly couple as senseless. Since they planned to be cremated, they could see no point to either embalming or a casket.

Finally, in frustration, the son told the mortician involved that he planned to write the Bay Area Funeral Society to see if they could help him. The undertaker then said he'd be happy to donate a coffin if Mr. Gates would forget the whole thing. Later, when the society arranged to handle all details for a total of $232 each, the San Luis Obispo mortician offered to meet the competition. The son refused. When his parents die, they will be transported to the Bay Area for cremation. There is, incidentally, no California law requiring a casket when people are cremated. . . .

The Bay Area group has attracted a number of zealous cohorts, but none more dynamic than Jessica Treuhaft, a born rebel at heart, a seeker after causes and a member of the famous English family of Mitfords. . . .

When I called on her in her Oakland house one afternoon, I found her sipping tea and quietly enjoying the latest issue of *Mortuary Management*. "This is a lovely magazine," she said. "Did you know that Dorothy Parker, when she was a magazine editor, used to subscribe to it and tack up articles on her bulletin board to entertain the staff?"

I picked up one of the back copies on her coffee table. My eye fell on an advertisement for a mortuary college in Boston. Two curvaceous majorettes, with dimpled knees, were beckoning the reader to join a seminar on such courses as "Color in the Funeral Service," "Embalming Problems" and "Tax Planning for Tangible Savings."

Over the teacups, Jessica Treuhaft revealed her experiences as an ardent researcher for the society. She had telephoned or visited in widow's weeds many funeral establishments to inquire about prices. In one place, having been shown a $515 casket, she tearfully asked the owner if he had something less expensive. She was told that he did have a "flattop," if she'd care to come out to the garage to look at it. "But I assure you," he added with distaste, "that you wouldn't be caught dead in it!"

On another occasion she played the role of a hard-as-nails relative shopping for a funeral for a "sister-in-law," who, she explained, was a terminal-cancer case in the hospital. She asked for the minimum price without a casket, since the sister-in-law was to be cremated. Three morticians she visited implied that it was illegal to cremate bodies without using a coffin. To a fourth she said that she planned to pick up the sister-in-law in her station wagon and take her personally to the crematory. "Is that legal?" she asked, knowing full well that it was.

There was a long pause. Finally the funeral director spluttered. "Madame," he said, "the *average* lady has neither the inclination nor the facilities to be carting dead bodies about."

In addition to being a tireless recruiter for the society, Mrs. Treuhaft has been a writer and speaker on the subject of the American funeral and a careful reader of the professional trade journals.

By subscribing to the publication, *Successful Mortuary Operation and Service*, she got a look at the high-powered salesmanship that lies behind the sedate facade of many funeral homes. In a series of selling tips this publication gave Jessica Treuhaft a few hints on how to sell a coffin.

"Never say to a client, 'I can tell by the fine suit you're wearing that you appreciate fine things and will want a fine casket for your father,'" advises the publication. Instead, it urged that the funeral director say, "Think of the beautiful memory picture you will have of your dear father in this beautiful casket." On another page it suggested, "After quoting a price, continue talking for a moment or two. And never use the dollar sign on a price tag!" Before appearing on the famous TV debate, Mrs. Treuhaft had read *Mortuary Management* so thoroughly that she was able to disconcert the opposition by quoting from the publication to show that a lively conflict exists between clergymen and morticians on the subject of keeping down the cost of funerals. The magazine had recently published a series of suggestions from funeral directors on how to handle clergymen who tried to influence parishioners to purchase less expensive caskets.

It was suggested by one mortician that the minister be invited into the mortician's office for coffee while the family is left in the showroom to make a selection. "This works *part* of the time," he wrote.

Another contributor reported, "We have this same problem of nosy clergymen in our town, and I am convinced there is nothing that can be done about the situation. We tried."

Statistical proof that such a cleavage does exist between clergymen and morticians was indicated in a poll that Dr. Robert L. Fulton, well-known Los Angeles State College sociologist, conducted for the industry in 1959. The poll revealed that a majority of Protestant ministers and 41 per cent of Catholic priests believed "American funeral directors exploited or took advantage of a family's grief in selling funeral services."

Some of the complaints made by clergymen were that funerals were "too solemn," "too expensive" and that there was too much "pagan display" with too little of the "meaning of death." Said the late Rev. Dr. Bernard Iddings Bell, the noted Episcopal clergyman, "By a conspiracy of silence and pretense, we make our funerals as unlike funerals as possible. . . . I have even seen the faces of corpses rouged. All this is macabre, morbid, indecent."

One of the most passionate critics of morticians was the late W. W. Chambers, a Washington, D.C., funeral director. The firm that bears his name conducts more funerals in the nation's capital than does any other firm and has handled five of them in the White House.

Testifying before a congressional committee in 1948 against a proposal to license undertakers, the late Mr. Chambers said, "The business is a mighty sweet racket." He said he got into it when he was working in a livery stable and saw a "poor broken widow" being sold a seventeen-dollar casket for $250. "It had the horse business beat a mile," he declared. During his testimony, Mr. Chambers made coast-to-coast headlines by insisting he could embalm an elephant for $1.50.

The High Cost of Dying

Ruth Mulvey Harmer

Ruth Harmer's book The High Cost of Dying *unfortunately came out in 1963, the same year as the publication of Jessica Mitford's macabre and wryly satiric best-seller,* The American Way of Death. *As a result, Harmer's straightforward, well-documented attack on the funeral industry, though it preceded Mitford's book by a few months, didn't receive its fair share of attention. For the passage below, we have combined passages from two chapters, "The Economics of Necrolatry" and "Requiem for Everyone."*

Criticism of the bizarre economics and the financially destructive aspects of funerals have come from many sources since Mark Twain made a sharp protest in *Life on the Mississippi*. When a child of one of Twain's Negro acquaintances died—a man who had never earned more than four hundred dollars a year—the father was charged twenty-six dollars for a plain wooden coffin. "It would have cost less than four," Twain noted witheringly, "if it had been built to put something useful into."

In the 1920's, the literary men, welfare workers, and clergymen who had been opposed chiefly to the vulgarity and paganism of the morticians' practices began to cast a cold eye particularly on the cruel exploitation of the urban poor. One of the pioneers was Rev. Quincy L. Dowd, whose *Funeral Management and Costs: A World Survey of Burial and Cremation*, published by the University of Chicago Press in 1921, took sharp issue with the economics—or lack of economy—prevalent in United States funeral customs. Foolish and costly excesses in this country were contrasted with more restrained practices in Europe, where public provisions had long existed and where the disposal of the dead has been regarded as a necessary public service for many years. Mr. Dowd's personal observation of the staggering effects of undertaking bills on many low income families had persuaded him of the need to speak out. Social workers in increasing numbers joined the chorus of protest since they, more readily than others, had accumulated concrete evidence with which to condemn the preposterous abstractions advanced by the trade about "signs of respect" and "necessary outlets for grief."

Touched by the misery he had witnessed in the Chicago slums, Graham Taylor mourned the exploitation of settlement clients in 1930 in a book called *Pioneering on Social Frontiers.* In it, he pointed out the "pathos" of funeral customs which confer after death the only distinction that is ever accorded the recipient. And he scored the cruelty of preying upon willing victims: "The living need protection from being sacrificed for the dead by the extravagant indulgence of their grief, as well as by the exactions of custom, the pride of benefit orders, and by the wasteful if not extortionate toll laid upon the bereaved by the unscrupulous funeral trades." Frequently, he said indignantly, "nothing is left to meet the immediate needs of the widow and dependent children."

Puckle had noted the same folly among the British poor in 1926, when he pointed out that in the slums an admirable opportunity was offered—thanks to the fierce pride of the poor, their fanatical insistence on "suitable" obsequies, and the readiness of money lenders to encourage them "at a penny a week interest on the shilling"—for one to see how generously these foolish notions were catered to.

An elderly woman I know, one of the first social workers at the Grand Street Settlement House in New York, still becomes excited at the way of death among her clients of thirty and forty years ago. One of the most memorable "cases" was an Italian family of three generations trying to encompass the necessaries of life within the bounds of a fifty-dollar-a-month welfare allotment and whatever odd jobs the social worker was able to find for the father and several of the older children in the job-scarce depression years.

When the grandmother died, she was invited to the funeral. "It was incredible," my friend told me. The center of interest in the two tenement rooms the family occupied on the lower East Side was a gleaming coffin lined with satin and white velvet. Candles shed a soft glow on the corpse, neatly arranged and wearing a new dress and veil for the viewing. The affair went on for several days, with much wine and food served to seemingly everyone who had ever known her and many who had not. "But when I looked at her feet, I really got mad," the social worker remembered the scene indignantly thirty years later. "The price tag still clinging to the new black shoes she had on read '$35.' My God, can you imagine it? Wearing $35 shoes to the grave when the kids were going to school with paper in the soles of theirs."

During the jazz age the most important of the criticisms made, because it was the most objective, most comprehensive, and from a most unexpected source, was John C. Gebhart's study of funeral costs, published in 1928. That study, financed by an initial grant of $24,000, later supplemented, by the Metropolitan Life Insurance Company, was a remarkably fair and inclusive one. It was conducted under an Advisory Committee on Burial Survey made up of forty-one social workers, economists, educators, attorneys, psychiatrists, research workers, clergymen representing the three major religious groups in the country, and six undertakers. . . .

The 15,000 funeral bills he studied indicated how severely survivors were penalized, particularly in the lower income groups. A study of estate settlements in New York, Brooklyn, Chicago, and Pittsburgh revealed that the average price of funerals for estates under $1000 ate up about 62 per cent of the total, averaging between $350 and $372. Estates valued at between $1000 and $5000 showed funeral bills that ranged from $484 (averaging 15 per cent of the gross estate) in Brooklyn to $541 (23.7 per cent of the net estate) in New York County.

The most startling findings were those revealed by a study of the funeral costs of policyholders of industrial insurance. Gebhart found that the average price of the 7,871 adult funerals he considered from that source was $363. The average amount of insurance carried was $308. That left an average balance for the workingman's family to meet—with the principal wage earner gone—of $55. Average funeral prices in eleven of eighteen states were greater than the insurance carried by as much as 64 per cent of the families. Gebhart concluded his study on a gloomy note, pointing out that "as long as the public is ignorant of what funeral service and merchandise should cost and as long as manufacturers, through shortsighted policy, encourage new members to enter the undertaking business to make it possible for inefficient and superfluous ones to continue, there is little hope of lowering funeral prices to the public or correcting the flagrant abuses that now exist."

He was right, of course. The Metropolitan Life Insurance Company, which had sponsored the study, was so concerned about the findings that it ordered its agents never to reveal to undertakers how much insurance the bereaved family had. That the measure was not outstandingly successful is not surprising. Without education, survivors have been easy and willing victims. To indicate to what extent the more things change the more they are the same, a union business agent in California told a group last year that he would never again tell an undertaker the amount of insurance held by a dead worker. "I thought they were asking to find out how much they could reasonably charge," he said. "Instead, I found that they were charging up to the very last cent the family got, and then some." . . .

In our Western culture, most persons are agreed that some kind of final acknowledgement is fitting and proper. . . . And it must be conceded that a funeral can be of value; it does provide during a period of crisis a set of customs and rituals that minimize the traumatic effect of the experience and offer other members of the group an opportunity for spiritual and secular communion. Bereavement for all who genuinely feel grief is a shock that disrupts and disturbs and devastates; for some, it is such an intolerable experience that their incoherent response may be suicide or moral and emotional disintegration. Funerals can help to alleviate the pain of individuals affected by offering a series of actions that must be performed and by offering the solace that grief is shared by others. The social unit—the family, the tribe, the nation, and even, as in the case of Mrs. Roosevelt's funeral, the community of nations—gains a feeling of cohesiveness and fraternity from participating in an affecting ritual.

Unfortunately, current funeral practices do not serve those ends, but negate them. They encourage irrational responses by enhancing the feeling of unreality survivors often experience when death occurs. By forcing bereaved persons to play publicly their parts as chief mourners during the first terrible wave of grief, funerals intensify their emotional shock and dislocation. The social value has also been minimized because the undertakers, the entrepreneurs, have appropriated the members' traditional roles and usurped their functions. Even though a number of mourners may show up somberly clad for the ceremony, they have surrendered to the florist the expression of their thoughts and feelings and to the mortician the expression of their ritualistic gestures. The occasion, therefore, merely isolates and alienates them from other members of the group. Spiritually, death is the one human event that makes us most acutely conscious of the dignity and divinity of man and most completely aware of the folly of our preoccupation with getting and spending. But a theatrical production starring a theatrically made-up corpse enhances the illusion of the importance of the world and the flesh and makes the spiritual realities of the occasion as remote as any Grade B motion picture does—all at tremendous cost to the living.

A first step has already been taken by many religious leaders to simplify the funeral service and strip it of its pagan emphasis on the material: the extravagant casket, the heaps of floral offerings, the embalmed corpse decked out brighter than life with fancy garb and layers of cosmetics. Most religious groups in the country have endorsed the idea that the funeral should be conducted in a church rather than in a commercial establishment and that the spiritual implications once again be emphasized so that the occasion may, as the Psalmist wrote, "teach us to number our days, that we may apply our hearts unto wisdom." Many churches are now precluding elaborate ceremonies conducted by fraternal organizations. A considerable number have also, like the Los Angeles Episcopal diocese, made it mandatory that the casket be closed before the beginning of the service on the grounds that it is pagan, just as parading past the open casket "is an ugly survival of paganism, when the mourners danced around the funeral pyre, beating their tom-toms."

Although some religions do not adapt themselves to the practice, many churches are encouraging the substitution of memorial services for elaborate funerals. At a specified time—a week, two weeks, or a month after death has occurred—members of the family and friends meet at the church or home to commemorate the person who has died. The delay is held important since it gives the persons most deeply affected an opportunity to appreciate the gathering of friends to honor the dead at a time when they are less likely to indulge in uncontrollable emotional outbursts. At the service, whatever is appropriate in the way of homage is paid to the person as an individual. "What is important," one Unitarian minister said, "is to express something true about the person, to acknowledge death as a deep break in the experience of the living. . . . In the frank acknowledgment of the meaning of death and in identifying the person who has died, what may be achieved is a celebration of life in its full dimension."

Squandering money on flowers that cannot be enjoyed by the recipient has become so repugnant to many that it has now become common practice to urge that instead of sending floral offerings to the funeral home or cemetery a check be sent to some worthwhile organization. Opportunities to make one's death a contribution to the living are numerous, although not all are of equal value since many of the charity promoters can put the funeral entrepreneurs to shame in the matter of exploiting decent human emotions. The most satisfactory solution is for the donor to select a charity he knows and approves. Although the family of the deceased may have specified the . . . . Fund, there is nothing to prevent the mourner from sending the five or ten or fifteen or more dollars he might have spent on flowers to the principal of a nearby school, for example, to be used to help some youngster achieve his goal. Such a gift could only add to the stature of the person thus commemorated.

If funeral services were simplified and limited to relatives and closest friends, the living might be better served. Grief and anguish are not buried with the corpse, and during the long period of adjustment that inevitably follows the day of the funeral, life might be made more bearable for the survivors by having those who would normally have attended the funeral spend that amount of time with them. By restricting attendance at the funeral, the persons closest to the dead would be freed from the obligation of putting on a show designed to impress casual on-lookers. Economically as well as emotionally the saving would undoubtedly be great; many an otherwise sensible person has indulged in extravagance against his or her better judgment and at great cost to the members of the family merely to protect the memory of the dead against the accusations of neighbors whose only standard of measurement about death as life is "How much did it cost?"

Post-funeral activities may also be simplified in the interests of the living and the dead. The bomb-proof vaults and elaborate air-tight caskets with and without hospital beds are an essential blasphemy—a denial of all of our philosophical and religious beliefs. To accept that dust shall be returned to dust is to commit ourselves to what we call our deepest beliefs—an acceptance that enables us to feel, like Socrates, that "neither in life, nor after death, can any harm come to a good man."

One of the great values of the memorial societies and the funeral cooperatives is that they encourage us to think in a realistic way about the practical aspects of death. By concerning ourselves with the economics, we are led to question the worth. From there, it is not a long step to making pertinent and ultimate inquiries about the meaning of death. When we have answered them in a reasonable way, we shall have gone far toward establishing the meaning of life and toward the establishment of a satisfactory conduct of life for ourselves and the world we live in. To do that is really to have lived.

In the Hands of the Embalmer

Jessica Mitford

When Jessica Mitford was in her teens, she ran off with a nephew of Winston Churchill to fight in the Spanish Civil War. (She was brought back by relatives.) In 1951, by then living with her husband in San Francisco, she was requested by the California Un-American Activities Committee to appear before them to explain her involvement in left-wing politics. In the early 1960s she threw herself into volunteer work for the Bay Area Funeral Society, an organization designed to reduce the price of funerals. Then in 1963 her attack on the funeral industry, The American Way of Death, *was published. Clearly, Mitford enjoys a good fight. And she fights well. With a deft hand for satire and an eye for the ridiculous, Mitford is probably the funeral industry's most effective critic.*

In an era when huge television audiences watch surgical operations in the comfort of their living rooms, when, thanks to the animated cartoon, the geography of the digestive system has become familiar territory even to the nursery school set, in a land where the satisfaction of curiosity about almost all matters is a national pastime, the secrecy surrounding embalming can, surely, hardly be attributed to the inherent gruesomeness of the subject. Custom in this regard has within this century suffered a complete reversal. In the early days of American embalming, when it was performed in the home of the deceased, it was almost mandatory for some relative to stay by the embalmer's side and witness the procedure. Today, family members who might wish to be in attendance would certainly be dissuaded by the funeral director. All others, except apprentices, are excluded by law from the preparation room.

A close look at what does actually take place may explain in large measure the undertaker's intractable reticence concerning a procedure that has become his major *raison d'être*. Is it possible he fears that public information about embalming might lead patrons to wonder if they really want this service? If the funeral men are loath to discuss the subject outside the trade, the reader may, understandably, be equally loath to go on reading at this point. For those who have the stomach for it, let us part the formaldehyde curtain. . . .

The body is first laid out in the undertaker's morgue—or rather, Mr. Jones is reposing in the preparation room—to be readied to bid the world farewell.

The preparation room in any of the better funeral establishments has the tiled and sterile look of a surgery, and indeed the embalmer-restorative artist who does his chores there is beginning to adopt the term "dermasurgeon" (appropriately corrupted by some mortician-writers as "demisurgeon") to describe his calling. His equipment, consisting of scalpels, scissors, augers, forceps, clamps, needles, pumps, tubes, bowls and basins, is crudely imitative of the surgeon's, as is his technique, acquired in a nine- or twelve-month post-high-school course in an embalming school. He is supplied by an advanced chemical industry with a bewildering array of fluids, sprays, pastes, oils, powders, creams, to fix or soften tissue, shrink or distend it as needed, dry it here, restore the moisture there. There are cosmetics, waxes and paints to fill and cover features, even plaster of Paris to replace entire limbs. There are ingenious aids to prop and stabilize the cadaver: a Vari-Pose Head Rest, the Edwards Arm and Hand Positioner, the Repose Block (to support the shoulders during the embalming), and the Throop Foot Positioner, which resembles an old-fashioned stocks.

Mr. John H. Eckels, president of the Eckels College of Mortuary Science, thus describes the first part of the embalming procedure: "In the hands of a skilled practitioner, this work may be done in a comparatively short time and without mutilating the body other than by slight incision—so slight that it scarcely would cause serious inconvenience if made upon a living person. It is necessary to remove the blood, and doing this not only helps in the disinfecting, but removes the principal cause of disfigurements due to discoloration."

Another textbook discusses the all-important time element: "The earlier this is done, the better, for every hour that elapses between death and embalming will add to the problems and complications encountered. . . ." Just how soon should one get going on the embalming? The author tells us, "On the basis of such scanty information made available to this profession through its rudimentary and haphazard system of technical research, we must conclude that the best results are to be obtained if the subject is embalmed before life is completely extinct—that is, before cellular death has occurred. In the average case, this would mean within an hour after somatic death." For those who feel that there is something a little rudimentary, not to say haphazard, about this advice, a comforting thought is offered by another writer. Speaking of fears entertained in early days of premature burial, he points out, "One of the effects of embalming by chemical injection, however, has been to dispel fears of live burial." How true; once the blood is removed, chances of live burial are indeed remote.

To return to Mr. Jones, the blood is drained out through the veins and replaced by embalming fluid pumped in through the arteries. As noted in *The Principles and Practices of Embalming*, "every operator has a favorite injection and drainage point—a fact which becomes a handicap only if he fails or refuses to forsake his favorites when conditions demand it." Typical favorites are the carotid artery, femoral artery, jugular vein, subclavian vein. There are various choices of embalming fluid. If Flextone is used, it will produce a "mild, flexible rigidity. The skin retains a velvety softness, the tissues are rubbery and pliable. Ideal for women and children." It may be blended with B. and G. Products Company's Lyf-Lyk tint, which is guaranteed to reproduce "nature's own skin texture . . . the velvety appearance of living tissue." Suntone comes in three separate tints: Suntan; Special Cosmetic Tint, a pink shade "especially indicated for young female subjects"; and Regular Cosmetic Tint, moderately pink.

About three to six gallons of a dyed and perfumed solution of formaldehyde, glycerin, borax, phenol, alcohol and water is soon circulating through Mr. Jones, whose mouth has been sewn together with a "needle directed upward between the upper lip and gum and brought out through the left nostril," with the corners raised slightly "for a more pleasant expression." If he should be bucktoothed, his teeth are cleaned with Bon Ami and coated with colorless nail polish. His eyes, meanwhile, are closed with flesh-tinted eye caps and eye cement.

The next step is to have at Mr. Jones with a thing called a trocar. This is a long, hollow needle attached to a tube. It is jabbed into the abdomen, poked around the entrails and chest cavity, the contents of which are pumped out and replaced with "cavity fluid." This done, and the hole in the abdomen sewn up, Mr. Jones's face is heavily creamed (to protect the skin from burns which may be caused by leakage of the chemicals), and he is covered with a sheet and left unmolested for a while. But not for long—there is more, much more, in store for him. He has been embalmed, but not yet restored, and the best time to start the restorative work is eight to ten hours after embalming, when the tissues have become firm and dry.

The object of all this attention to the corpse, it must be remembered, is to make it presentable for viewing in an attitude of healthy repose. "Our customs require the presentation of our dead in the semblance of normality . . . unmarred by the ravages of illness, disease or mutilation," says Mr. J. Sheridan Mayer in his *Restorative Art*. This is rather a large order since few people die in the full bloom of health, unravaged by illness and unmarked by some disfigurement. The funeral industry is equal to the challenge: "In some cases the gruesome appearance of a mutilated or disease-ridden subject may be quite discouraging. The task of restoration may seem impossible and shake the confidence of the embalmer. This is the time for intestinal fortitude and determination. Once the formative work is begun and affected tissues are cleaned or removed, all doubts of success vanish. It is surprising and gratifying to discover the results which may be obtained."

The embalmer, having allowed an appropriate interval to elapse, returns to the attack, but now he brings into play the skill and equipment of sculptor and cosmetician. Is a hand missing? Casting one in plaster of Paris is a simple matter. "For replacement purposes, only a cast of the back of the hand is necessary; this is within the ability of the average operator and is quite adequate." If a lip or two, a nose or an ear should be missing, the embalmer has at hand a variety of restorative waxes with which to model replacements. Pores and skin texture are simulated by stippling with a little brush, and over this cosmetics are laid on. Head off? Decapitation cases are rather routinely handled. Ragged edges are trimmed, and head joined to torso with a series of splints, wires and sutures. It is a good idea to have a little something at the neck—a scarf or high collar—when time for viewing comes. Swollen mouth? Cut out tissue as needed from inside the lips. If too much is removed, the surface contour can easily be restored by padding with cotton. Swollen necks and cheeks are reduced by removing tissue through vertical incisions made down each side of the neck. "When the deceased is casketed, the pillow will hide the suture incisions . . . as an extra precaution against leakage, the suture may be painted with liquid sealer."

The opposite condition is more likely to present itself—that of emaciation. His hypodermic syringe now loaded with massage cream, the embalmer seeks out and fills the hollowed and sunken areas by injection. In this procedure the backs of the hands and fingers and the under-chin area should not be neglected.

Positioning the lips is a problem that recurrently challenges the ingenuity of the embalmer. Closed too tightly, they tend to give a stern, even disapproving expression. Ideally, embalmers feel, the lips should give the impression of being ever so slightly parted, the upper lip protruding slightly for a more youthful appearance. This takes some engineering, however, as the lips tend to drift apart. Lip drift can sometimes be remedied by pushing one or two straight pins through the inner margin of the lower lip and then inserting them between the two front upper teeth. If Mr. Jones happens to have no teeth, the pins can just as easily be anchored in his Armstrong Face

Former and Denture Replacer. Another method to maintain lip closure is to dislocate the lower jaw, which is then held in its new position by a wire run through holes which have been drilled through the upper and lower jaws at the midline. . . .

If Mr. Jones has died of jaundice, the embalming fluid will very likely turn him green. Does this deter the embalmer? Not if he has intestinal fortitude. Masking pastes and cosmetics are heavily laid on, burial garments and casket interiors are color-correlated with particular care, and Jones is displayed beneath rose-colored lights. Friends will say, "How *well* he looks." Death by carbon monoxide, on the other hand, can be rather a good thing from the embalmer's viewpoint: "One advantage is the fact that this type of discoloration is an exaggerated form of a natural pink coloration." This is nice because the healthy glow is already present and needs but little attention.

The patching and filling completed, Mr. Jones is now shaved, washed and dressed. Cream-based cosmetic, available in pink, flesh, suntan, brunette and blond, is applied to his hands and face, his hair is shampooed and combed (and, in the case of Mrs. Jones, set), his hands manicured. For the horny-handed son of toil special care must be taken; cream should be applied to remove ingrained grime, and the nails cleaned. "If he were not in the habit of having them manicured in life, trimming and shaping is advised for better appearance—never questioned by kin."

Jones is now ready for casketing (this is the present participle of the verb "to casket"). In this operation his right shoulder should be depressed slightly "to turn the body a bit to the right and soften the appearance of lying flat on the back." Positioning the hands is a matter of importance, and special rubber positioning blocks may be used. The hands should be cupped slightly for a more lifelike, relaxed appearance. Proper placement of the body requires a delicate sense of balance. It should lie as high as possible in the casket, yet not so high that the lid, when lowered, will hit the nose. On the other hand, we are cautioned, placing the body too low "creates the impression that the body is in a box."

Jones is next wheeled into the appointed slumber room where a few last touches may be added—his favorite pipe placed in his hand or, if he was a great reader, a book propped into position. (In the case of little Master Jones a Teddy bear may be clutched.) Here he will hold open house for a few days, visiting hours 10 A.M. to 9 P.M.

Death, Here Is Thy Sting

Deborah Wolters

In this short informal essay, originally published in The Progressive *in 1978, Deborah Wolters wryly describes the ever-expanding services of the undertaker. Like the local gas station that brags about being a full service station, Wilbert Incorporated is proud of being a "full service funeral company." All the better to serve you, my dear.*

When I was a child, my parents would take me along on their duty calls to the undertaker, where they would pay their last respects to ancient relatives, friends of relatives, and relatives of friends, who had passed on. (Often these last respects were also first respects, but, as Mother said, it was the thought that counted.)

A scant twenty years later, duty calls are all that remain of the old-fashioned, affordable funeral syntax. Today it is the cost—not the thought—that counts. And the cost of being counted is mounting.

It used to be that a body needed only one funeral service—and that directed by a clergyman. But undertakers, eschewing their Charonic image, have become impresarios, and today provide and preside over a host of professional services. Now, "professional" is always an expensive adjective. (In the funeral biz, it connotes a costly undergraduate degree in a competitive field of "mortuary science.") But the real syntactic coup has been the change from service to services. The inspired addition of a single letter has been the *sine qua non plus*—the without which nothing extra—of funerals.

Wilbert Incorporated of Forest Park, Illinois—"the full service funeral service company"—thoughtfully provides a directory to all the services you might otherwise never suspect you need:

First, there is the rental of the funeral home. Syntactical initiative in this area has brought the terminology almost full circle from the old days, when funerals actually were held in homes but people had no rental expenses because the homes were their own. Then undertakers—they were still undertakers—convinced the public that home parlors were onerous (not to mention odorous), and that a rented room specially designed for funerals—a "funeral parlor"—was required for any civilized (not to mention deodorized) send-off.

In recent years, several rooms have been added to the parlor, rooms you will—for an added price—not be permitted to do without. "The advantages made possible by the funeral home," Wilbert soothingly explains, include "spacious facilities" with "appropriate" furnishings.

Among the spacious facilities is the casket showroom, appropriately furnished with "a complete selection" of caskets—formerly called coffins—in "a wide variety of styles and features." From this selection, says Wilbert, you will make the "appropriate" choice. ("Appropriate" is another one of those expensive adjectives. It replaces the more efficient but less costly modifier "only.")

Funeral fashion dictates that shrouds are out. But Wilbert advises not to worry if the deceased owns no "suitable" (read "appropriate") clothing, for "funeral directors do offer a line of burial garments."

You will also have to select a burial vault. On Pages 31 to 37 of the Wilbert directory—called *Facts Every Family Should Know*—are illustrated displays of the Wilbert line. ("WILBERT brand burial vaults are chosen more often than any other brand.") At the top of the line is the "Triune," which features a sixteen-ounce copper inner lining, a Strentex outer lining, and a custom-crafted exterior. For a bit less, you may purchase the "SST/Triune," with an inner lining of stainless steel. The "Venetian" and "Continental" models lack inner linings, but still offer the Strentex outer lining (or a subvariation, the Marbelon) and custom-crafted exteriors. At the bottom of the line is the "Monticello," a concrete box with Strentex lining—period.

Like most professionals, your funeral director has connections. For a fee, he will place the order for flowers since, Wilbert notes, "it has become customary [read "appropriate"] to place a floral spray from the family on the casket." If you are not affiliated with a church, he can suggest a clergyman. (Members of the clergy have been relegated to the role of outside consultant in the funeral service known as "the tribute.")

Your funeral director can also obtain a flag for a veteran without charge from the Veterans Administration. (The flag is free, but the obtaining is a service, and therefore costs.) He can even arrange for burial plots.

"Possibly not until after the funeral service," Wilbert chides, "will you fully appreciate the vast amount of detail, the numerous specialized services and the tremendous responsibility the funeral director has assumed in serving your family at this time of need. . . ." To stimulate your full appreciation there will be a bill. Wilbert's catalogue discreetly omits specific dollar amounts but offers extensive advice on how to induce Social Security to share your appreciation as much as possible.

Although funerals have traditionally been go now, pay later affairs, cost accounting has come to the funeral business, and Wilbert includes a short section on pay-as-you-go and prepaid options. (The ancient Greeks also had a prepaid option: The dead were buried with coins on their tongues to bribe Charon into ferrying them across the river Styx. Mythic images are not always easy—or profitable—to eschew.) . . .

The Wilbert directory has received the Good Housekeeping Seal of Approval.

The Pros

De Mortuis

J. H. Plumb

"De Mortuis" originally appeared in Horizon *in 1967. In it J. H. Plumb argues that the traditional funeral has a long line of historical antecedents. Plumb further suggests that something deep in the human psyche—the urge to "obliterate death by extending life"—is the unconscious and entirely honorable motive behind the traditional funeral service.*

The British have hilarious fun over the quaint funerary habits of the Americans. The death of Hubert Eaton, the world's greatest entrepreneur of death, and the recent discovery of a funeral home for pets, by a wandering British journalist, released another gale of satirical laughter in the English press. The mockery was hearty and sustained; yet was it deserved? Well, certainly much of Mr. Eaton's Forest Lawn is hard to take—the wet, nursery language for the hard facts of dying ("the loved one" for the corpse, "leave taking" for burying, and "slumber" for death), the cosmetic treatment (the contortions of death waxed away, replaced by rouge and mascara and fashionably set hair)—all of this is good for a gruesome joke. The place names of Forest Lawn appall—Lullabyland, Babyland. The piped guff, the music that flows like oil, and the coy fig-leaved art give one goose flesh.

One turns, almost with relief, to a harsh fifteenth-century representation of the dance of death—livid corpses, jangling bones, and skulls that haunt. How wholesome, after Hubert Eaton, seem the savage depictions by Bonfigli of the ravages of plague, or even the nightmares of death painted by Hieronymus Bosch. And how salutary in our own age to turn from Forest Lawn to the screaming, dissolving bodies of a Francis Bacon painting, for surely this is how life ends for most of us, in pain, in agony.

And if Forest Lawn nauseates, what of the Pets Parlor? "Blackie" combed and brushed, stretched out on the hearth rug before a log fire, waits for his sorrowing owners. The budgerigar is wired to its perch. The Ming Room houses the Siamese cats, and if you want to do your kitty proud, you can spend three hundred dollars or so on a stately laying out, a goodly coffin (if you're worried about its fun in the afterlife, you can put an outsize rubber mouse in with it), and naturally a special plot in Bide-A-Wee, the memorial park for pets. Vice-President Nixon's dog, Checkers, had the treatment: he lies among the immortals in Bide-A-Wee, like Hubert in Forest Lawn.

However, this will become a mere second-class death if deep-freezing really catches on, as it shows every sign of doing. The Life Extension Society is spreading, and the entrepreneurs have smelled the profit in immortality. As soon as the breath goes, get yourself encapsulated in liquid nitrogen and stored in one of the specially constructed freezers that are springing up all over America from Phoenix to New York. And so wait for the day when they can cure what you died of, or replace what gave way—the heart, the brain, the liver, or the guts—or rejuvenate your cells.

None of this is cheap: the capsule costs four thousand dollars, and then there are the freezing costs and who knows what they may be in fifty years, so it would be imprudent not to make ample provision. Forest Lawn may be death for the rich; this is death for the richer, death for the Big Time. But in America there are a lot of very rich, so maybe soon now, outside all the large cities, there will be refrigerators as huge as pyramids, full of the frozen dead. This surely must be a growth industry.

Perhaps by the year 2000 Hubert Eaton will seem but a modest pioneer of the death industry, for who does not crave to escape oblivion? The rich have always tried to domesticate death, to make death seem like life. The American way of death is not novel: seen in proper historical perspective it reaches back not only down the centuries but down the millenniums, for it is a response to a deep human need.

Some of the earliest graves of men, dating from paleolithic times, contained corpses decked out with bits of personal finery and sprinkled with red ocher, perhaps the symbol of blood and life, done in the hope of a future resurrection. After the neolithic revolution, which created much greater resources and considerable surplus wealth, men went in for death in a very big way. Doubtless the poor were thrown away, burned or exposed or pushed into obscurity, back to the anonymous mind from which they came.

The rich and the powerful, high priests and kings, could not die; they merely passed from one life to another. Because the life hereafter was but a mirror image of life on earth, they took with them everything they needed—jewels, furniture, food, and, of course, servants. In the Royal Graves at Ur, some of the earliest and most sumptuous of tombs ever found, a row of handmaidens had been slaughtered at the burial—death's necessities were life's. No one, of course, carried this elaboration of funerary activity further than the Egyptians. And the tombs of Pharaohs and the high officials of the Egyptian kingdom make Forest Lawn seem like a cheap cemetery for the nation's down-and-outs.

What should we think of vast stone mausoleums outside Washington, stuffed with personal jewelry from Winston's, furniture from Sloane's, glassware by Steuben, food from Le Pavillon, etc., etc., and in the midst of it all the embalmed corpse of a Coolidge or a Dulles? We should roar with laughter. We should regard it as vulgar, ridiculous, absurd. Pushed back three millenniums, such habits acquire not only decorum but also majesty, grandeur, awe.

The Egyptians were as portentous in death as in life, and their grave goods only occasionally give off the breath of life, unlike the Etruscans, who domesticated death more completely and more joyously than any other society. A rich caste of princes built tombs of singular magnificence, filling them with amphorae, jewels, and silver. And they adorned their walls with all the gaiety that they had enjoyed alive. There was nothing solemn about their attitude to death. In their tombs they hunted, played games, performed acrobatics, danced, feasted; their amorous dalliance was both wanton and guiltless. Deliberately they banished death with the recollected gusto of life. No society has brought such eroticism, such open and natural behavior, to the charnel house. But in the annals of death, Etruscans are rare birds.

How different the grandiose tombs of medieval barons, with their splendid alabaster or marble effigies. There they lie, larger than life, grave, portentous, frozen in death, a wife, sometimes two, rigidly posed beside them, and beneath, sorrowing children, kneeling in filial piety, the whole structure made more pompous with heraldic quarterings. Yet these are but another attempt to cheat death, to keep alive in stone what was decaying and crumbling below. And even here a breath of life sometimes creeps in. The Earl and Countess of Arundel lie side by side, dogs beneath the feet, pillows under the head, he in armor, she in her long woolen gown. But, movingly enough, they are holding hands. The sons of Lord Teynham cannot be parted, even in death, with their hawk and hound. Nor were these tombs so cold, so marmoreal, when they were first built. They were painted, the faces as alive with color as the corpses in the parlors of Forest Lawn.

Seen in the context of history, Forest Lawn is neither very vulgar nor very remarkable, and the refrigerators at Phoenix are no more surprising than a pyramid in Palenque or Cairo. If life has been good, we, like the rich Etruscans, want it to go on and on and on, or at the very least to be remembered. Only a few civilizations have evaded expensive funerary habits for their illustrious rich, and these usually poverty-stricken ones. For all their austerity, the Hindus, burning bodies and throwing the ashes into the Ganges, have maintained distinction in their pyres. Not only were widows coaxed or thrown onto the flames, but rare and perfumed woods were burned to sweeten the spirit of the rich Brahman as it escaped from its corrupt carapace. Cremation à la Chanel!

What is tasteless and vulgar in one age becomes tender and moving in another. What should we say if we decorated our tombs with scenes from baseball games, cocktail bars, and the circus, or boasted on the side of our coffins of our amatory prowess, as erect and as unashamed in death as in life. And yet when the Etruscans do just these things, we are moved to a sense of delight that the force of life could be so strong that men and women reveled in it in their graves.

So the next time you stroll through Forest Lawn, mildly repelled by its silly sentimentality, think of those Etruscans; you will understand far more easily why seven thousand marriages a year take place in this California graveyard. After all, like those Arundels, Eros and Death have gone hand in hand down the ages. The urge to obliterate death is the urge to extend life, and what more natural than that the rich should expect renewal. How right, how proper, that Checkers should be waiting in Slumberland.

Funerals Are Good for People

William M. Lamers, Jr.

William Lamers, Jr., a psychiatrist from California, argues, largely through illustration, that the quick disposal of the corpse that is favored by memorial societies is not good for the mourners from a psychological standpoint. According to Lamers, the mourners need to confront the reality of death; it is through this confrontation that they are able to release their grief. "Funerals Are Good for People" was originally published in Medical Economics *in 1969.*

While attending a medical meeting about a year ago, I ran into a fellow I'd known in residency. "What are you doing here, Bill?" he asked. "Giving a talk on the responses to death," I replied. "It will cover the psychological value of funerals as well as—"

"Funerals!" he exclaimed. "What a waste *they* are! I've made it plain to my wife that *I* don't want a funeral. Why spend all that money on such a macabre ordeal? And why have the kids standing around wondering what it's all about?"

"Look, Jim," I said patiently, "I've seen case after case of depression caused by the inability of patients—young and old—to work through their feelings after a death. I've found that people are often better off it they have a funeral to focus their feelings on. That lets them do the emotional work necessary in response to the loss." My friend still looked doubtful. And, as we parted company, I wondered how many other physicians are also overlooking the psychological value of funerals.

Their value is brought home time and time again in my own practice. Consider the woman who called me recently after making a suicide attempt. She was a divorcée and the mother of three sons, the youngest of whom had died of encephalitis about two months before. She was very much attached to her sons and highly dependent on them emotionally. The youngest had been her pet, and her grief at his loss was overwhelming.

Well-meaning friends persuaded the woman to have an immediate cremation and memorial service rather than go through the pain of a funeral. As a result, within a few hours after the boy's death, his body was cremated. Two weeks later a memorial service was held. The mother went around smiling to show people how well she'd adjusted to the boy's death. There was a small rock 'n' roll band and several poetry recitations. It was very pleasant and happy and likely provided some beautiful memories. Yet it was all only frosting on an under-baked cake.

Within a few weeks the mother became extremely depressed. She was afraid to express her true feelings from fear of offending the friends who had planned the memorial service. She didn't want them to feel it wasn't good enough, and she tried to cover up her tremendous unresolved grief. All that was a prelude to her suicide attempt. This woman still had doubts that her son was dead. I'm convinced that, had she gone through a formalized funeral experience and been allowed to vent her grief, her son's death would have held some finality for her. And her feelings wouldn't have healed superficially while the core still continued to fester.

I see constant evidence that the problems resulting from a serious separation—through death, divorce, or other means—can have great psychological impact. If these problems remain unresolved, grave emotional trouble can result later. That's what happened to a patient I saw several years ago. She'd been married and divorced four times, each time to men at least 20 years older than she. And all were men who were gone from home most of the time—sea captains, traveling men, and the like.

She began to develop ulcers, high blood pressure, and had made several suicide attempts. When referred to me, she was about to divorce her fifth husband and marry a sixth. Apparently she also went through psychiatrists as fast as husbands: I was the fourth she'd seen. In consultation she told me she couldn't remember anything before the age of 10. Two or three sessions with her brought no results. Finally, trying to get at her early childhood through the back door, I said, "Tell me about your mother and father." She told me she'd been brought up in Europe and that her father had died in the early days of World War II.

Slowly, more of the story came out. One day, her father came back from the mountains—he was a guerrilla leader—to a triumphant reception in the village. Apparently he was also under strong suspicion of collaborating with the Germans. He'd been home less than an hour when some of his soldiers came and, on a ruse, took him away. Minutes later, my patient painfully recalled, she and her mother were summoned to the village square. There, with no explanation from the villagers, her father was shot before her eyes.

In that village it was the custom for villagers to file through the home to view the body and express condolences. Then there would be a funeral service, a procession, and a gathering afterwards. In this instance, however, my patient and her mother were carted away to another town. No one knows what happened to the father's body, but there was no funeral. Possibly as a direct result, my patient had never been able to accept emotionally the fact of her father's death.

In my office she finally wept. The extent of her reaction indicated that at last she was beginning to express the feelings that might have been more properly handled about 20 years earlier. From then on, she was gradually able to understand that, in marrying older men who were away most of the time, she'd been searching for her father. Today, she's settled down considerably. But I can't help believing that a funeral, with its acknowledgement of death, would have contributed to her emotional well-being years earlier.

When a death occurs, most people feel a need to *do* something. And the doing can come out in several ways—in crying, in the funeral and burial, perhaps in informing others that the death has occurred, perhaps in assuring themselves that what was seen and heard was, in fact, a true happening. The funeral makes these things easier by providing the setting in which people can begin to resolve their feelings about death.

Children, of course, are especially vulnerable to the suffering that results from unresolved grief situations. So we do them a tremendous injustice when we don't let them know the facts or we lie—describing "the trip" Grandfather has gone on, for example. We need to answer their questions about death in a straightforward manner and give them the opportunity to talk about death and to express their feelings toward it. Many parents don't seem to understand this. They're not doing their children a favor by sheltering them.

A case in point is that of a 7-year-old girl whose mother brought her to me shortly after the death of the father. The little girl had become despondent, and her mother couldn't understand why. As the mother explained it, she'd done everything to protect her daughter's feelings. She'd kept almost all knowledge of the death from the child and hadn't allowed her to participate in the services or the burial.

Their first visit to me occurred about a week before President John F. Kennedy's assassination. Shortly after the assassination, the mother called to tell me her daughter had run away. Desperately, she asked me what to do, but I couldn't be of much help.

A few days later the girl returned home. She'd been at a friend's house where for the entire weekend she'd watched the Kennedy funeral on TV—a steady, continuous ritual of mourning. When the little girl came home, she told her mother: "Everything's O.K. now. I know what happened to Daddy."

Are there any satisfactory funeral substitutes—a memorial service, for example? In my opinion, there aren't. Though a memorial service is a response to loss and can be extremely satisfying for many, it's not ideal because it lacks several basic elements. First, a memorial service usually doesn't take place when feelings are most intense, which is shortly after the death. Second, members of the family aren't involved in communication, participation, and repeated exposure to the fact that death has occurred. These things force people to acknowledge the reality of loss. Finally, a memorial service doesn't include the presence of the body, which means people aren't given as great an opportunity to fix the fact of death in their minds.

In contrast to the memorial service, which is a one-time gathering, the traditional funeral as we know it in this country is a continuum of things. It includes visitations at the funeral home, usually with the remains lying in state. Frequently, there are religious services there as well as in the church, a procession to the place of burial, and committal service. Afterward, there's often a gathering of close friends and relatives. Throughout these events there's a repeated acceptance of condolences, acknowledgement of the fact of death, sharing of grief feelings, and encouragement for the future.

Since I'm so profuneral, you may wonder how I feel about those attacks on the funeral profession in recent years. Let me make it plain that I don't own a funeral home. Some funeral directors *are* guilty of abuse and of taking advantage of the public. I contend, however, that they're in the minority and that criticism of the funeral business has been blown out of proportion. In time of need, the majority of the directors provide an effective means of helping families through a lot of turmoil.

What can we, as physicians, do to steer families of dying patients in the right direction? Naturally, we can't actively impose our beliefs on others. In other words, it's unwise to steer a family toward a particular kind of funeral or service. If they prefer to have a memorial service held, then this may well be the most satisfactory for them.

On the other hand, a family that's avoiding the reality of death, trying to seal it over without allowing normal emotional responses to come to the surface, may need guidance. In that case, we doctors have an obligation to point out the possible consequences and to make ourselves available to discuss the situation. We do patients a disservice when we oversedate or overtranquilize them so that they're unaware of what's happening or unable to experience normal feelings of grief.

In short, we should encourage the practice of something as psychologically economical as funerals. They do a therapeutic job, and in most cases they can do it for a lot less money than we psychiatrists could.

The Reality of Death: What Happens When It Is Ignored?

Ralph A. Head

One of Ralph Head's arguments for the traditional funeral is unique among its supporters in this chapter. Essentially his argument is this: Only the traditional funeral treats man as a "total being" by displaying the corpse. The memorial service, Head says, lacks the presence of the corpse and thus denies the Christian concept of the dual nature of man—spirit and flesh.

Head's article originally appeared in Casket & Sunnyside, *a funeral trade publication, in 1971.*

... In 1959 a college professor, Leroy Bowman, published the first modern critique on "The American Funeral," further described as a "Study in Guilt, Extravagance, and Sublimity," motivated by his experience as a student working parttime at a mortuary. Like his contemporaries who would follow, Bowman presented the value of speedy disposition of the body as emphasizing the reality of the loss and the acceptance of that separation. Today we have every reason to deny this assumption with mounting evidence that immediate disposal of the body actually represents an escape mechanism, a means for evading reality and avoiding the pain of loss.

In 1963 Jessica Mitford made little pretext at presenting a social scientific study, but relied heavily on satire to attract public readership. In this respect she was quite successful. Mrs. Mitford levied her attack both at the funeral industry and at the funeral itself and offered the conclusion that the best way to eliminate the latter was to exterminate the former. Almost completely absent from Mrs. Mitford's analysis was the possibility that the funeral could be a religious service. She refused to recognize the humanitarian possibility that the funeral might be a way of relieving family suffering.

In the same year, Ruth Harmer, an instructor at California Polytechnic College, published a more moderate yet critical study of funeral service titled, *The High Cost of Dying*. Unlike Mrs. Mitford, Mrs. Harmer was willing to recognize that there was a connection between the funeral and the culture, but in a totally negative sense.

She wrote, "The American funeral with its vulgarity, sacrifice of human values to materialistic trappings, immature indulgence in primitive spectacles, unethical business practices, and overwhelming abnegation of rational attitudes, has become for many students of the national scene a symbol of cultural sickness."

Not only were these books widely read, but they were followed by innumerable magazine and newspaper articles and reports, many taking basically the same position. Altogether and almost in concert they narrowed their focus on the economic aspects of the funeral, and while this limited profile destroyed practically all of their objectivity, many of the public were more than willing to assign funerals to that category entitled "The High Cost of Everything."

It must be admitted that there is always validity for concern about the cost of dying just as there is today about the cost of medical care, the cost of housing, transportation, foods, and government, but if the other values of the funeral . . . values of a social nature, psychological nature, and religious nature are not considered . . . then the studies are just as materialistic as the critics claim the modern funeral itself to be. . . .

How, then, should we evaluate a funeral service, and what should a funeral accomplish?

It should provide a means by which the family knows of the willingness of the community to share its loss. There should be every opportunity for the group to symbolize its respect for the memory of the deceased through the sending and displaying of flowers.

The funeral should express an understanding of the social, fraternal and religious relationships of the living to the deceased.

The funeral must assist the family in the recognition of the reality of death.

The funeral should offer an opportunity of expression of feelings by the bereaved.

The funeral should enable the family to have access to all religious sources for understanding loss and suffering.

The funeral should develop a perspective for the meaning of life and death in light of the contingency created by death.

The funeral should assist the family and the community to comprehend the nature of man and his relationship to God.

The valuation of a funeral by these standards sharpens the contrast with what is currently termed the memorial service. The advocates of the immediate disposition of the body and the memorial service in place of the funeral contend that the absence of the body emphasizes the spiritual rather than the material. They further contend that the memorial service is less emotional than the funeral. Because the body is not present, the service may proceed on an intellectual basis rather than on an emotional level. Advocates of the memorial service contend that the absence of the body makes it easier to avoid the severity of death. The fundamental argument in favor of the memorial service is economy, but the end result is that the appeal of saving money becomes the major factor favoring immediate disposition with the result that the memorial service with all its supposed benefits seldom takes place.

The belief in the resurrection of the body has been a part of the Christian understanding of life and death and life after death from the beginning of the Church nearly 2,000 years ago. The biblical view of total embodiment relates to life and death and new life after death as part of the whole man. What we call a man's body is no less a part of him than is his spirit.

The memorial service preceded by disposition of the body immediately after death prevents the presentation of man as a total being, because a portion of the person has been voluntarily removed and isolated. The funeral represents man as a whole affirming him in the Christian concept both as flesh and spirit.

The memorial service and disposition procedure restrains and may even prevent the release of the feelings and emotional sensibilities which constitutes one of the values of the funeral. The funeral may direct sensitivity into patterns of release that help to share a common loss. The funeral stimulates a recollection and memory of the deceased and what he contributed to the community. The funeral presents realistically the separation which death brings. The memorial service inhibits the feelings of the family, the friends, and the community.

Closely akin to the memorial service is the private funeral, advocated by those who contend that mourning is a private matter and not subject to public display.

To the contrary, a funeral should be a group sharing of the sorrows of its members and in such a form that provides the widest possible social participation. There should be developed a strong sense of involvement in the death experience, so that those who attend not *only* observe but actually participate in the ceremony. Out of this evolves a true group experience.

The memorial service and the private service discourage if not deny the display of flowers, yet flowers provide a method by which persons who cannot attend the funeral may be symbolically represented. For those who can and do attend the funeral, the presence of flowers is further evidence of participation.

Beyond the funeral is the decision on the disposition of the body.

Archaeological studies indicate that earth burial is the oldest method of disposition. There are several symbolic meanings in this. In one connotation, burial is a natural unity with the familiar "earth to earth, ashes to ashes, and dust to dust." Burial provides a locality, an ambit, a point of reference for remembering the one who lived and then died. The site of burial can be revisited as a provocation for reviewing memories of the deceased and reminiscing on relationships with him. There are values and purposes for burial as there are for funeral: the committal and the burial comprise the natural denouement for the funeral. It represents the finale of the ritual and the emblematic conclusion of natural life. It denotes that the last act has been performed, the curtain has fallen, and the separation has been accomplished.

Whether final disposition is by burial, by entombment, or by cremation is not of substantial importance if the decision is made in the proper perspective. What is important is the acceptance of the reality of death. Burial is wrong if based on a belief the body is symbolically preserved for eternity and that there still exists some form of personification. Cremation is wrong if it is used to escape the absolutism of death.

The combination of the temporary presence of the body and the final disposition is an effective means for both recalling the significance of the body as a representation of the total whole man in body and spirit and for recognizing that relationships as they did exist are now terminated.

The funeral must make it clear that disposing of the body is not tantamount to abandoning or discarding it as we would an empty shell or box.

The body is the extension of the person who died. If we proclaim the eminence of a person, we cannot disdain any aspect of that person.

This then is one value of the funeral: an affirmation and an awareness that death has taken place, a willingness of family and community to accept the pain of mourning, and the acknowledgement that the relationship with the deceased has ended. . . .

Four Undertakers

Dotson Rader

Naturally, justification for the traditional funeral service from inside the industry is not impartial testimony. But it is necessary testimony for any well-rounded portrait of the funeral industry. What is immediately apparent from the following comments by undertakers is that they are proud of their work and eager to give people, as Vincent Pucherelli says, a "better impression of death."

Paul Norwood, Norwood-Welch Funeral Home, Broken Bow, Oklahoma.

"Cosmetics and reconstruction of a face is what I'm proudest of. 'Cosmetology' is what we call it. Many bodies we have to reconstruct maybe the eyes, the nose, the mouth. Maybe an ear.

"I always enjoy taking someone that's maybe been in a wreck and reconstructing their face so the family can come in and say, 'My, that looks just like 'em!' Gunshot wounds, car wrecks . . . I enjoy what we do after it's finished, how the body looks. I take pride in that. Oh, we've had a few cremations. We go to Dallas, Texas, for that, take the body up there, you know. I don't really care for it. I don't care for burning up the body. After you do your reconstruction and cosmetics, all that hard work, and then see all your proud work going up in flames, why, in a few minutes, destroyed!"

Marguerite Marshall Blake, M. Marshall Blake Funeral Home, New York, New York.

"Funerals are show, a show for the living.

"You get a feeling about a person when you see their body. You can visualize what they were like. As you work with it they begin to mold themselves, the expression just molds itself; you get a sense of him. And I guess that's because you love the work and have the touch.

"I always want faces to keep a nice, tight look, the beautiful, youthful appearance that's so important. In our everyday work we do extra things in filling out a face, in giving it that certain look, that the average commercial embalmer won't bother with in the restorative arts. As a painter and artist would look at a portrait, we do too. We put so much of ourselves into it, to get that little something extra. Even when I visit other funeral parlors and view the remains, I know I would have put a crease differently here or there, given the dead person a slightly different expression, tightened things up a bit. Some people are so taut, as if they hated the world when they died.

"When I die I want my funeral done elegantly. Oh, I want it done right. I will have a cement vault. A fine casket with sealer. I will be laid out in elegant clothes, because I love soft, beautiful things so much. I love jewelry, and I would want to be laid out in my jewelry."

Reverend Reuben Ruiz, Coffey-Ruiz Funeral Home, Idabel, Oklahoma.

"I am minister at the Central Assembly Church. I also direct the funeral business, dealing with people in sorrow and distress whose loved ones have gone on. I don't do the embalming myself. I carry smelling salts.

"My best-selling casket is the Batesville Moniseal. It costs an average of eleven hundred and fifty dollars. Its best points are the sealing quality, and the fact that every single one comes with a mattress and box spring. Just like your bed at home. There are cheaper caskets with just cotton-and excelsior beds in them, but I think to a lot of families this is the cheaper route and they don't want to go that way.

"Most funeral homes are drab and have no color. We're trying to make ours look more like home, so people feel welcome and at home here with a little brighter colors, because actually, to the Christian, death is a bright experience. My wife selected all the furniture and did all the interior decorating. We meet friends here. We have coffee and chat. Sometimes church groups will meet here.

"Here, in a small town, you have to handle the deceased with a lot more care. If you make an error then everyone knows about it, you see, and this is the reason we have to be a whole lot more careful in a small town."

Vincent Pucherelli, Horne-Dannecker Funeral Home, New York, New York.

"It's a nerve-racking business. People are too damn demanding. When they have a death in the family they expect you to do the impossible. They think it's a very simple matter to get a body out of a hospital. I got news for them, it isn't. They don't realize there's goddamn paper work involved, doctors to handle. The doctor may hold up a body for a couple hours. By the time we get it and prepare it, which is a big job, we can't have it on display right away. But they want it *now*, on view. I haven't the vaguest idea why. There's a lot of pressure. You have to get the hairdressers, fight the traffic and stuff. Boy, it's a killer.

"What is our service? We give people a better impression of death, especially if the body is deteriorating. When we finish with them they do have a lifelike appearance, they do seem to be about twenty or thirty years younger, the embalming fluids seem to put the albumin back in the skins. Formaldehyde. Firms things up when they're deteriorating, just like clockwork.

"The future of the profession is still good. As long as you have Catholics and Protestants and Jews and whatnot, you need us. Today the pricing is lower, only we're selling real estate instead of merchandise. You go into a parlor today and you pay three hundred dollars to walk into the chapel and three hundred dollars to talk to the funeral director. If you do a volume business, two or three thousand funerals a year, you can give your merchandise at cost because you're still selling your room and your directors. The younger generation doesn't want to pay x amount of dollars on a casket. Fine. But they will fork over three hundred dollars for your professional services. They will give you three hundred dollars for your chapel. It's still the nine-hundred-dollar casket with the hidden chapel charge and service fee.

"Funeral directors have a good sense of humor. But we don't make jokes about the business. No way."

The Role of the Mortician

Richard Huntington and Peter Metcalf

*Huntington and Metcalf, both anthropology professors, say that the unifor-
mity of funeral customs in the United States reveals widespread support for
the traditional funeral. Furthermore, they say, the limited success of reformist-
minded "memorial societies" shows that the public continues to approve of the
"American way of death." For the sake of uniformity with other essays in* The
Freshman Reader, *we have removed most of the article's citations that called
attention to literature in the field of anthropology. We have inserted ellipses
to indicate places where citations stood in the original.*

As the critics have shown, funeral directors have not failed to exploit
their position in order to make a profit. [Ruth Harmer's *The High Cost
of Dying* and Jessica Mitford's *The American Way of Death*] are full of
examples of such opportunism. For example, Mitford describes how
funeral directors regularly play upon the emotional state of their customers in order to get them to purchase a more expensive coffin than
they had intended. As she points out, the morticians' customers are
almost by definition "impulse buyers." . . . Again, cemetery landsca-
pers are in a particularly favorable position vis-à-vis their customers:
They collect payment on plots that they will not have to provide for
perhaps many years, leaving themselves with interest-free capital in
the interim. . . .

The National Funeral Directors Association has frequently exercised
a powerful political influence. It maintains well-financed lobbies in
Washington and the state capitals. Occasionally it has been able to
secure legislation favorable to the business interests of its members.
For instance, the association has steadily opposed cremation, and in
some states has supported laws that make it unnecessarily expensive
by requiring that a coffin be provided and burned up with the
corpse. . . .

However, in comparative perspective the proportion of available
resources committed to death ritual does not seem exceptional: Cer-

Peter Metcalf, "Conclusion: American Deathways," in Richard Huntington and Peter
Metcalf, *Celebrations of Death: The Anthropology of Mortuary Ritual.* Copyright © 1979 by
Cambridge University Press. Reprinted by permission of the publisher and the
authors.

tainly the Berawan and the Malagasy use up more. Moreover, the amount spent each year on funerals in the United States is considerably less than the amount spent on weddings, yet few condemn the materialism of weddings. Charges of exploitation are not leveled at the dressmaking industry, or the Brewers' Association of America on the grounds that they make a profit out of these festive events. . . . Presumably this is because the critics regard weddings as socially'useful and funerals as useless. But who is to judge the value of a ritual?

The same kind of overstatement has occurred in connection with conspicuous consumption at American funerals. Certainly, commercialism is noticeable, but it is not unlimited. For example, sumptuous flower arrangements surrounding the coffin are a feature of the "viewing," and it could be argued that the mourners compete to display their affluence in such gifts. However, very nice distinctions of status govern the size of floral tributes. It would be entirely tactless for a mere acquaintance or a distant relative to offer too large a wreath. In general, the impression is of a striving to find the *correct* level of expenditure in funeral accoutrements, rather than the most *impressive.* . . .

The same tendency is noticeable in the funeral cavalcade. Although it is common for close relatives to request that the hearse drive past the deceased's former residence or work place, the display at such times is modest by comparison with, say, nineteenth-century England. In *The Victorian Celebration of Death*, J. S. Curl presents a remarkable photograph from England of a six-horse hearse, heavily draped in black crepe, the horses decorated with black-dyed ostrich feathers, and attended by a dozen or so equerries. The striking feature of the picture is the obvious poverty of the neighborhood to which this apparition has been summoned. By comparison, the dark American hearse and line of cars is positively spartan. In grave markers also, the prevalent trend is toward simple horizontal tablets. Clearly, wealth and social class *are* expressed in funerals, as they are in other phases of American culture, such as housing, clothing, and automobiles. However, there is little evidence of the manipulation of the dead for status-climbing purposes.

Considering the economic explanation as a whole, there is no doubt that the existence of a tightly organized group of specialists who control every phase of the disposal of corpses is the most significant single feature of American funerals. It explains why funerals cost what they do, and why nonspecialists, such as kin and clergy, appear only in passive roles.

But it does not explain everything about them. Why do they have the ritual form they do? There are other things that could be done to the corpse that would be just as expensive and therefore just as profitable. The very uniformity of funeral rites places limits on the economic explanation because merchandisers usually try continually to add new products to tickle the fancy of consumers. There has been, it is true, some gimmickry in the funeral industry—drive-in funeral parlors are a recent example—but the overall form of the rites has remained remarkably stable for several decades.

Moreover, it is clear that Americans are not just passive consumers of the only services available to them; they actively approve of them. A survey in several midwestern cities revealed that a majority of respondents felt that contemporary funerals are appropriate, and that the funeral director has an important role to play in comforting the bereaved. . . . P. Silverman concludes in "Another Look at the Role of the Funeral Director" (1974) that the widows she worked with in Boston received more help and comfort from the funeral director than from either physician or clergyman. This tacit approval is also manifest in the limited success of movements to reform funeral practices. Nonprofit funeral and memorial societies have had some success, and certainly provide much cheaper funerals, but their membership remains small. Some unions have established funeral plans for members, but their experience has been that the cheapest variety does not sell. Their blue-collar clientele still demands all the elements found in the commercial funeral. . . .

A final piece of evidence: Modern-style embalming, with its associated rites, has been practiced for nearly a century now. During that time, the United States has continued to receive immigrants from many different cultural backgrounds. The statistics quoted in the preceding section indicate that the majority have adopted American deathways, just as they have absorbed other aspects of national culture. Had it been otherwise, institutions would surely have sprung up to cater to their needs. This shows that funerals somehow fit into a peculiarly American ideology; that funerals express something. Economics is powerless to explain what.

Suggestions for Writing

Naturally, before you write you should have a clear idea of what type of paper you are going to write. That knowledge will largely determine the style and tone of your prose, and your techniques of documentation. Because we have included a wide variety of writing assignments based on the essays in this chapter, we have divided those assignments into "types": the personal essay, the textual analysis, the research report, and the research argument.

The Personal Essay

The personal essay is a relatively short (sometimes as short as a single typed page), informal, and subjective response by the writer. Although it doesn't depend on research and documentation, it does use, in an informal way, other people's ideas for support or illustration. (More about that later.)

What makes the personal essay personal is that it is not afraid of revealing the writer's biases. (Indeed, it sometimes glories in those biases, especially the small benign ones.) And it doesn't hesitate to use the writer's own experiences as supporting details.

In tone, the personal essay is intimate and usually friendly. Its informal style permits contractions, short and simple sentences, and an occasional colloquialism. It can argue a point, illustrate an idea, or describe a scene. In any case, the writer first looks into his or her heart, and then writes.

In dealing with the following personal essay topics, you can use whatever ideas you need from the essays in this chapter. But if you do paraphrase or quote from these works, you are obliged to give the author credit within your text. You can do this by simply mentioning the author's name and work in your introduction to the quote: "An early critic of the funeral industry, Ruth Harmer, wrote in 'The High Cost of Dying' that. . . ." (The personal essay rarely uses footnotes.)

If you read at least the essays by Harmer and Lamers in this chapter before you write, your personal essay will probably be more well informed and detailed. Here, then, are a few personal essay topics:

1. Write about your experiences in a funeral home. Weave a description of the surroundings into your essay, but focus your attention on how you felt. Arrive at a thesis if you can.

2. Assume that our civilization has collapsed, leaving only a primitive farming economy. There are no funeral directors or funeral homes. How do you think the physical fact of death should be coped with under these circumstances? Assume that you are in charge of a dead person, and describe in detail the procedure you would follow.

3. Making the same assumption about the collapse of our civilization called for in the previous writing assignment, describe the rituals you would have enacted for a dead person to demonstrate your sense of the spiritual dimension of life.

4. If you have recently attended a traditional funeral, tell about your satisfaction or dissatisfaction with the way it was conducted. Focus your attention on its usefulness to the mourners. Did the services help to make a dreadful occasion endurable? Or did they, in Ruth Harmer's words, merely serve to "intensify shock and dislocation"?

The Textual Analysis

The textual analysis is an examination of what another writer says or the way he says it. It is usually an analysis of a single piece of writing, though it occasionally treats two works (sometimes more) when the purpose of the analysis is comparison.

The textual analysis is not primarily a research paper. That is, the writer doesn't go out and read a variety of sources and combine those sources in his writing. Instead, he uses his own resources—his sensitivity to language and his analytical skills—to understand and communicate to readers the ideas and techniques of a work.

In tone, the textual analysis is objective and relatively formal (at least when compared with the personal essay), though there remains plenty of room for the writer's "personality" to shine through.

We have given equal space below to suggestions for essays that examine ideas and essays that examine techniques.

1. Jessica Mitford's "In the Hands of the Embalmer" is a description of the practice of embalming; it is also, quite obviously, a criticism of the practice. How does Mitford communicate her distaste for embalming without overtly criticizing?

2. Discuss the tone of "De Mortuis." Is it ironic, dignified, pompous, scholarly, cold, heated, formal, informal, coy, wry, sour, rea-

soned? Support your points by citing words, sentences, and passages.

3. Contrast the tone and style of "The Bier Barons," written for a general audience, with the tone and style of "The Role of the Mortician," written for a specialized audience. Consider diction, sentence structure, the use of details and examples, documentation, and anything else you can think of.

4. In "De Mortuis," J. H. Plumb shows that the traditional funeral is not an anomaly, and he defends it on the grounds that it has honorable historical precedents. Is this a reasonable defense?

5. Write a short satiric essay based on this statement by Reuben Ruiz in "Four Undertakers": "My best-selling casket is the Batesville Moniseal. Its best points are the sealing quality, and the fact that every one of them comes with a mattress and box springs. Just like your bed at home." Don't use words like "ridiculous," "unreasonable," and "foolish" to describe Ruiz's comments. That's not satire. Instead, use a gentle touch and satirize by indirection. You might use a persona—perhaps the corpse itself, a casket salesman, a naive customer, a dog, a worm, a visitor from outer space, or an archeologist who digs up a Moniseal coffin a thousand years from now.

6. Write an essay in which you show that Ruiz's statement above is not so foolish as it first appears to be.

Research Writing Skills

There are a few special problems connected with the next types of papers, the research report and the research argument. So we need to spend a little time here, before we offer the rest of the suggestions for writing, discussing those problems. Naturally, our purpose is not to cover all of the problems connected with research writing—only to take you far enough so that you can get some practice in handling multiple sources and in documenting those sources in footnotes.

Footnoting

The research paper requires that every time you borrow either an idea or words from the writings of others, you will have to acknowledge that borrowing with a footnote. (There is an exception: Generally known facts, such as the invention of the telephone by Alexander Graham Bell, do not need to be footnoted.) The purpose of a footnote is to give readers information about your sources so that they can locate them easily in a library; they may want to read further into the topic, or they might wish to check you for fairness and accuracy.

To simplify matters, we have listed the ten works in this chapter in their proper footnote format. When you footnote a source for the first time in your paper, use the forms below. A second reference to the same source is even easier: Merely write the last name of the author and the new page number (Harmer, p. 65). We have left off the original page numbers. You will have to pretend that the page numbers used in this book, *The Freshman Reader*, are the numbers of the original sources. Naturally, your footnote numbers will not correspond to the numbers we have used below. The first footnote you use in a paper will be numbered "1," the next will be "2," and so on throughout your paper.

[1]Ruth Mulvey Harmer, "The High Cost of Dying," in *The High Cost of Dying* (New York: Collier Books, 1963), p. _____.

[2]Ralph A. Head, "The Reality of Death," *Casket and Sunnyside*, June 1971, p. _____.

[3]Richard Huntington and Peter Metcalf, "The Role of the Mortician," in *Celebrations of Death* (New York: Cambridge University Press, 1979), p. _____.

[4]William M. Lamers, Jr.,"Funerals Are Good for People," *Medical Economics*, 23 June 1969, p. _____.

[5]Jessica Mitford, "In the Hands of the Embalmer," in *The American Way of Death* (New York: Simon & Schuster, 1963), p. _____.

[6]Al Morgan, "The Bier Barons," *Playboy*, June 1960, p. _____.

[7]J. H. Plumb, "De Mortuis," *Horizon*, Spring 1967, p. _____.

[8]Dotson Rader, "Four Undertakers," *Esquire*, February 1975, p. _____.

[9]Roul Tunley, "Can You Afford to Die?" *The Saturday Evening Post*, 17 June 1961, p. _____.

[10]Deborah Wolters, "Death, Here Is Thy Sting," *The Progressive*, May 1978, p._____.

Note that titles of magazine articles are always placed within quotation marks and titles of books are underlined, whether you cite them in your text or in a footnote.

Introducing Quotations

Let's say that you are arguing in a research paper that extravagance in funerals is nothing new, and you have found in your research a passage in the essay "De Mortuis" that you think would support your point nicely. This is what your citation, complete with transitional "bridge," would look like:

A
There is really nothing terribly extravagant about our funeral customs. As a matter
B
of fact, *those who have compared them with funeral customs of the past usually*
discover how spare and stingy ours are, not how extravagant they are. *One*
C   **D**   **E**
historian, J. H. Plumb, says *that* "the tombs of the Pharaohs . . . make Forest
F
Lawn [*a particularly rich and successful Hollywood cemetery*] seem like a cheap
cemetery for the nation's down-and-outs."

Here is an explanation of the various techniques used in the preceding passage:

A. This is your own prose as it moves its way down the page, making points and developing ideas. But at this point you begin to feel the need to cite evidence from a source to support one of those developing ideas.

B. Here is the first span of the bridge. It shows the reader the relationship between your idea (that there is nothing terribly extravagant about traditional funerals) and the quotation you are about to use.

C. This is an identification of the author whose quote you are about to use. You will always want to identify the author, even if that identification is as slight as "One critic of the funeral industry," or "a journalist for *Time*," or even "One author."

D. This is the spot where your words stop and the quotation begins. Notice that when you go into a quotation directly from a "that," you need no comma. If you had stopped one word earlier with "says," you would have needed a comma immediately following "says."

E. These dots, called ellipsis points, are used when you wish to leave extraneous material out of a quotation. Three dots are used when you leave something out of the middle of a quotation, and four are used when you leave something out at the end. Ellipses are rarely used at the beginning of a quotation. When you want to omit the beginning of a quotation, you can simply use a "that" bridge (see "D") and go directly into the middle of a quotation.

F. Brackets are used when you want to insert your own words within a quote. In this case, many readers would not have understood the implications of Forest Lawn Cemetery, so the reference to it needed a note of explanation. A pronoun like "it" within a quotation might also require clarification within brackets if the pronoun refers to something in your source material appearing before the portion you're quoting.

Introducing Paraphrases

A paraphrase, which is simply a borrowing that you have put into your own words, also needs to be footnoted. (Remember, you have to give credit for ideas as well as for words.)

Naturally, you don't need to place quotation marks around a paraphrase as you must around quotations, but otherwise requirements for the construction of the transition bridge remain the same. A bridge plus a paraphrase of the same passage quoted above would look something like this:

> There is really nothing terribly extravagant about our funeral customs. As a matter of fact, those who have compared them with funeral customs of the past usually discover how spare and stingy ours are, not how extravagant they are. One historian, J. H. Plumb, says that Forest Lawn resembles a pauper's cemetery when it is compared with the lavish tombs of the Egyptian Pharaohs.

Now it's your turn. If you need further information about research writing, you can probably find it in a grammar textbook. Most have a special section devoted to the research paper.

The Research Report

The report is an impartial and broad overview of a subject. Unlike the writer of the textual analysis, the writer of a report reads a wide variety of works, synthesizes those works, and then communicates that synthesis to the reader. The report writer may occasionally reach a modest conclusion at the end of the report, but that conclusion is relatively detached and basically noncontroversial, and is the direct, visible result of the information that lies in the report itself.

The writer of the report says, essentially, "I am going to illustrate, not argue, an idea by using bits and pieces from a variety of works." Naturally, when the writer of the report deals with controversy, his purpose is to explain to a reader what the controversy is all about, not to persuade the reader that one of the sides is the correct one.

Like the personal essay, the research report gives credit to others' ideas within the text, but the writer gives the complete documentation to these borrowings in footnotes, either at the bottom of the page or on a separate page at the end of the report. (In the latter case they are called "notes," not "footnotes.") Here, then, are a few research report topics:

1. Write a report on the controversy surrounding embalming. Use Mitford and Harmer to represent one side, and Rader's four morticians and Head to represent the other.
2. When Ruth Harmer calls the traditional funeral "pagan" in its emphasis, what does she mean? Use passages from three or more essays to help explain her meaning.
3. Write a report on the controversy over the role of the mortician. Is he a necessary evil or is he not? Remember, don't take a side. Merely report objectively what the controversy is about.
4. Contrast the view of William Lamers, Jr., on the memorial service with that of Ruth Harmer. Use two or three additional essays to clarify the contrast.

The Research Argument

Unlike the report, the argumentative research paper takes a side in a controversy from the beginning, and its purpose is to show that one side is superior to another. The writer of the research argument says, "I have already reached a conclusion on the basis of my thinking and reading. I will explain enough of other views to fill you in on what the controversy is all about (or to rebut those views), but my overriding purpose is to show you why I am right and those other views are wrong."

Like the research report, the research argument is an investigative paper, but its purpose is not merely to illustrate: it wants to persuade. Also like the report, the research argument documents borrowings in footnotes.

The writer of the argumentative paper may argue a side strenuously, but he tries to give the appearance of objectivity. He is not detached, but he is fair.

Here are some topics to use for research arguments:

1. Write a short argumentative research paper in which you use at least six of the essays in this chapter. Your topic will be: "The Role of the Undertaker: High-Priced Superfluity or Necessary Evil?"

2. Do the same with this topic: "Are Funerals Good for People?"
3. Try to convince your readers that people should or should not be buried with a traditional funeral service. Use four or five of the articles in this chapter, including at least one that argues the opposing view.
4. Attack the practice of embalming, using the views of Mitford and Harmer as support and the four undertakers' comments in "Four Undertakers" and Head's article to represent the opposing side.
5. Ruth Harmer says that an extravagant funeral is a "blasphemy," a "denial of all our philosophical and religious beliefs." Attack or defend her statement, using the materials from this chapter.
6. Write a research paper on whether people should or should not know about what happens to the body in a traditional funeral. Use passages from four or five essays in this chapter to illustrate your argument.
7. First consider Vincent Pucherelli's statements from "Four Undertakers": "We give people a better impression of death, especially if the body is deteriorating. When we finish with them. . . they do seem to be about twenty or thirty years younger." Then support or attack his view of his function, using at least four different articles from this chapter to support and illustrate your observations.
8. Attack Mitford's and Harmer's position on embalming by using Ralph Head's arguments, especially his statement that "the body is the extension of the person who died. If we proclaim the eminence of a person, we cannot disdain any aspect of that person."

Index

Abbey, Edward ("The Right to Arms"), 239–241

Abbey, Edward ("The Spadefoot Toad"), 28–29

"The Abyss" (Rachel Carson), 36–38

"Americans and Russians" (Alexis de Tocqueville), 115 [*Model Comparison Paragraph*]

"Back to Reticence!" (Lance Morrow), 195–197

Berg, David ("The Right to Bear Arms"), 244–246

"The Bier Barons" (Al Morgan), 252–256

"The Bird and the Snake" (Loren Eiseley), 50–52

Bronowski, Jacob ("Man and the Grunion"), 117–118

"Building a Fire with Buffalo Chips" (William Clayton), 96 [*Model Process Paragraph*]

"California Dreaming" (Joan Didion), 83–86

Campbell, Joseph ("The Witch in the Nervous System"), 80–81

"Can You Afford to Die?" (Roul Tunley), 257–260

"The Candy Man" (Alexander Theroux), 153–156

Carson, Rachel ("The Abyss"), 36–38

Catton, Bruce ("A Watery Grave and the Stars"), 67–71

Churchill, Winston ("Their Finest Hour"), 230 [*Model Paragraph Based on an Emotional Appeal*]

Clayton, William ("Building a Fire with Buffalo Chips"), 96 [*Model Process Paragraph*]

"Communication Among the Naked Apes" (Desmond Morris), 149–151

"Conundrum" (Nora Ephron), 88–91

Cousins, Norman ("Where Hell Begins"), 163–164

"Cruel Lib" (D. Keith Mano), 211–213

"De Mortuis" (J. H. Plumb), 276–279

"Death, Here Is Thy Sting" (Deborah Wolters), 272–274

"Dialects: What They Are" (Roger Shuy), 166–169

Didion, Joan ("California Dreaming"), 83–86

"Do We Survive Death?" (Bertrand Russell), 205–208

Eiseley, Loren ("The Bird and the Snake"), 50–52

Ephron, Nora ("Conundrum"), 88–91

"Faces in the Crowd", 140–142

Faulkner, William ("The Nobel Prize Address"), 173–174

"Female Athletes: They've Come a Long Way, Baby" (P. S. Wood), 129–133

Fern, George ("Of Pigeons, Fish, and Gulls"), 138–139 [*Model Classification Paragraph*]

"The '51 Merc" (William Jeanes), 26–27 [*Model Description Paragraph*]

Forster, E. M. ("My Wood"), 180–182

Forster, E. M. ("Voltaire and Frederick the Great"), 120–123

"Four Undertakers" (Dotson Rader), 288–290

"Funerals Are Good for People" (William M. Lamers, Jr.), 280–283

Ganger, Marilyn ("The Meeting"), 48–49 [*Model Narrative Paragraph*]

Grant, Ulysses S. ("Such a Climate!"), 179 [*Model Cause-and-Effect Paragraph*]

Harmer, Ruth Mulvey ("The High Cost of Dying"), 261–266

Hayakawa, S. I. ("How Dictionaries Are Made"), 98–99

Head, Ralph A. ("The Reality of Death: What Happens When It Is Ignored?"), 284–287

"Here Come the Voutians," 162 [*Model Definition Paragraph*]

"The High Cost of Dying" (Ruth Mulvey Harmer), 261–266

"How Dictionaries Are Made" (S. I. Hayakawa), 98–99

"How It Feels to Be Shot" (George Orwell), 32–34

"How to Say Nothing in Five Hundred Words" (Paul Roberts), 5–16

"How to Tell Bad from Worse" (Michael Levin), 125–127

Hume, David ("Which Is the Greater Miracle?"), 203 [*Model Paragraph Based on an Appeal to Reason*]

Huntington, Richard, and Peter Metcalf ("The Role of the Mortician"), 291–293

"I Have a Dream" (Martin Luther King, Jr.), 231–234

"In the Hands of the Embalmer" (Jessica Mitford), 267–271

"Is a Crime Against the Mind No Crime at All?" (Judith Plotz), 215–219

Jeanes, William ("The '51 Merc"), 26–27 [*Model Description Paragraph*]

King, Martin Luther, Jr. ("I Have a Dream"), 231–234

King, Martin Luther, Jr. ("Three Ways of Responding to Oppression"), 144–146

Lamers, William M., Jr. ("Funerals Are Good for People"), 280–283

"The Law of Human Nature" (C. S. Lewis), 221–224

"Leftovers" (E. B. White), 75 [*Model Illustration Paragraph*]

Levin, Michael ("How to Tell Bad from Worse"), 125–127

Lewis, C. S. ("The Law of Human Nature"), 221–224

Lincoln, Abraham ("Second Inaugural Address"), 236–237

"Linking 'A' to 'Aleph'" (Faye Moskowitz), 61–65

Macrorie, Ken ("Telling Truths"), 17–22

Madson, John ("On the Trail of the Curly Cows"), 40–43

"The Maker's Eye: Revising Your Own Manuscripts" (Donald M. Murray), 106–110

"Man and the Grunion" (Jacob Bronowski), 117–118

Mano, D. Keith ("Cruel Lib"), 211–213

"The Meeting" (Marilyn Ganger), 48–49 [*Model Narrative Paragraph*]

Metcalf, Peter (and Richard Huntington), "The Role of the Mortician," 291–293

Mitford, Jessica ("In the Hands of the Embalmer"), 267–271

Model Cause-and-Effect Paragraph: Ulysses S. Grant, "Such a Climate!," 179

Model Classification Paragraph: George Fern, "Of Pigeons, Fish, and Gulls," 138–139

Model Comparison Paragraph: Alexis de Tocqueville, "Americans and Russians," 115

Model Definition Paragraph: "Here Come the Voutians," 162

Model Description Paragraph: William Jeanes, "The '51 Merc," 26–27

Model Illustration Paragraph: E. B. White, "Leftovers," 75

Model Narrative Paragraph: Marilyn Ganger, "The Meeting," 48–49

Model Paragraph Based on an Appeal to Reason: David Hume, "Which Is the Greater Miracle?," 203

Model Paragraph Based on an Emotional Appeal: Winston Churchill, "Their Finest Hour," 230

Model Process Paragraph: William Clayton, "Building a Fire with Buffalo Chips," 96

Morgan, Al ("The Bier Barons"), 252–256

Morris, Desmond ("Communication Among the Naked Apes"), 149–151

Morrow, Lance ("Back to Reticence!"), 195–197

Moskowitz, Faye ("Linking 'A' to 'Aleph'"), 61–65

Murray, Donald M. ("The Maker's Eye: Revising Your Own Manuscripts"), 106–110

"My Wood" (E. M. Forster), 180–182

"The Nobel Prize Address" (William Faulkner), 173–174

"Of Pigeons, Fish, and Gulls" (George Fern), 138–139 [*Model Classification Paragraph*]

"On Natural Death" (Lewis Thomas), 76–78

"On the Trail of the Curly Cows" (John Madson), 40–43

"Once More to the Lake" (E. B. White), 54–59

Orwell, George ("How It Feels to Be Shot"), 32–34

Paul ("Tongues of Men and Angels"), 171

"The Perfect Crime" (Tom Wolfe), 189–193

Plotz, Judith ("Is a Crime Against the Mind No Crime at All?"), 215–219

Plumb, J. H. ("De Mortuis"), 276–279

"The Preying Tree" (Joseph Wheelwright), 103–104

Rader, Dotson ("Four Undertakers"), 288–290

"The Reality of Death: What Happens When It Is Ignored?" (Ralph A. Head), 284–287

"The Right to Arms" (Edward Abbey), 239–241

"The Right to Bear Arms"(David Berg), 244–246

Roberts, Paul ("How to Say Nothing in Five Hundred Words"), 5–16

"The Role of the Mortician" (Richard Huntington and Peter Metcalf), 291–293

Russell, Bertrand ("Do We Survive. Death?"), 205–208

"Second Inaugural Address"
(Abraham Lincoln), 236–237

Shuy, Roger ("Dialects: What They
Are"), 166–169

"The Spadefoot Toad" (Edward
Abbey), 28–29

"Such a Climate!" (Ulysses S. Grant),
179 [*Model Cause-and-Effect
Paragraph*]

"Telling Truths" (Ken Macrorie), 17–
22

"Their Finest Hour" (Winston
Churchill, 230 [*Model Paragraph
Based on an Emotional Appeal*]

Theroux, Alexander ("The Candy
Man"), 153–156

Thomas, Lewis ("On Natural
Death"), 76–78

"Three Ways of Responding to
Oppression" (Martin Luther King,
Jr.), 144–146

de Tocqueville, Alexis ("Americans
and Russians"), 115 [*Model
Comparison Paragraph*]

"Tongues of Men and Angels"
(Paul), 171

Tunley, Roul ("Can You Afford to
Die?"), 257–260

Twain, Mark ("The War Prayer"),
185–187

Umlauf, Hana, and Barry
Youngerman ("An Exercise in
Levitation"), 101–102

"Voltaire and Frederick the Great"
(E. M. Forster), 120–123

"The War Prayer" (Mark Twain),
185–187

"A Watery Grave and the Stars"
(Bruce Catton), 67–71

Wheelwright, Joseph ("The Preying
Tree"), 103–104

"Where Hell Begins" (Norman
Cousins), 163–164

"Which Is the Greater Miracle?"
(David Hume), 203 [*Model
Paragraph Based on an Appeal to
Reason*]

White, E. B. ("Leftovers"), 75 [*Model
Illustration Paragraph*]

White, E. B. ("Once More to the
Lake"), 54–59

"The Witch in the Nervous System"
(Joseph Campbell), 80–81

Wolfe, Tom ("The Perfect Crime"),
189–193

Wolters, Deborah ("Death, Here Is
Thy Sting"), 272–274

Wood, P. S. ("Female Athletes:
They've Come a Long Way,
Baby"), 129–133

Youngerman, Barry (and Hana
Umlauf), "An Exercise in
Levitation," 101–102